JESUS ONLY

PAUL'S LETTER TO THE ROMANS

JESUS ONLY

PAUL'S LETTER TO THE ROMANS

ERWIN R. GANE

ROSEVILLE, CA

Amazing Facts, Inc.
P.O. Box 1058
Roseville, CA 95678-8058
www.amazingfacts.org

Unless otherwise stated, the Bible quotations are taken from the New King James Version.

Cover Design: Steve Miljatovic – Branch 7 Design
Text Design and Layout: Greg Solie – Altamont Graphics
Final Copy Editing by Tarah Solie – Altamont Graphics

Library of Congress Cataloging-in-Publication Data

Gane, Erwin R.
Jesus only : Paul's letter to the Romans / Erwin R. Gane.
p. cm.
ISBN 1-58019-187-8 (alk. paper)
1. Bible. N.T. Romans–Criticism, interpretation, etc. I. Title.

BS2665.52.G35 2004
227'.107--dc22

2004027228

---

04 05 06 07 08 • 5 4 3 2 1

Contents

Preface

Each chapter of this book was originally a radio talk broadcast by KNDL Angwin, California. Special thanks are due to David Shantz, the manager of the station, who graciously granted me two half-hour segments of time each week to present the gospel. In response to requests that I put my talks into book form, I have prepared this volume.

Because each chapter was originally a radio talk, the language of the book is more akin to that of the spoken word than that of a literary work. I have not attempted to titillate my listening audience or my readership with fascinating eloquence or, for that matter, with technical scholarship. Although I have endeavored to follow the best scholarship in my approach to the Bible text, I have written for the average reader. The great apostle Paul didn't write his epistle to the Romans primarily for scholars. He wrote for the express purpose of leading sinners to accept Jesus Christ as Savior and Lord. And that has been my motivation as I have spoken on the radio and as I have prepared this book. My great concern has been to bring to light the exalted spiritual message of every chapter of Paul's letter to the Romans.

This letter is Paul's most systematic presentation of the gospel, and although he often expresses himself as a learned rabbi, in the final analysis his message is profoundly simple and delightfully consistent with the teachings of Jesus Christ as expounded in the four Gospel accounts. The message that the righteousness of Jesus is available to every repentant, believing sinner is the message that must span the world before the second coming of Jesus. This message will transform lives, because Jesus' presence in the heart is His Spirit in the heart, the Deity in the heart, and His presence brings righteousness to the heart. The righteousness of Jesus is the qualification for heaven.

I am greatly indebted to Bruce Babienco, whose e-mail service, *News and Views*, provides stories used by permission from various publishers. A number of the stories I have used as illustrations have come from this source. Others have been taken from the *Encyclopedia of 7,700 Illustrations: Signs of the Times* (Rockville, Md.: Assurance Publishers, 1979), edited by Paul Lee Tan. Yet other stories have come from the Internet Web site www.sermonillustrations.com. A few other stories have been adapted from published books that have been acknowledged in the notes at the end of the chapters. Every attempt has been made to respect the rights of copyright holders. I welcome hearing from any copyright holders inadvertently ignored. Omissions will be corrected in subsequent printings.

I am especially grateful to my wife, Winsome, who has carefully read each chapter and offered helpful suggestions for change. My deep gratitude is also extended to Sandra Blackmer for her most efficient copy editing.

My fond prayer and earnest hope is that the readers of this volume will be inspired to enter into fellowship with Jesus Christ, accepting His power to overcome sin and to reflect His loving character.

— Erwin R. Gane

Chapter One

Introduction to Romans

Romans 1:1–7

Our study of the Bible book of Romans begins with an overview of the author's life and briefly looks at his introduction to his letter.[1] Paul was born of Jewish parents in the city of Tarsus in Cilicia, southern Asia Minor, known today as Turkey (Acts 21:39). He belonged to the tribe of Benjamin and so was a loyal Jew; but he was also a Roman citizen (Philippians 3:4–6; Romans 11:1; Acts 22:28). In the Bible book of Acts, he is called Saul up to Acts 13:9, but after that he is referred to as Paul. Saul means "asked of God," or "lent of God." This was his Hebrew name and was used in his home and in his contacts with the Jews. His Greco-Roman name, the Latin name Paulus, meaning "little," or "small," was used in his contacts with the Greeks and other Gentiles. According to tentative Bible chronology, Paul was probably born about A.D. 10. His early training in Tarsus as a tent maker enabled him later in life to support himself financially as he conducted his various evangelistic campaigns (Acts 18:1–3; 20:34; 1 Corinthians 4:12). As a young man of possibly 18 or 20, Paul traveled to Jerusalem where he was trained as a rabbi by the famous Rabbi Gamaliel (Acts 22:3). As a Pharisee, Paul adhered to the strictest rules of that sect (Acts 26:5). As a young man, he distinguished himself for scholarship and zeal for Jewish causes; so much so that he was highly regarded by the Sanhedrin, at that time the supreme religious council of the Jews. Of course the Romans were in control of Palestine in those days, but, with Roman permission, the Sanhedrin to some extent directed the religious and political life of the Israelite nation.

When the Christian preacher Stephen was stoned to death because of his faith in Christ, Paul took care of the coats of those who stoned him. Acts 7:58 says that those casting the stones at Stephen, "laid down their clothes at the feet of a young man named Saul." That was Paul. Then Saul (or Paul) "made havoc of the church, entering every house, and dragging off men and women, committing them to prison" (Acts 8:3). Paul was very zealous for his Jewish faith. He didn't accept Jesus as the Messiah, and he thought that those who did accept Him were traitors to the Israelite faith. So he did all he could to have them arrested, thrown into prison, and even put to death.

Acts 9:1, 2 records that "Saul [or Paul], still breathing threats and murder against the disciples of the Lord, went to the high priest and asked letters from him to the synagogues of Damascus, so that if he found any who were of the Way [that is, any who were Christians], whether men or women, he might bring them bound to Jerusalem." As Saul (or Paul), with his companions, was approaching Damascus, suddenly a blinding light shone around him. In terror, he fell to the ground and heard a voice saying to him, " 'Saul, Saul, why are you persecuting Me?' And he said, 'Who are You, Lord?' And the Lord said, 'I am Jesus, whom you are persecuting' " (Acts 9:3, 4).

Trembling with fear and astonishment, Paul said, " 'Lord, what do You want me to do?' And the Lord said to him, 'Arise and go into the city, and you will be told what you must do' " (Acts 9:6). The men traveling with Paul stood trembling as all this was going on. They heard a voice, but were not aware of what was happening.

When Paul arose from the ground, he was blind. They led him by the hand into Damascus where for three days he remained blind and neither ate nor drank (Acts 9:9). Now it so happened that there was a faithful Christian in Damascus named Ananias. The Lord spoke to him in a vision and said: "Arise and go to the street called Straight, and inquire at the house of Judas for one called Saul of Tarsus, for behold he is praying" (Acts 9:11). Ananias objected. He said: "Lord, I have heard from many about this man, how much harm he has done to Your saints in Jerusalem. And here he has authority from the chief priests to bind all who call on Your name" (Acts 9:13, 14). But the Lord responded: "Go, for he is a chosen vessel of Mine to bear My name before Gentiles, kings, and the children of Israel. For I will show him how many things he must suffer for My name's sake" (Acts 9:15, 16).

Ananias obeyed the Lord, went to the house where Paul was staying, and laying his hands on him, said: " 'Brother Saul, the Lord Jesus, who appeared to you on the road as you came, has sent me that you may receive your sight and be filled with the Holy Spirit.' Immediately there fell from his eyes something like scales, and he received his sight at once; and he arose and was baptized. And when he had received food, he was strengthened. Then Saul spent some days with the disciples at Damascus" (Acts 9:17–19).

Paul immediately began preaching in the synagogues in and around Damascus that Jesus is the Messiah, that He died for the sins of the world, that He rose from the dead, and is now our Advocate in heaven. Then he spent some time in Arabia studying the Old Testament prophecies about the Christ and receiving from God the message that he was to present to the Gentile world (Galatians 1:15–17).

Paul returned to Damascus and continued preaching the Christian gospel. The Bible says that he "increased all the more in strength, and confounded the Jews who dwelt in Damascus, proving that this Jesus is the Christ" (Acts 9:22). So effective were Paul's evangelistic endeavors that the Jews in Damascus plotted to kill him. The Christian believers took him one night and let him down over the wall of the city in large basket.

Paul traveled to Jerusalem and tried to link up with the disciples of Jesus. But they were afraid of him and didn't accept that he was really a believer. Barnabas, a friendly Christian, intervened by introducing Paul to the apostles. After Paul had told them the story of his conversion, they accepted him, and he went on preaching the Christian good news in and around

Jerusalem. But again there was an attempt to kill him. "When the brethren found out, they brought him down to Caesarea and sent him out to Tarsus" (Acts 9:30).

For the next 6 years, from approximately A.D. 38 to 44, Paul witnessed for Christ in Tarsus. Then Barnabas traveled from Syrian Antioch to Tarsus, met Paul, and persuaded him to return with him to Antioch. Paul preached there for a time, until the Holy Spirit inspired the church to send him and Barnabas on a missionary tour of southern Asia Minor (Acts 13:1–4).

That was the beginning of Paul's great evangelistic endeavors that took him during three missionary journeys not only to Asia Minor but also to Greece. On his third missionary journey he was in Corinth for three months. This was the year A.D. 57 or 58. During that three-month stay in Corinth, Paul wrote his famous epistles to the Romans and the Galatians.

Then he returned to Jerusalem, was arrested, and thrown into prison in Caesarea for two years (A.D. 58–60). Finally he was sent to Rome as a prisoner where for two years (A.D. 61–63) he witnessed from his prison to as many as were willing to hear the story of Jesus. About A.D. 63, he was tried by Nero and released. He traveled around again, preaching the gospel, but again was arrested, taken to Rome, tried a second time before Nero, and in the year A.D. 67 or 68 was condemned and beheaded.

Just before his execution, Paul wrote to his fellow worker Timothy: "I have fought the good fight, I have finished the race. I have kept the faith. Finally, there is laid up for me the crown of righteousness, which the Lord, the righteous Judge, will give to me on that day, and not to me only but also to all who have loved His appearing" (2 Timothy 4:7, 8).

Thus ended the life of one of the greatest Christians of all time. The letter to the Romans, which he wrote from Corinth in A.D. 57 or 58 a few years before his death, is a brilliant, systematic presentation of the good news about Jesus Christ. It outlines the manner in which our loving God takes sinners and, because of Jesus' sacrifice on the cross, transforms them into living saints.

We begin our study of this inspired letter by considering the first few verses of chapter 1. Romans 1:1 reads, "Paul, a servant of Jesus Christ, called to be an apostle, separated to the gospel of God." As a servant of Christ, Paul was totally committed to the work of proclaiming the good news that salvation is readily available because of Jesus' death on the cross and His resurrection from the dead. In all his letters the fact of his complete dedication to the work of Christ comes through forcefully. For example, he wrote to the Corinthians, "For I determined not to know anything among you except Jesus Christ and Him crucified. I was with you in weakness, in fear, and in much trembling. And my speech and my preaching were not with persuasive words of human wisdom, but in demonstration of the Spirit and of power, that your faith should not be in the wisdom of men but in the power of God" (1 Corinthians 2:2–5).

In his second letter to the Corinthians, Paul tells us what was involved for him in being a servant of Jesus Christ. He wrote: "From the Jews five times I received forty stripes minus one. Three times I was beaten with rods; once I was stoned; three times I was shipwrecked; a night and a day I have been in the deep; in journeys often, in perils of waters, in perils of robbers, in perils of my own countrymen, in perils of the Gentiles, in perils in the city, in perils in the wilderness, in perils in the sea, in perils among false brethren; in weariness and toil, in sleeplessness often, in hunger and thirst, in fastings often, in cold and nakedness—besides the other things, what comes upon me daily; my deep concern for all the churches" (2 Corinthians 11:24–28).

Romans 1:1 says: "Paul, a servant of Jesus Christ, called to be an apostle." What does the word *apostle* mean? Who can be considered an apostle? The Greek word translated "apostle" means an "ambassador," an "envoy," a "messenger." Literally the word means "one who is sent." Every Christian is an ambassador of Jesus Christ. We are all sent to make known to the world the love of Jesus by the way we live and the things we teach.

But an apostle in the New Testament often refers to those special people who were chosen by Christ to be the leaders of

His church. A number of times the Bible speaks of an apostle as one who has received special revelations from God. The twelve apostles of Jesus received special revelations from Jesus Christ during the three and one-half years of His ministry on this earth. Later they and others received visions and dreams in which Christ revealed His will for them and for the church. The apostle Paul himself received special revelations from Christ. In 2 Corinthians, chapter 12, Paul refers to the "visions and revelations of the Lord" that were given to him in abundance (vs. 1–7). Also in 1 Corinthians 9:1, he writes: "Am I not an apostle? Am I not free? Have I not seen Jesus Christ our Lord?" Because Paul had received direct revelations of Christ and from Christ, his message was as authoritative as the messages of the other apostles.

That's why we should read carefully and prayerfully the writings of the Bible's authors. They were inspired apostles who were given messages for you and me directly from God. The Bible is a series of letters inspired by God and written down by those He chose to give those messages to us (2 Timothy 3:16; 2 Peter 1:20, 21). If you want to know how the God of the universe would have you live, read the Bible. No one can afford to ignore its messages. Through the Bible, God speaks directly to you; He lets you know that He loves you infinitely, that He wants to save you from sin, and that He wants you to live for eternity.

Romans 1:1–3 reads: "Paul, a servant of Jesus Christ, called to be an apostle, separated to the gospel of God which He promised before through His prophets in the Holy Scriptures, concerning His Son Jesus Christ our Lord, who was born of the seed of David according to the flesh."

The good news about Christ was "promised before through His prophets in the Holy Scriptures." Old Testament prophets predicted the birth, life, death, and resurrection of Jesus Christ. Hundreds of years before Christ's day the prophets of the Old Testament were told about His coming, where He would be born, the kind of ministry He would conduct, His death for the sins of the world, and His resurrection and subsequent work in heaven.

One of the main reasons we can believe that the Bible is God's inspired book is that it contains hundreds of prophecies that were literally fulfilled. Jesus Christ was the long-promised Messiah who died for the sins of the world. "God so loved the world that He gave His only Son, so that everyone who believes in Him may not perish but may have eternal life" (John 3:16, NRSV). And that fact was known centuries before His day by those who took time to read the writings of the Old Testament prophets.

Romans 1:3 says that "Jesus Christ our Lord … was born of the seed of David according to the flesh." And that's exactly true! As a human being Jesus was a descendant of David. The Gospel of Matthew, chapter 1, verse 1, says: "The book of the genealogy of Jesus Christ, the Son of David, the Son of Abraham." As a descendant of David "according to the flesh," Jesus Christ was fully human. He was a human being in every sense except that in Him there was no sin (1 John 3:5; 1 Peter 2:21, 22).

Moreover, Jesus was Deity also in the fullest sense. Romans 1:4 says that He is "the Son of God with power, according to the Spirit of holiness, by the resurrection from the dead." Colossians 2:9 speaks of Jesus as "the fullness of the Godhead bodily."[2] Micah 5:2, predicting Jesus' birth in Bethlehem, says that His "goings forth have been from of old, from everlasting" [or "from the days of eternity"]. In other words, as God, there never was a time when Christ did not exist. As God, He has *eternity* of existence. Jesus claimed equality with the Deity, because He was Deity. John 5:18 says that He made "Himself equal with God." As recorded in John 8:58, Jesus claimed to be the I AM. That was the name for Himself that Jehovah related to Moses centuries before. God instructed Moses: "Thus you shall say to the children of Israel, 'I AM has sent me to you' " (Exodus 3:14). Jesus Christ was and is that I AM. He was and is God in the fullest sense, in the flesh of a human being in the fullest sense. He was and is a God-man, the only God-man who has ever lived.

That's why the Bible says we should worship Him. Philippians 2:9–11 teaches: "God also has highly exalted Him and given Him the name which is above every name, that at the name of Jesus every knee should bow, of those in heaven, and of those on earth, of those under the earth, and that every tongue should confess that Jesus Christ is Lord, to the glory of God the Father."

According to Romans 1:5, through this God-man "we have received grace and apostleship for obedience to the faith among all nations for His name." In other words, through Christ we receive grace, or power, to obey God's will. What is God's will? Basically His will is expressed in the Ten Commandments. Christ doesn't give us His grace so that we will be free from obedience to the commandments of God. He gives us His grace, His spiritual power, to keep, to observe, to obey His commandments.

Romans 3:31 says: "Do we then make void the law through faith? Certainly not! On the contrary, we establish the law." The law is established in our hearts. Romans 3:20 makes it clear that the purpose of the law is to point out our sin. Romans 7:7 says: "I would not have known covetousness unless the law had said, 'You shall not covet.' " And Romans 8:3, 4 announces that Christ died "so that the righteous requirement of the law might be fulfilled in us who do not walk according to the flesh but according to the Spirit."

That's simply telling us that the Holy Spirit, Christ's representative in our hearts, gives us the power to turn away from sin and to live for Him (compare Romans 8:9, 10). Are you struggling with sin in your life? The sin problem is the universal human problem. We are all fallen human beings with biases, propensities, to sin. But Romans 1:5 reminds us that through Christ we have the grace, the power, "for obedience to the faith." How do you get this power? By exercising faith in Jesus Christ. How do you do that? First, you give Him your life. You say, "Lord, all I am and have are Yours. Take my life and lead me according to Your will." Then you read the Bible every day to receive His messages for you. Through the Bible He speaks to your mind and heart. He inspires you, encourages you, strengthens you to face the struggles of every day. Every day you bow in prayer and commune directly with Jesus. You invite Him to take charge of your mind and your program for that day. Then during the day when you are tempted to do something or say something that you know is wrong, you pray: "Lord, I'm helpless. I can't overcome this in my own strength. Please give me Your power. Thank You, Jesus, thank You." Praise Him for the victory, even before you experience it, and He will give it to you. That's faith.

That is what 1 John 5:4, 5 is talking about: "For whatever is born of God overcomes the world. And this is the victory that has overcome the world—our faith. Who is he who overcomes the world, but he who believes that Jesus is the Son of God?"

So by believing in Jesus and by faith receiving His power, you and I can be victors over sin, and we can live happy, joy-filled lives. We can have grace and peace "from God our Father and the Lord Jesus Christ" (Romans 1:7).

To bring the message right down to where we are, it's like this: You're stranded along life's highway, and Jesus comes along, gets your car going, and sends you on your way rejoicing. Then when you meet other stranded sinners, Jesus uses you to help them also to get moving toward heaven.

It reminds me of the story of two young men, Jim and Jon, both seventeen years of age. It was autumn in southwest Georgia. Jon was an expert auto mechanic. He'd been working on cars since he was ten years old. He had a 1955 Oldsmobile four-door sedan. He and Jim would drive around for a while after school and then head off to work.

One afternoon they were driving south on US 19 when they came upon a battered 1958 Chevrolet station wagon. The rusty vehicle was parked on the shoulder and the hood was raised. The car was loaded withe luggage and cardboard boxes. The wagon was carrying a family of migrant workers traveling from Detroit, Michigan, to Orlando, Florida, where they were hoping to find work.

The two boys pulled in behind the broken-down automobile, got out, and introduced themselves. "You have car trouble?" Jon asked. The driver, a short, wiry man, told the boys that the engine had suddenly started making a terrible clattering noise.

Jon noticed a dimple on the left valve cover. With tools from his trunk, Jon removed the valve cover. Sure enough, there was one push rod lying over at a crazy angle. Jon fished out the steel pencil-like push rod and began fixing it. Then he replaced the valve cover and pronounced the repair finished.

Jim noticed that there were two small children sitting on a blanket in the rear of the wagon. He asked the mom, "When was the last time your family had something to eat?" Lowering her head, she replied, "Yesterday." Then she added, "We have no money, and we have just enough gas to get to Orlando."

Jim reached into his wallet and pulled out a ten-dollar bill, all the money he had on him. He knew that Jon had a five-dollar bill for his supper that evening. Jim turned to him and said, "Hand it over, bud, so those kids can get something to eat." Jon did so, and then he reached over inside the wagon and turned the key to start the engine. It ran smoothly.

The couple thanked the boys profusely. The husband said, "There's no way we can ever repay you." Jim said, "Don't worry about it. Help somebody else down the road." With a final wave, the family drove back onto the southbound lane.

That's what Jesus does for us. He comes to our rescue when we're stranded in life's journey. Then he says, "Help somebody else down the road." Being a Christian is exciting because it means having power from Christ and having the joy of using that power in service for Him and for others.

Endnotes

1. Some helpful commentaries on the Epistle to the Romans that include information on Paul's life as well as expositions of the Bible text are as follows:

Barrett, C. K. *The Epistle to the Romans.* New York: Harper & Row, 1957.

Bruce, F. F. *The Epistle of Paul to the Romans.* Tyndale Bible Commentaries, vol. 6. Grand Rapids, MI.: Eerdmans, 1963.

Calvin, John. *The Epistles of Paul the Apostle to the Romans and to the Thessalonians.* Grand Rapids, MI.: Eerdmans, 1540, 1973.

Davis, Thomas A. *Romans for the Everyday Man.* Washington, D.C.: Review and Herald, 1971.

Dodd, C. H. *The Epistle of Paul to the Romans.* London: Hodder and Stoughton, 1932, 1960.

Erdman, Charles R. *The Epistle of Paul to the Romans.* Grand Rapids, MI.: Baker, 1983. Godet, F. *Commentary on the Epistle to the Romans.* Grand Rapids, MI.: Zondervan, 1883, 1956.

Lloyd-Jones, D. M. *Romans.* 7 vols. Grand Rapids, MI: Zondevan, 1986.

Loane, Marcus. *The Hope of Glory: An Exposition of the Eighth Chapter in the Epistle to the Romans.* Waco Texas: Word Books, 1968.

Luther, Martin. *Luther's Works: Lectures on Romans.* Vol. 25. Saint Louis: Concordia, 1972.

Murray, John. *The Epistle to the* Romans. 2 vols., Grand Rapids, MI.: Eerdmans, 1959.

Newell, William R. *Romans: Verse by Verse.* Chicago: Moody Press, 1918.

Nygren, Anders. *Commentary on Romans.* Philadelphia: Fortress Press, 1944, 1949.

Price, Walter K. *Revival in Romans.* Grand Rapids, MI.: Zondervan, 1962.

Rhys, Howard. *The Epistle to the Romans.* New York: Macmillan, 1961.

Sanday, William and Headlam, Arthur C. *A Critical and Exegetical Commentary on the Epistle to the Romans.* Edinburgh: T. & R. Clark, 1895, 1964.

Stott, John R. W. *Men Made New: An Exposition of Romans 5–8.* London: Inter-Varsity Fellowship, 1966.

The Interpreter's Bible. Vol. IX. New York: Abingdon Press, 1954.

The Seventh-day Adventist Bible Commentary: Acts to Ephesians. Vol. 6. Washington, D.C.: Review and Herald, 1957.

2. The Greek word translated "fullness" in Colossians 2:9 is *pleroma,* meaning, according to the best Greek lexicons, "the sum total," "the full measure." See William F. Arndt and F. Wilbur Gingrich, *A Greek-English Lexicon of the New Testament and Other Early Christian Literature* (Chicago: Chicago University Press, 1957), article *pleroma.*

Chapter Two

The Righteousness of God is Power

Romans 1:8–17

Jean Thompson stood in front of her fifth-grade class on the very first day of school in the fall and told her children something she didn't really believe. She said that she loved them all the same and that she would treat them all alike. But that was impossible because there in front of her, slumped in his seat on the third row, was a little boy named Teddy.

Mrs. Thompson had watched Teddy the year before and noticed that he didn't play well with the other children, that his clothes were unkempt, and that he constantly needed a bath. And Teddy was unpleasant. It got to the place in the first few months that she would actually take delight in giving him an F for his assignments. Because Teddy was so sullen and unpleasant, no one else seemed to enjoy his friendship.

When Mrs. Thompson opened Teddy's file she was in for a surprise. His first-grade teacher had written: "Teddy is a bright, inquisitive child with a ready laugh. He does his work neatly and has good manners. He is a joy to be around." His second-grade teacher had written: "Teddy is an excellent student, well-liked by his classmates, but he is troubled because his mother has a terminal illness, and life at home must be a struggle." His third-grade teacher wrote: "Teddy continues to work hard, but his mother's death has been hard on him. He tries to do his best, but his father doesn't show much interest, and his home life will soon affect him if some steps aren't taken." Teddy's fourth-grade teacher wrote: "Teddy is withdrawn and doesn't show much interest in school. He has become a problem."

At Christmastime, Mrs. Thompson's students brought her beautiful presents, all nicely wrapped; all except for Teddy's. His present was clumsily wrapped in heavy, brown paper. Mrs. Thompson took pains to open it in the middle of the other presents. Some of the children laughed when she found a rhinestone bracelet with some of the stones missing, and a bottle that was one-quarter full of cologne. But she stifled the children's laughter and dabbed some of the perfume on her wrist.

Teddy stayed behind after school just long enough to say, "Mrs. Thompson, today you smelled just like my mom used to."

After the children left, she cried a little. From then on she was not merely teaching reading, writing, and math. She began to teach children. And she paid particular attention to Teddy. As she worked with him, his mind seemed to come alive. The more she encouraged him, the faster he responded. On days when there would be an important test, Mrs. Thompson would wear that special cologne.

By the end of the year, Teddy was one of the best students in the class, and he had become the teacher's "pet."

A year later she found a note under her door from Teddy, telling her that of all the teachers he'd had in elementary school, she was his favorite. Six years went by, and she received another note from Teddy. He wrote that he had finished high school third in his class, and she was still his favorite teacher. Four years later she got another letter, saying that he was graduating from college with highest honors. He assured Mrs. Thompson that she was still his favorite teacher. Then four more years passed and yet another letter came. She was still his favorite teacher, but now the letter was signed, Theodore F. Stoddard, M.D.

And that's not all. The next spring there was another letter. Teddy was getting married. His father had died a couple of years before, and he was wondering if Mrs. Thompson might agree to sit in the pew usually reserved for the mother of the groom. And guess what—she did, and she wore some of that special cologne.

A little love and caring changed the course of a boy's life. And it was the love and caring of the Lord Jesus Christ that changed the life of the apostle Paul. He had been a legalistic killer. But Jesus' love made him a gentle, caring soul winner. Saul the killer became Paul the great Christian apostle to the Gentiles. And Jesus' love will change your life also. You give Him your heart and let Him be your Savior and Lord, and things will change for you. His love in your heart will make you a caring, loving person. Jesus makes us like Himself in disposition when we allow Him to live in our lives.

The first chapter of Romans reveals Paul, who was possessed by Jesus' love, as the most compassionate, caring pastor. He had never met many of the people in the church of Rome, but he wrote to them with great concern for their spiritual welfare. He wrote: "I thank my God through Jesus Christ for you all, that your faith is spoken of throughout the whole world. For God is my witness, whom I serve with my spirit in the gospel of His Son, that without ceasing I make mention of you always in my prayers, making request if, by some means, now at last I may find a way in the will of God to come to you. For I long to see you, that I may impart to you some spiritual gift, so that you may be established; that is, that I may be encouraged together with you by the mutual faith both of you and me" (Romans 1:8–12).

You see, Paul was a man of prayer. His great concern was that the Roman Christians would be true to Christ and to the lifestyle that He wanted them to live. Paul prayed for them "without ceasing." That means that he spoke to God in prayer constantly for the Roman Christians.

Paul wanted to be able to visit Rome so that he could impart to the believers there the wonderful truths that Jesus Christ had given him. He wrote: "Now I do not want you to be unaware brethren, that I often planned to come to you (but was hindered until now), that I might have some fruit among you also, just as among the other Gentiles" (Romans 1:13). Paul was writing from Corinth about A.D. 57 or 58. He had often wanted to visit Rome but had been prevented by the enormous needs of the churches in Asia Minor and Greece. His earnest pastoral care of those churches had kept him from traveling to Italy. But now he saw some hope at last of breaking loose and visiting the Christians in Rome.

Paul wrote: "I am debtor both to the Greeks and to barbarians, both to wise and to unwise" (Romans 1:14). He was in debt to all people because Jesus had saved him from a life of sin, and he felt a deep, inner conviction that he must repay Jesus as best he could by working for others who needed the same salvation. That's why he said, "I am a debtor."

Then he added: "So much as is in me, I am ready to preach the gospel to you who are in Rome also" (Romans 1:15). Did you get that? "So much as is in me," Paul said. That means, to the extent of my ability and powers, I am ready to preach the gospel to you in Rome. In other words, I am willing to give all of myself to the task. And that was Paul's characteristic attitude. He wasn't a preacher to make money. In fact, he supported himself by working as a tent maker. He wasn't interested in fame or glory or an easy life. He was willing and ready to give all his time, strength, and talent to the work that Christ had committed to him. And that work was leading other sinners to Jesus so that they too could have the wonderful gift of eternal life.

Paul said, "I am a debtor" and "I am ready." Then he added: "For I am not ashamed of the gospel of Christ" (Romans 1:16). He was not ashamed of the good news of salvation; he was proud of it! Why? Because there was power in that good news to change people from being degraded sinners to happy, vibrant Christians. He said: "I am not ashamed of the gospel of Christ, for it is the power of God to salvation for everyone who believes, for the Jew first and also for the Greek. For in it [that is, in the gospel] the righteousness of God is revealed from faith to faith; as it is written, 'The just shall live by faith' " (Romans 1:16, 17).

Paul wasn't ashamed of the gospel because there is power in it to change people's lives. There is power in the good news of salvation through Christ to enable people to live righteous lives by faith in Jesus Christ. Christ's love, manifested when He died for our sins on the cross, makes it possible for us to rise above our weaknesses and sins and to live spiritually victorious lives. You may think you are living now. But if you don't know Jesus as your Savior and Lord, you are, in fact, afflicted by a living death. Without Christ, you don't have the power to resist and overcome the habits and practices of your life of sin. You are an orphan without God, without true love in your life, without genuine fulfillment and satisfaction. But when you find Jesus, you have a heavenly Father, you have deliverance from evil thought, evil speech, evil habits, and selfish ways. You become pure, kind, and thoughtful of others. If you are a married person, your marriage is enriched. If you are a parent, your children become more important to you, and you show them more love. If you are a single adult, you know that you are not alone, that Christ loves you infinitely and will walk and talk with you every day.

Larry was an orphan who lived in an orphanage with other parentless children. Often Larry and the other children would lean against the gate and watch "luckier" children go by, children who had mothers and fathers, who would stare wide-eyed at the orphans. At such times a mantle of loneliness and hurt would fall over the boys within the enclosure.

One day Larry saw a boy outside staring in. Larry fiercely expressed his resentment. He ran to the gate and yelled, "Go away!" The boy outside recoiled a little. Then he said: "My name is Thaddeus. Can I come in and play?"

"No," said Larry, angrily. "You go home. Only boys without fathers and mothers can play in here."

The stranger looked disappointed. But he didn't leave. He kept calling to them until finally one of the boys helped him climb the fence. It wasn't long before their differences were forgotten, and even Larry made friends with the newcomer. Later, after the game, Thaddeus said: "Can't I stay with you? I like it here." Larry stared in amazement. He said: "If I had folks, I wouldn't want to stay here."

Suddenly Thaddeus had tears in his eyes. He replied: "It isn't so nice at home. My mom and dad are always fighting. They are out every night, and they don't have any time for me."

So the boys smuggled Thaddeus into the orphanage dormitory for the night. The next day, Larry said to Thaddeus, "You better go home. The supervisor will be around soon, and he'll find you here."

Then Thaddeus had a bright idea. "Why don't we change places? You come home with me, and you can stay there with my mom and dad. And I'll come back here and take your place in the orphanage." So together they sneaked out and went to Thaddeus's home. There was a police officer, a minister, and a crowd of people.

Thaddeus's father shook his son and shouted: "Where have you been? We thought you were kidnapped!" His mother, her face pale with relief, took him in her arms.

Thaddeus said: "I just went to the orphanage. I know you don't want me, so I'm going to live there, and Larry is coming to live here." There was a frozen silence. Thaddeus's father shouted at Larry: "Did you put this idea into his head?" "No," said Larry. "And I've changed my mind. I don't want to trade with him. The orphanage *is* nicer than here."

The anger in the father's face faded and only pain was left. He was overwhelmed with shame. Then suddenly Thaddeus, his mother, and father were embracing and weeping in a tangled group.

The minister took Larry back to the orphanage. He told the minister, "Someday, I'll marry and have children. And believe me, my kids will know they're loved and wanted. I know what it means!"

When we neglect our children, shout at them because they do wrong things, and blame them when, in the final analysis, we are to blame, we are driving them away from love. We are driving them away from Christ. But when Jesus is living in our lives, and His Spirit is in charge of our minds, we love one another, and we love our children. Then the gospel becomes to us and to our children the power of God unto salvation. It's Jesus' love that binds us together as families. It's His love that makes us loving husbands and wives, and loving parents.

The apostle Paul wrote: "For I am not ashamed of the gospel" (Romans 1:16). What does he mean by the gospel? Writing to the Corinthian Christians, Paul spoke of the gospel he had taught them. First Corinthians 15:3, 4: "For I delivered to you first of all that which I also received: that Christ died for our sins according to the Scriptures, and that He was buried, and that He rose again the third day according to the Scriptures." So the good news is that Christ died for our sins on Calvary's cross and that He arose from the dead and that today He is our living Savior.

The gospel is the story of the cross. But the gospel is also the good news of what happens to us when we accept Jesus as Savior and Lord. Writing to the Galatians, Paul explained that years before he had presented to the apostles in Jerusalem the gospel he preached among the Gentiles (Galatians 2:2). And that gospel he spelled out in his message to the Galatians. Galatians 2:16 presents that gospel: "Knowing that a man is not justified by the works of the law but by faith in Jesus Christ, even we have believed in Christ Jesus, that we might be justified by faith in Christ and not by the works of the law; for by the works of the law no flesh shall be justified."

So we are justified, or made right with God, by faith in Jesus Christ. When we respond to the conviction of the Holy Spirit, Jesus gives us faith. Then we surrender our lives entirely to Him, and we are justified, or made right with God.

Justification includes three acts of God on our behalf. First, because of the cross, God forgives all our sins. Acts 13:38, 39 tells us: "Let it be known to you, brethren, that through this Man is preached to you the forgiveness of sins; and by Him everyone who believes is justified from all things from which you could not be justified by the law of Moses."[1] The point is that the forgiveness of sins is justification, and this is God's gift to us when we believe in Jesus.

Second, justification is the righteousness of Christ put to our account in heaven. Romans, chapter 4, teaches that Abraham's faith in God "was accounted to him for righteousness" (Romans 4:22). Then Paul adds: "Now it was not written for his sake alone that it was imputed to him, but also for us. It shall be imputed to us who believe in Him who raised up Jesus our Lord from the dead, who was delivered up because of our offenses, and raised because of our justification" (Romans 4:23, 24). In other words, the righteousness of Jesus is imputed, counted, reckoned to us.[2] The legal reckoning of Christ's righteousness to us is accompanied by the bestowal of His righteousness upon us by the gift of the Holy Spirit.

Third, justification is the righteousness of Christ bestowed upon us in the new-birth experience. That's the message of Titus 3:5–7: "Not by works in righteousness which we have done, but according to His mercy He saved us, through the washing of rebirth and renewing of the Holy Spirit, whom He poured out upon us richly through Jesus Christ our Savior, so that having been justified by His grace, we should become heirs according to the hope of eternal life."[3] The point is that Jesus' act of saving us is the same thing as His justifying act, and this is by the washing of rebirth, by the bestowal of the Holy Spirit upon us in the new-birth experience.

So the good news is what Jesus accomplished by dying for us on the cross. And the good news includes what He does for us when He justifies us. He forgives our sins; He counts His perfect righteousness for us; and He bestows His righteousness upon us by giving us the Holy Spirit to dwell in our hearts.

That's why the gospel is "the power of God to salvation for everyone who believes" (Romans 1:17). In the gospel "the righteousness of God is revealed" to our hearts by the Holy Spirit. Romans 1:17 reads: "For in it [in the gospel] the righteousness of God is revealed from faith to faith." That word *revealed* is used elsewhere in the New Testament to refer to what God bestows upon us when we believe in Jesus.[4] For example, Paul wrote to the Corinthians: " 'Eye has not seen, nor ear heard, nor have entered into the heart of man the things which God has prepared for those who love Him.' But God *has revealed* them to us through His Spirit" (1 Corinthians 2:9, 10). Then in verse 12 Paul adds: "Now we have received, not the spirit of the world, but the Spirit who is from God, that we might know the things that have been freely given to us by God." God revealed divine truths to our hearts by giving us the Holy Spirit. The revelation is a spiritual experience. It is the experience of receiving the presence of Christ into our hearts by the indwelling of the Holy Spirit. The revealing is a bestowal.

Jesus prayed: "I thank You, Father, Lord of heaven and earth, because you have hidden these things from the wise and prudent and have revealed them to babes" (Matthew 11:25). The divine truths Jesus taught are revealed to our minds and hearts by the Holy Spirit. Jesus wasn't talking about academic knowledge. He was talking about a spiritual experience. Just so, in Romans 1:17, the gospel reveals to our hearts "the righteousness of God." The righteousness of God becomes our righteousness because God the Holy Spirit comes to live in our lives, and we grow from one level of faith to another.

Then Paul concludes this theme of the book of Romans by saying: "The just shall live by faith" (Romans 1:17). The just! Who are the just? The Greek of the passages translates simply, "The righteous person shall live by faith."[5] That means that if you are living by faith in Jesus, you are a righteous person. It means that if you are a righteous person, it is because you are living by faith. The righteousness of Jesus Christ has become your righteousness. It is counted for you in heaven, and it is bestowed upon you by the gift of the Holy Spirit. And His righteousness is the power to live as God wants us to live. The Spirit of God in our hearts is Christ in our hearts, is righteousness in our hearts (Romans 8:9, 10). And now we are living the victorious life of faith.

Hudson Taylor, the famous 19th century missionary to China, lived by faith in Jesus Christ. That's why he was so successful in founding the China Inland Mission and in leading hundreds of

Chinese to accept Jesus Christ as Savior and Lord. When he first went to China, Taylor traveled in a sailing vessel. One day there was no wind to fill the sails and make progress possible. The ship was dangerously close to an island inhabited by cannibals, and the ship was slowly drifting toward the shore. The savages were waiting on the beach, anticipating a feast.

The captain came to Mr. Taylor and urged him to pray for God's help. "I will," said Taylor, "provided you set your sails to catch the breeze." The captain declined to make himself a laughing stock by unfurling the sails when there was no wind. Taylor insisted: "I will not undertake to pray for the vessel unless you will prepare the sails."

So it was done. Then Hudson Taylor devoted himself to prayer that the Lord would send a wind so that the ship could move. While he was praying, there came a knock at the door of his cabin. "Who is there?" he called. And the captain's voice responded. "Are you still praying for wind?" the captain asked. "Yes," was Taylor's reply. "Well," said the captain, "you'd better stop praying, for we have more wind than we can manage."

And that is how it is when you come to Jesus and accept Him as your Savior and Lord. He gives you more blessings than you can manage all at once. You have faith in Jesus and His life becomes your life, His Spirit comes into your life, and His righteousness becomes your righteousness. His power to overcome sin becomes your power. You become a new person. The righteous person lives by faith. That's the message of Romans 1:16, 17. That's why "I am not ashamed of the gospel of Christ, for it is the power of God to salvation for everyone who believes, for the Jew first and also for the Greek. For in it [in the gospel] the righteousness of God is revealed from faith to faith; as it is written, 'The just [the righteous person] shall live by faith.' "

Come, my friend, to Jesus today, and let Him produce in your life the mighty transformation this passage is promising.

Endnotes

1. The Greek verb "to justify" (*dikaioo*) is used twice in the passage as an explanation of forgiveness (*aphesis*).

2. The verb "to reckon" used in these verses may also be translated "to impute" or "to count." These English words translate the Greek verb *logizomai.* This verb and its Hebrew equivalent *chashav* sometimes refer to a legal accounting of something. These verbs may also refer to a gift of something to someone. Both ideas are contained in a number of uses of *chashav* in the Hebrew Bible and of *logizomai* in the Greek translation of the Old Testament (the Septuagint). For example, 2 Samuel 4:2 reports that "Beeroth also was reckoned to Benjamin" (KJV). The word "reckoned" in the Hebrew original is *chashav*, and in the Septuagint it is *logizomai.* In the apportioning of the land to the various tribes, the town Beeroth was legally imputed, or reckoned, to the tribe of Benjamin. This legal accounting amounted to the gift of the town Beeroth to Benjamin. Another Old Testament example of the use of the verb "to impute" is found in Numbers 18:27, 30. The tithe imputed to the priests was an actual gift of produce to them, one-tenth of which they paid as tithe and nine-tenths of which they and their families consumed.

   In Romans, chapter 4, Paul takes the Old Testament concept of imputation and applies it to Christ's gift of His righteousness to the believer. Paul quotes Genesis 15:6: "For what does the scripture say? 'Abraham believed God, and it was reckoned to him as righteousness' " (Romans 4:3). Abraham's faith union with God was reckoned, imputed, or counted, as righteousness because God's righteousness was given to him by the Holy Spirit. (See Galatians 3:1–14.) The legal reckoning of the righteousness of God to the believer is accompanied by the gift of His righteousness to the heart by the presence of the Holy Spirit.

   The point is that imputation of righteousness is not merely a legal accounting in heaven; it involves the righteousness of Christ being bestowed upon the believer's heart by the gift of the Holy Spirit.

3. My translation. The text says: "He saved us … so that having been justified …" Christ's saving act is His justifying act. He saved us by giving us the new-birth experience, by pouring out the Holy Spirit upon us. The text speaks of Christ saving us by "the washing of rebirth" (*paliggenesias*). Since the saving is the justifying, He justifies us by the new-birth experience, by pouring out the Holy Spirit upon us. Justification is not

only a legal declaration that Christ's righteousness is counted for us; it is also the transforming new-birth experience that we enjoy when the Holy Spirit brings the presence of Christ to our hearts. Thus Paul repeated Jesus' message to Nicodemus (John 3), using different imagery, but identifying his imagery with that used by Jesus.

4. The Greek word translated "revealed" in Romans 1:17 is *apokalupto.* This word is used elsewhere in the New Testament to refer to spiritual life and truth revealed to the hearts of believers by the Holy Spirit. See, for example, 1 Corinthians 2:9, 10. Paul's point in Romans 1:17 is that the righteousness of God is revealed to our hearts, or bestowed upon us, by the gift of the Holy Spirit.

5. The famous phrase, "the just shall live by faith," translates the Greek, *Ho de dikaios ek pisteos zesetai.* Simply and accurately translated it reads, "The righteous [person] shall live by faith." It means that if you are a righteous person, it is because you are living by faith; and if you are living by faith, you are a righteous person. Believers are not righteous independently of Christ, but righteous in two senses: (1) the righteousness of Christ is accounted for them, and (2) the righteousness of Christ is bestowed upon them by the Holy Spirit. Compare Romans 8:9, 10.

Chapter Three

The Guilty May Know Him

Romans 1:18–32

Many years ago in England a young man was employed as a houseboy by a retired lady-in-waiting of Queen Victoria. She took pity on him, and he lived there for two or three years. One day when the young man was about eighteen years old, this poor woman was found dead, killed with an axe, and the axe was found hidden in the boy's closet. They found blood on his clothes—all the circumstantial evidence they needed to convict him of murder. He denied that he had done it, said that he was asleep in his room at the time, that he loved the woman because of her kindness to him, and that he was absolutely innocent. But the old English judge put on the black cap, pronounced him guilty, and passed sentence upon him to be hanged by the neck until he was dead. And the judge added, "May the Lord have mercy on your soul!" So the young man was taken down to the prison.

Finally the day came for the execution. The time appointed was Friday at eight o'clock in the morning. A large crowd had gathered outside the prison walls. The black flag was to go up on the prison as soon as the sentence of death was executed. The crowd waited—five, ten, fifteen, twenty minutes past eight, but that flag didn't appear. The newspaper reporters ran across the street to the telegraph office, and in about an hour the newspapers were on the street with an account of what had happened.

The night before the execution was to take place, the young man had a dream. He dreamed that the next day—the day of his execution—had come, and that they led him out of his cell. They walked down the hall, then turned in a certain direction and went outside along the side of the prison—inside the walls, but outside the prison building. Soon they came to a cottage and then to a flower garden, neither of which he had ever seen before. Then they turned to the right and into another door, and finally mounted the thirteen steps to the place of execution. But he dreamed that the execution never took place, that he was innocent, and that God delivered him.

The young man told his dream to the chaplain. "Of course," he said, "it's only a dream." The next day they took him out to be hanged, and as they walked along in the solemn procession of the condemned, he was suddenly aware of the strangely familiar path and garden—the same path and garden that he had seen in his dream. This gave him hope.

As they went over those very steps and saw the other things that he had seen in his dream, it brought courage to his heart. Finally he stood on the gallows. The last words were spoken, and the rope was pulled—but nothing happened. They had the young man get off the platform so they could examine it. Everything worked all right. They put some more oil on the drop and placed the boy on the trap. He had to go through all that agony again. Again they pulled the rope, but it wouldn't work. Then they put a sack of sand on the drop, and it worked all right. They put the young man back on and tried the third time. It wouldn't work. You might say that young man suffered three times for his crime.

Then they telegraphed to the authorities in London—to Queen Victoria. The word came back that since they had tried three times, and there was no mechanical or scientific reason for the trap not to work, the sentence was commuted to life imprisonment. So the young man was marched down the hall, back down the steps, and into the prison where he was to stay for many years. His dream was true indeed!

Finally, in that town a woman died who had been a servant in the same home when the murder was committed. On her deathbed, she confessed to this murder and told how she had placed the axe in the boy's room and put the blood on his clothes. The British government gave the man a large sum of money as partial compensation for his years of confinement, and he married his sweetheart who always believed him innocent and who had waited for him all those years. The story is that they went away to Australia, and, according to the best tradition, lived happily ever after![1]

Now the point is that the young man was innocent all along, during his trial, while they were trying to execute him, and for those long years of imprisonment. He was innocent all the time. Someone else had committed the crime for which he had been condemned. But he wasn't free to leave the prison until the judge pronounced him innocent.

The Bible says that, because Jesus paid the penalty for our sins on the cross, when we come to him with belief and repentance, God regards us as innocent. Romans, chapter 8, verse 1, says: "There is therefore now no condemnation to those who are in Christ Jesus, who do not walk according to the flesh, but according to the Spirit." So, if we believe in Jesus, we are now innocent because Jesus suffered for our sins on the cross. We are innocent, but still bound in this old world of sin. But the Bible says that one day soon Jesus will return with a glorious second coming, and those who are innocent because they believe in Him will be taken from this old prison house of a world and given immortality and eternal life in His kingdom.

The Bible says: "The Lord Himself will descend from heaven with a shout, with the voice of the archangel, and the trumpet of God. And the dead in Christ will rise first. Then we who are alive and remain shall be caught up together with them in the clouds to meet the Lord in the air. And thus we shall always be with the Lord" (1 Thessalonians 4:16, 17).

Those who are innocent in Christ will be taken to heaven to be with Him at His second coming. Right now, we are innocent in Christ, but bound to this old prison house of a world. But soon the Lord will come and we will be free at last, both innocent and free.

But those who refuse to accept Christ as Savior and Lord remain in their guilt and will be held guilty when He appears the second time. The Bible says that they will be put to death by the brightness of His coming (2 Thessalonians 1:8–10). There is terrible danger in clinging to our sin and refusing to allow God to forgive us because of Jesus' sacrifice on the cross. That's what Romans, chapter 1, verses 18 and following, are talking about.

The passage says: "The wrath of God is revealed from heaven against all ungodliness and unrighteousness of men, who suppress the truth in unrighteousness" (Romans 1:18).[2] The wrath of God is being revealed in various ways now, but it will ultimately be revealed when Jesus comes the second time. We have the chance to repent now, but when Jesus appears in the clouds of heaven, it will be forever too late. The probation of unbelievers will have closed, and God will destroy them. God wants to have a perfect universe free from sin and sinners. If we identify ourselves with sin, there will be no hope for us.

The passage goes on to say that unbelievers will be rejected by God, "because what may be known of God is manifest in them, for God has shown it to them. For since the creation of the world His invisible attributes are clearly seen, being understood by the things that are made, even His eternal power and Godhead, so that they are without excuse" (Romans 1:19, 20). That simply means that we have sufficient evidence in the order of the natural world and universe to indicate that there is a God who loves and cares for us. We have every reason to believe in the Creator God, because the obviously planned order of created things points to Him as the Creator.

In his book, *Stones and Bones,* Carl Wieland points out: "In the U.S. alone, it is conservatively estimated that there are upwards of 10,000 professional scientists (the vast majority not officially linked to creation organizations) who believe in Biblical Creation. ... Most university science professors have one earned doctorate; the late Prof. A. E. Wilder-Smith, a pioneer of creation thinking in the latter part of the twentieth century, held three. Physicist Dr. Saami Shaibani, who holds four earned science degrees from the University of Oxford, and has published over 100 scholarly articles, believes Genesis as a historical, factual account. Almost all branches of modern science were founded, co-founded, or dramatically advanced by scientists who believed in the biblical account of special creation and the worldwide Flood of Noah."[3]

People who reject God usually believe in evolution. They believe that since nobody made us, nobody owns us, so nobody can set the rules except us. There is no logical reason to be bound by the biblical commandment not to steal, if other parts of the Old Testament are rejected as cultural myths.

The simple fact is that evolution is not based on science; it's a religion based on faith—faith in an interpretation of history that cannot be established by the scientific method. The evolutionist responds that belief in creation is also a religion based on faith. Quite so, but the scientific facts that are available point convincingly to the existence of a Designer who planned and created the universe and our world.

Dr. Carl Wieland writes: "Consider the incredible improbabilities involved in getting the whole evolutionary show started in the first place. People talk as if it were somehow an observed *fact*—but the fact is that no one really has any sort of scientific explanation for how the complicated, information-bearing molecules required for even the simplest conceivable 'first life' could have arisen without outside intelligence. And there are good scientific reasons for believing this to be impossible."[4]

The Bible says, in the first chapter of Romans, that God can be known by the things He has made (Romans 1:20). In other words, the created world and universe reveal the existence of God. And I would rather believe God than some scientist who can't even effectively apply the scientific method to prove his theory of evolution. It remains a theory, unproven, believed in by millions who would rather have faith in an unscientific theory than faith in the living God.

Romans 1:21–23 tells us: "Although they knew God, they did not glorify Him as God, nor were thankful, but became futile in their thoughts, and their foolish hearts were darkened. Professing to be wise, they became fools, and changed the glory of the incorruptible God into an image made like corruptible man—birds and four-footed beasts and creeping things." So human beings who knew in their hearts of God's existence substituted idols for God as objects of worship. And today, although the idols unbelievers worship come in different forms, they are just as powerless to bring peace, joy, and happiness to the human heart.

Because many people have rejected God, He withdraws from their lives. The result is stated clearly in Romans 1:24–27: "Therefore God also gave them up to uncleanness, in the lusts of their hearts, to dishonor their bodies among themselves, who exchanged the truth of God for the lie, and worshiped and served the creature rather than the Creator, who is blessed forever. Amen. For this reason God gave them up to vile passions. For even their women exchanged the natural use for what is against nature. [That's talking about lesbianism.] Likewise also the men, leaving the natural use of the woman, burned in their lust for one another, men with men, committing what is shameful, and receiving in themselves the penalty for their error which was due." [That's talking about homosexuality and its terrible results.]

So the result of atheism, evolution, and idolatry is sexual perversion of the worst kind. When humans turn away from God, He leaves them to their own predilections, their own evil desires, and the result is homosexuality, bestiality, moral perversion. Instead of being a child of God, governed and controlled by the Holy Spirit, the unbeliever is driven from one level of perversion to another until mind and body are destroyed by the fires of lust.

Long ago God condemned homosexuality as an evil way of life, contrary to His will. In Leviticus 18:22–25, we read: "You shall not lie with a male as with a woman. It is an abomination. Nor shall you mate with any beast, to defile yourself with it. Nor shall any woman stand before a beast to mate with it. It is perversion. Do not defile yourselves with any of these things; for by all these the nations are defiled, which I am casting out before you. For the land is defiled; therefore I visit the punishment of its iniquity upon it, and the land vomits out its inhabitants."

God instructed ancient Israel that homosexuality and other modes of sexual perversion practiced by surrounding nations had resulted in punishment being meted out upon them. And God says: "Therefore you shall keep My ordinance, so that you do not commit any of these abominable customs, which were committed before you, and that you do not defile yourselves by them: I am the Lord your God" (Leviticus 18:30).

Paul concludes chapter 1 of Romans by reiterating the terrible results of atheism, idolatry, and homosexuality. He writes: "And even as they did not like to retain God in their knowledge, God gave them over to a debased mind, to do those things which are not fitting; being filled with all unrighteousness, sexual immorality, wickedness, covetousness, maliciousness; full of envy, murder, strife, deceit, evil-mindedness; they are whisperers, backbiters, haters of God, violent, proud, boasters, inventors of evil things, disobedient to parents, undiscerning, untrustworthy, unloving, unforgiving, unmerciful; who, knowing the righteous judgment of God, that those who practice such things are worthy of death, not only do the same but also approve of those who practice them" (Romans 1:28–32).

That passage reads like a graphic description of our own society. When God is forgotten, sin reigns. When people turn away from the conviction of the Holy Spirit, impurity, vice, and crime pervade society.

But there is hope! Romans 2:4 asks the pertinent question: "Do you despise the riches of His goodness, forbearance, and longsuffering, not knowing that the goodness of God leads you to repentance?" God's goodness, His power, His grace will transform our lives if we accept Jesus Christ as our Savior and Lord.

A story is told of the emperor Napoleon. One day as he was reviewing his troops, riding along on his white charger, his horse suddenly took fright. The horse reared dangerously and jerked the reins out of Napoleon's hands, and the emperor of France was in momentary danger of losing his life.

In front of him was a solid wall of infantrymen trained to stand at attention, presenting arms. As the horse raced down past this line of men, one of the privates, disregarding all discipline and order, threw down his musket, leaped forward out of the line, grasped the flying reins, and brought the horse to a standstill. Then he handed the reins back to the thankful emperor, who said, "Thank you, *Captain*." The private, standing there in the plain uniform of an infantryman, asked, "Of what regiment?"

"Of my guards," replied the emperor.

Then the young man left the line and started off across the field in his old muddy infantry uniform, with no hat, to join the group of officers over on the hill at staff headquarters. They looked askance at him, and finally one said, "What are you doing here?"

He replied, "I am captain of the guards."

"Captain of the guards! Whatever makes you think you are captain of the guards?"

He just pointed to the emperor who was riding by and replied, "He said so."

It wasn't the uniform, not the sword or medals, but the word of the emperor that made him captain of the guards.[5]

Jesus Christ's Word makes it clear that, when you come to Him in surrender and submission, when you accept Him as your Savior and Lord, you are a saved soul who has the gift of eternal life. Jesus says: "He who hears My word and believes in Him who sent Me has everlasting life, and shall not come into judgment, but has passed from death into life" (John 5:24). That's a wonderful assurance. You don't have to go through life in your old sin-stained garments. Jesus gives you the robe of His righteousness, and you become one of His special subjects with the gift of eternal life.

Many years ago in Texas, a man named Buckner and his wife ran an orphanage in which they housed two or three hundred little orphan children. Mamma and Papa Buckner used to gather orphans from one end of the state to the other, take them home, take care of them, and give them a father's care and a mother's love. Their orphanage was a real home, not a mere institution, and they gave the children what they longed for, the love of a father and a mother.

One day in a little town way out in the Panhandle of Texas, a fire broke out and in a few minutes destroyed a humble home. Everyone in that home was burned to death except one little girl, seven-year-old Mary. Her face was badly burned and so were her hands. Neighbors had barely saved her life by pulling her out of a window.

After a few weeks had gone by, and her burns had healed, the town's people decided to send her to the Buckners' orphan home, where she could get love and protection from Papa and Mamma Buckner. So they packed a few belongings for her, put a tag on her, and put her on a train. They explained: "Now, Mary, the conductor will tell you when to get off the train, for this little tag that we are putting on you tells where you are going. When you see a big man with a smile on his face at the station, that will be Papa Buckner."

So Mary rode all day on the train, and you can just imagine how she felt having left the only town she had ever known, her mamma and papa being dead. You can imagine the fear and sorrow in her heart as she traveled to some town she knew nothing about and to the home of people she had never met.

Along toward evening the train stopped, and she got off. And sure enough, there was a big man with a smile on his face. Mary went up to him timidly and asked, "Are you Papa Buckner?" "Oh yes," he said, and threw his arms around her and patted her and loved her. He took little Mary home with him, and before long she loved the place and all the other children and the good people who took care of her.

One day Mr. Buckner went on a trip and was gone for several weeks. Whenever he would come home from one of his frequent trips, the children would all run to meet him. And this time was no different. When the children saw him coming, they all ran down the path laughing and shouting, "Here comes Papa!" There was a regular tribe of children welcoming him home. When they met, he threw his arms around them, one after another, and gave them each a kiss. But little Mary stood back; she didn't go up to greet Papa Buckner as the other children had, and Papa Buckner was surprised and disappointed. He said, "Mary, come here; come close to me." He looked at her lovingly and asked, "What's the matter, Mary? Don't you love Papa? Why don't you come and give me a hug and a kiss?"

Mary just burst out crying, and Papa Buckner went to her and drew her up close and patted her. He led her off alone, and asked: "What's the matter, Mary? Why don't you come and give me a welcome like the other children?"

Mary sobbed, "Oh, Papa Buckner, all the other children are so pretty with their nice white faces and wavy hair, and I'm so ugly. I just looked in the mirror this morning, and I am so awfully ugly. I don't see how you could love me. The fire burned my face and my hair, and I'm so ugly, and the other children are all so pretty."

Then she started to cry some more. And do you know what that father did? He just drew her close to his big chest, gave her a hug and a kiss, and loved her more than ever. Then he took her in to Mamma Buckner, and they both loved her especially because she had been burned. They made her know that they loved her for what she was and not for what she looked like.[6]

You and I have been burned by sin, and the miserable old devil tries to tell us that God won't love us because we have done so many wrong things. But that's a shocking lie! The Bible says that God is love. He loved us so much that He gave up His life on Calvary's cross so that we can be forgiven and cleansed. There is a great father-heart of love who cares for us even more because we have been scarred and broken by sin. The Bible says it clearly: "God demonstrates His own love toward us, in that while we were still sinners, Christ died for us" (Romans 5:8).

Endnotes

1. Adapted from H. M. S. Richards, *Revival Sermons* (Washington, D.C.: Review and Herald, 1947), pp. 446–448.
2. The Greek of Romans 1:18 reads: *Apokaluptetai gar orge Theou,* which is translated, "For the wrath of God is being revealed." The wrath of God is ultimately revealed at the second coming of Jesus (2 Thessalonians 1:7–10; Revelation 6:12–17; 19:11–21) and at the end of the millennium (Revelation 20:1–15). But the tense of the verb in Romans 1:18 is present. The present tense in New Testament Greek is usually a continuous tense. Hence, the text means that the wrath of God is continuously being revealed "from heaven against all ungodliness and unrighteousness of men, who suppress the truth in unrighteousness." In other words, the wrath of God is being revealed now against those who persistently choose a life of sin.
3. Carl Wieland, *Stones and Bones: Powerful Evidence Against Evolution* (Acacia Ridge D.C., Qld, Australia: Answers in Genesis Ministries, 1994, 2001), pp. 5, 6.
4. *Ibid.*, p. 32.
5. Adapted from H. M. S. Richards, *Revival Sermons*, pp. 290, 291.
6. *Ibid.*, pp. 272–274.

Chapter Four

How God Judges

Romans 2

Once there was a little boy who wanted his dad to teach him how to play catch. One sunny day the little boy's father was sitting on the couch drinking a beer, while watching a baseball game. The boy rushed into the house exclaiming, "Daddy, Daddy, show me how to play catch!" Blankly staring at the television screen, the father replied, "In a little while, son. Let me finish watching this inning. Come back in five minutes."

"Okay, Daddy," said the boy, and he ran out of the room. Five minutes later, the boy returned screaming, "Daddy, let's go play some catch now!" The father turned to the boy and said, "Hold on, son, the inning isn't quite over. Come back in five more minutes."

"Okay, Daddy," the boy said as he shuffled out of the room. Five minutes later he returned, ball and glove in hand, eagerly waiting for his father to play some catch. "Daddy, let's go. I want to pretend I am a baseball star!" shouted the boy.

By this time, the father had cracked open another cold one, and another inning was being played. Frustrated by the boy's constant interruptions, the dad scanned the room and noticed a magazine underneath the coffee table. On the cover of the magazine was a large picture of the world. The father, who was angered and annoyed, began tearing the magazine cover into small pieces. After a few moments of shredding up the magazine cover, the father placed the torn pieces in the hands of his son and said, "Son, once you put this picture of the world back together, we can play catch, but don't interrupt me again until you're finished!"

Sadly, the boy took the magazine and shuffled off into his room, as he sobbed, "Okay, Daddy, I won't." But a few minutes later the boy returned and said, "I'm done, Daddy, can we play catch now?" Stunned, the father glanced toward his boy, and there in his hands was the magazine with the world pieced together perfectly. Amazed, the dad asked his child how he put the world together so quickly.

"It was simple," the boy said. "On the back of the world was a picture of a person, and once I put the person together, that's when the world came together."

When we see Jesus, the world comes together. If that father had taken a good look at Jesus, he would have put away his beer, and he would have modified his television watching so that he could give his son some much-needed attention. Our world is so fragmented because people don't see Jesus and live for Him. If everyone in our world could catch a vision of Jesus, of His love and concern for all humanity, the world would be a different place. There wouldn't be selfishness or hate or violence or promiscuity or war anymore. There would truly be peace on earth. Because when the people of the world see Jesus and respond to His love, the world will come together.

That's a summary of the apostle Paul's message in his epistle to the Romans. What he is virtually saying to us is, "Look to Jesus. He's the answer to the sin problem. He's the answer to your personal spiritual need. When you see Him and give Him your heart and life, you have forgiveness and peace of mind, and you have the power to live a truly meaningful, productive life."

Romans, chapter 1, tells us that everyone is a sinner in need of a Savior. Chapter 2 tells us how God judges human beings. People who, themselves, are not serving Christ are sometimes the most judgmental of others who are not serving Christ. God judges such judgmental people as guilty. Romans, chapter 2, verses 1–3, makes the point clearly:

"Therefore you are inexcusable, O man, whoever you are who judge, for in whatever you judge another you condemn yourself; for you who judge practice the same things. But we know that the judgment of God is according to truth against those who practice such things. And do you think this, O man, you who judge those practicing such things, and doing the same, that you will escape the judgment of God?"[1]

So God rejects self-righteous people, who themselves are not right with Him. Then Paul asks the crucial question: "Or do you despise the riches of His goodness, forbearance, and longsuffering, not knowing that the goodness of God leads you to repentance" (Romans 2:4)?[2] Sinful persons who are sitting in judgment on others may not be aware that God in His infinite love and goodness is waiting to give them the gift of repentance. You see, the Bible doesn't say you must repent *before* you can come to God. The Bible teaches that you come to Him just as you are, in all your sinful need, and He will then give you repentance. Repentance is true sorrow for sin and turning away from it. And repentance is not something you do for yourself. God makes us sorry for the past and gives us the power not to repeat past failures when we come to Him just as we are and accept Jesus Christ as our Savior and Lord.

Romans, chapter 2, verses 6–10, emphasizes that God judges all people according to their works. The passage reads: God " 'will render to each one according to his deeds': eternal life to those who by patient continuance in doing good seek for glory, honor, and immortality; but to those who are self-seeking and do not obey the truth, but obey unrighteousness—indignation and wrath, tribulation and anguish on every soul of man who does evil, of the Jew first and also of the Greek; but glory, honor, and peace to everyone who works what is good, to the Jew first and also to the Greek."[3]

So God decides whether we will be saved or lost on the basis of whether our works, our deeds, have been good or bad. But the Bible teaches that we are not saved by our works; we are saved by God's grace. Ephesians, chapter 2:8–10, makes the point: "For by grace you have been saved through faith, and that not of yourselves; it is the gift of God, not of works, lest anyone should boast. For we are His workmanship, created in Christ Jesus for good works, which God prepared beforehand that we should walk in them." So we are saved by grace and grace alone. But when we are saved by grace, we do works that God accepts as good. So, you see, when God judges us by our works, He is simply judging whether or not we have received His grace as the power to do good works. If we are saved by God's grace, our works will be good works. If we are not saved by God's grace, our works will be sinful works. That's why God judges us by our works.

But someone is sure to ask. What about people who do good works even though they have never heard or understood the good news about Jesus Christ? There are many in our world who have no idea that Jesus Christ bore the punishment for their sins on Calvary's cross. Is there no hope for these people? The apostle Paul answers that very question in verses 12–16 of Romans, chapter 2.

In a nutshell his message is that people who don't have the Bible and don't know about Jesus Christ may, in fact, be living up to all the light that God has been able to give them. Paul says, "For when Gentiles, who do not have the law [that is, the Bible], by nature do the things contained in the law, these, although not having the law, are a law to themselves, who show the work of the law written on their hearts, their conscience also bearing witness" (Romans 2:14, 15).

There are people who are serving God on the basis of the light given to them by the Holy Spirit, even though they have never heard a Christian preacher or had the chance to read the Bible. These people have the will of God written on their hearts by the Holy Spirit. And the Bible says, if they live up to all the knowledge God has given them, they are counted as believers and saved for eternity. They are judged on the basis of what understanding they have received. But if they reject the voice of the Holy Spirit and don't live up to the truth He has given them, they will be lost.[4]

Sometimes people are kind to others because the Holy Spirit is moving them to be kind, even though they haven't had the opportunity to accept the good news about Jesus Christ.

A young man named Kurt was a stock boy working in a supermarket. He was busily working when he heard a new voice over the speaker asking for a carry-out at check register 4. Kurt answered the call. As he approached the checkout stand a distant smile caught his eye. The new checkout girl was beautiful.

She was an older woman, maybe 26, and he was only 22, but he fell in love at first sight. Later that day, after his shift was over, he waited by the punch clock to find out her name. She came into the break room, smiled softly at him, took her card, punched out, and left. Then Kurt looked at her card. Her name was Brenda.

The next day, Kurt waited outside as she left the supermarket and offered her a ride home. He looked harmless enough, so she accepted. When he dropped her off, he asked if maybe he could see her again, outside of work. She simply said it wasn't possible. He pressed, and she explained that she had two children, and she couldn't afford a baby-sitter. He offered to pay for the baby-sitter. Reluctantly she accepted his offer for a date for the following Saturday night.

That Saturday night he arrived at her door only to have her tell him that she was unable to go with him because the baby-sitter had called and canceled. To which Kurt simply said, "Well, let's take the kids with us."

She tried to explain that taking the children was not an option, but again he pressed her, not taking no for an answer. Finally Brenda brought him inside to meet her children. She had a daughter who was just as cute as could be. Then Brenda brought out her son—in a wheelchair. He was born a paraplegic with Down Syndrome.

Kurt said, "I still don't understand why the kids can't come with us." Brenda was amazed. Most men would run away from a woman with two kids, especially if one had disabilities. That's what her first husband, the father of her children, had done.

Kurt and Brenda loaded up the kids in the car and went to dinner. When her son needed anything, Kurt would take care of him. When he needed to use the rest room, he picked him up out of his chair and took him. The kids loved Kurt.

Brenda and Kurt fell deeply in love, and a year later they were married. Kurt adopted both her children, and since then they have had two more kids.

So what became of the stock boy and the checkout girl? Well, Mr. and Mrs. Kurt Warner moved to St. Louis, where Kurt was employed by the St. Louis Rams as the quarterback. And he has given large amounts of money to organizations that are working for disabled children.

I have no idea whether or not Kurt is a professed Christian. But this I do know, that his kindness and unselfishness are motivated by the Holy Spirit of God. His works are giving evidence that Jesus has given him understanding, and he is following it.

Paul proceeds in Romans, chapter 2, to underline the point that Jews are just as sinful in the sight of God as Gentiles, and they have the same need of salvation that Gentiles have. Paul writes: "Indeed you are called a Jew, and rest on the law, and make your boast in God, and know His will, and approve the things that are excellent, being instructed out of the law, and are confident that you yourself are a guide to the blind, a light to those who are in darkness, an instructor of the foolish, a teacher of babes, having the form of knowledge and truth in the law. You, therefore, who teach another, do you not teach yourself? You who preach that a man should not steal, do you steal? You who say, 'Do not commit adultery,' do you commit adultery? You who abhor idols, do you rob temples? You who make your boast in the law, do you dishonor God through breaking the law? For 'the name of God is blasphemed among the Gentiles because of you,' as it is written" (Romans 2:17–24).

Paul's point is that all human beings are sinners in need of a Savior, whether they happen to be Gentiles or Jews. The Jews can't claim that they are superior because they are children of Abraham. Their salvation doesn't depend on their being descendants of Abraham. They are saved in exactly the same way that Gentiles are saved, by faith in Jesus Christ.

Paul tries to convince his Jewish brethren and sisters that following the stipulations of the ceremonial law does not save them. He writes: "For circumcision is indeed profitable if you keep the law; but if you are a breaker of the law, your circumcision has become uncircumcision" (Romans 2:25). For centuries the Israelites had practiced male circumcision as a religious rite. They tended to argue that because they were circumcised Israelites, they were saved, whereas the uncircumcised Gentiles were excluded from God's favor.

Paul tried to correct this misconception. He wrote: "Therefore, if an uncircumcised man keeps the righteous requirements of the law, will not his uncircumcision be counted for circumcision" (Romans 2:26)? In other words, if a Gentile who has not been circumcised obeys the requirements of the Ten Commandments, God will accept him despite the fact that he has not been circumcised—not because he is saved by works of law, but because his works give evidence that he is saved by grace.

Paul continues: "And will not the physically uncircumcised, if he fulfills the law, judge you who, even with your written code and circumcision, are a transgressor of the law?" The Israelites had the law of God, but many of them were not obeying it. Paul's point is that in that case their circumcision counted for nothing. The Gentile who was living by faith and obeying the law of God was accepted by God even though he was uncircumcised.

Then Paul makes a crucial point that goes to the heart of the issue. He writes: "For he is not a Jew who is one outwardly, nor is that circumcision which is outward in the flesh; but he is a Jew who is one inwardly, and circumcision is that of the heart, in the Spirit, and not in the letter; whose praise is not from men but from God" (Romans 2:28, 29). As far as God is concerned, the spiritual state of a person's heart is the important consideration. Outward circumcision was intended to be a ceremonial sign of a heart relationship with God. But if the heart relationship were lacking, outward circumcision as a religious rite was meaningless.

Paul's discussion raises the whole question of God's intention in giving circumcision as a religious ceremony in the first place. The first mention of circumcision in the Bible as a religious ceremony is in Genesis, chapter 17, which describes the covenant agreement between God and Abraham. God said to Abraham: "As for you, you shall keep My covenant, you and your descendants after you throughout their generations. This is My covenant which you shall keep, between Me and you and your descendants after you: Every male child among you shall be circumcised: and you shall be circumcised in the flesh of your foreskins, and it shall be a sign of the covenant between Me and you" (Genesis 17:9–11).

Paul tells us what this covenant between God and Abraham was all about. In Romans, chapter 4, verses 11 and 12, he writes: "And he [Abraham] received the sign of circumcision, a seal of the righteousness of the faith which he had while still uncircumcised, that he might be the father of all those who believe, though they are uncircumcised, that righteousness might be imputed to them also, and the father of circumcision to those who not only are of the circumcision, but who also walk in the steps of the faith which our father Abraham had while still uncircumcised."

Now that's a simple way of saying that the covenant agreement between God and Abraham was a righteousness-by-faith agreement. That means that because Abraham believed, God gave him the gift of righteousness. This involved three things: (1) Abraham's sins were forgiven; (2) God's righteousness was put to Abraham's account in heaven; and (3) God's righteousness was bestowed upon him by the gift of the Holy Spirit. This meant that Abraham had salvation before he was circumcised. So Abraham is the spiritual father of the Gentiles who also believe in God, even though they have not been circumcised. Then Abraham, who was already enjoying the gift of righteousness by faith, was given the rite of circumcision as a sign of the gift that he was enjoying. Thus Abraham was also the spiritual father of the Israelites, who practiced circumcision as a national sign of their covenant relationship with God.

Paul was at great pains to point out that now, because Christ has died, circumcision, like other aspects of the ceremonial law, has no significance for Christian believers. He wrote to the Galatian Christians: "For in Christ Jesus neither circumcision nor uncircumcision avails anything, but faith working through love" (Galatians 5:6).

Some dispensationalist Christians would have us believe that before the cross, people were saved by law keeping, whereas after the cross they are saved by faith. They would have us believe that this is why Paul speaks in Romans 2:29 of circumcision of the heart as the important experience. I would point out that God emphasized circumcision of the heart as His will for His people *before the cross.* Deuteronomy 10:16 records God as saying to His people: "Therefore circumcise the foreskin of your heart, and be stiff-necked no longer." Again in Deuteronomy, chapter 30, verse 6, we read: "And the Lord your God will circumcise your heart and the heart of your descendants, to love the Lord your God with all your heart and with all your soul, that you may live." Again in Jeremiah 4:4 we read: "Circumcise yourselves to the Lord, and take away the foreskins of your hearts, you men of Judah and inhabitants of Jerusalem."

The point is that circumcision of the heart was just as much an Old Testament teaching as it is a New Testament teaching. Circumcision of the heart is the new-birth experience (compare John, chapter 3). And in every era of history, God has wanted His people to believe in Him so that He could give them transformation of heart by the gift of the Holy Spirit.

As we look to Jesus, we see the Light of the world. When we accept Him as Savior and Lord, our hearts are transformed by the new-birth experience. We are born of the Spirit, and Jesus reigns supreme in our lives. This is what the Bible means by circumcision of the heart.

A pastor of a church on the coast of Scotland watched as the rain lashed against the window of his house. He knew he had a service to conduct that night, but he thought to himself, "Why go out tonight? There won't be a person there." It was one of the stormiest nights of the winter. But somehow he felt he must conduct that evening service. So he put on his raincoat, took his lantern, and stepped out into the blackness. The water almost blinded him as he plunged into the teeth of the gale.

On and up he plodded until he came to his church, which stood on a high hill along the Scottish coast. When he had opened the door, he set the lantern on a windowsill and then sat down to wait for his congregation to arrive. But no one came.

At last, seeing he would be quite alone, he sang a hymn and knelt and prayed. Then, his duty performed, he locked the church and went down the hill. Had it all been a waste of time? the pastor wondered. But the next morning he heard a different story. The night before, when the storm was at its worst, a fishing vessel had been trying to make the harbor. The skipper was floundering around in the blackness until he saw the small light in the old church.

Without that lantern shining its light over the sea, that little ship surely would have been carried onto the rocks. But thanks to those steady beams, the pilot had brought his boat safely to port. It was a lesson to the pastor. After that, he knew that any light he might throw into this world's darkness would never be entirely lost.

When we see the light of Jesus' love, when we see what He has done for us and realize what He is doing for us now, we can see our way to the harbor of salvation. Jesus is wanting you to look to Him and be saved. Outward ceremonies will never do. Mere profession of faith is not enough. Jesus wants your heart. He wants to come into your life and transform you by the wonderful gift of His Holy Spirit. Jesus wants to be your Savior right now today.

Endnotes

1. Compare Matthew 7:1–5 and Romans 14:10. We have no right to condemn others, since we are also guilty of sin.
2. Compare 2 Timothy 2:25 and Acts 5:31. Repentance includes both sorrow for sin and turning away from it. Repentance is not our achievement; it is God's gift.
3. Many passages of Scripture teach that God judges us by our works. (See Psalm 62:12; Matthew 16:27; 1 Peter 1:17; Revelation 20:12; 22:12.) Salvation is by grace alone; but God works in and through the believer

(Philippians 2:13; Galatians 2:20). Good works provide evidence that God's grace is present in the life (James 2:18).

4. Ellen G. White's writings emphasize the Bible teaching that some will be saved for eternity who never had the opportunity to read a Bible or hear a Christian preacher. See *Christ's Object Lessons*, p. 385; *The Desire of Ages*, p. 638.

Chapter Five

God's Solution to the Sin Problem

Romans 3

The true story is told of a thirteen-year-old farm boy who, walking home from school, fell and scratched his knee. He was a husky, healthy lad, and he didn't think anything of it and didn't say anything about it to anyone. But when he was crawling into bed that night in the room that he shared with his five brothers, he noticed a jab of pain from that knee. The next morning his leg was painful, but he ignored it, didn't tell anyone, and went about his farm chores as usual.

But by the weekend his leg ached so badly that he could hardly drag himself into the barn to do his chores. The whole family went off to church, but the boy couldn't go because his leg was so painful. When his mom and dad came home, his foot had swollen so much that they had to cut the shoe off his discolored leg. Obviously the knee was badly infected, and the infection was moving down the leg and up toward his thigh.

Mother bathed the knee and foot and thigh, applied poultices, and wiped the boy's sweating forehead with a moist, cool cloth. She had already lost one son, and she was determined not to lose this one. Finally she called the doctor. He looked at the boy's leg, pursed his lips, and said, "It's not likely we can save it!"

At that the boy sat up in bed and asked, "What does that mean?"

"It means," explained the doctor gently, "if things get worse, we'll have to amputate."

"No, you won't," shouted the boy, "I won't have it! I'd rather die!"

"The longer we wait, the more we will have to take off," urged the doctor.

"You won't take any off!" exclaimed the boy.

The doctor stalked out, nodding to the mother to follow him. As he stood in the hallway explaining to both parents what could and probably would happen, they could hear the boy calling for his brother: "Ed! Ed! Come up here, will you?"

Ed stomped in, and then they heard the sick lad's voice, high pitched with pain: "If I go out of my head, Ed, don't let them cut off my leg. Promise me, Ed—promise!"

In a moment Ed came out and ran to the kitchen. When he returned his mother said, "Ed, what's your brother asking for?"

"A fork!" Ed said, "to bite on, to keep him from screaming."

Then Ed stood outside the bedroom door, his arms folded. Quite clearly he was standing on guard. When the doctor appeared, Ed announced, "Nobody's going to saw off that leg!"

"But, Ed—you'll be sorry," gasped the doctor.

"Maybe so, Doc, but I gave him my word." And nothing changed that.

Ed stood his ground for two days and two nights, even sleeping at the threshold of the room, not even leaving to eat. And Mother and Father went along with Ed, because they were not convinced that amputation was necessary. The boy's fever mounted, and he babbled in torment. The discoloration of the swollen leg was creeping toward the pelvis, just as the doctor had predicted. But Ed remained firm. Once, in a helpless rage, the doctor shouted, "It's murder!" and slammed the front door as he left the house. Nothing but a miracle could save the boy now. Then the parents remembered. The sick boy's grandfather was a minister who always believed in healings wrought by faith. Now, in their desperate need, Mother, Father, and Ed went to their knees at the boy's bedside.

They prayed in turn constantly. They kept up a prayer vigil. And the other four brothers joined in. The next morning when the faithful doctor stopped by again, his experienced eye saw a sign. The swelling was going down! The doctor closed his eyes and offered a prayer of his own—a prayer of thanksgiving. But even after the boy dropped into a normal sleep, one member of the family after another kept the prayer vigil.

It was nightfall again and the lamps were lighted when the boy opened his eyes. The swelling was way down now, and the discoloration of the leg had almost faded. In three weeks—pale and weak, but with eyes clear and voice strong—the boy could stand up. And shortly he was able to begin life again.

That boy was Ike Eisenhower. If his parents and brothers had not prayed for God to heal him, you and I would probably never have heard of President Eisenhower.

You see, God is well able to heal physically. He doesn't always choose to heal in that way. But He often does. And not only can He heal physically but He can heal spiritually, and He is always willing to do that. When you think all is lost because you can't overcome your addictions and obsessions, God has the answer. He will give you the power to live a new life, with freedom from habits that have been destroying you. God's healing power is the answer to the sin problem.

And that's the message of Romans, chapter 3.[1] In this chapter, the apostle Paul summarizes his first major point in his epistle to the Romans. He reemphasizes that all human beings are sinners in need of a Savior. Jews and Gentiles, whoever they are, and wherever they are, need the power of God to save them from sin. And only through the sacrifice and atoning ministry of Jesus Christ can we be saved from sin and given the power to live as God has in mind for us.

Paul writes: "We have previously charged both Jews and Greeks that they are all under sin" (Romans 3:9). Then he adds a passage from Psalm 14 and Psalm 53. "There is none righteous, no, not one" (Romans 3:10).

What Paul means is that there is no person who does not know Christ as a personal Savior who is righteous. Righteousness is a gift from God to those who believe in Jesus Christ. Paul says it himself in Romans 1:17 (NRSV): "In it [that is, in the gospel] the righteousness of God is revealed through faith for faith; as it is written, 'The one who is righteous will live by faith.' "

That means that if you are living by faith, you are a righteous person; and if you are a righteous person, you are living by faith. Again Paul speaks of justified, born-again Christians in Romans 6:18: "Having been set free from sin, you became slaves of righteousness." That means that those who are justified, born again, are willing slaves of righteousness. Again in Romans 8:9, 10, Paul points out that the Holy Spirit in your heart is Christ in your heart, is righteousness in your heart.

So when Paul says in Romans 3:10 that "there is none righteous, no, not one," he means that there is no unjustified, unborn-again person who is righteous. But the believer in Jesus Christ who is indwelt by His Holy Spirit has the gift of His righteousness.[2]

Then in Romans 3:11, Paul adds: "There is none who understands." But elsewhere, Paul makes it clear that those who believe in Jesus Christ, who have His Holy Spirit as their Teacher and Guide, do understand the things of God. 1 Corinthians 2:10 says that God reveals His mysteries to us "through His Spirit." And in Ephesians 3:16–19, Paul says that he prays "that He would grant you, according to the riches of His glory, to be strengthened with might through His Spirit in the inner man, that Christ may dwell in your hearts through faith; that you, being rooted and grounded in love, *may be able to comprehend with all the saints* what is the width and length and depth and height—to know the love of Christ which passes knowledge; that you may be filled with all the fullness of God."

So believers who are indwelt by Christ's Holy Spirit do understand God's will and have the power to follow it. So when Paul says in Romans 3:11, "There is none who understands," he means that there is none who is not surrendered to Jesus Christ who understands.

Likewise when he says: "There is none who seeks after God" (Romans 3:11), he is referring to unjustified people who do not believe in Jesus Christ. And when he says in verse 12, "There is none who does good, no, not one," he is referring to unbelievers who do not have the power to do works that are good in the sight of God. But believers in Jesus Christ do have that power. 1 John 2:29 says: "If you know that He is righteous, you know that everyone who does righteousness has been born of him."[3] So the born-again Christian does works that in the sight of God are righteous.

Then in Romans 3, verses 13–18, Paul continues quoting the Old Testament to describe the lost state of those who have not accepted Jesus Christ as Savior and Lord. He writes: "Their throat is an open tomb; with their tongues they have practiced deceit; the poison of asps is under their lips; whose mouth is full of cursing and bitterness; their feet are swift to shed blood; destruction and misery are in their ways; and the way of peace they have not known. There is no fear of God before their eyes" (Romans 3:13–18; compare Psalms 5:9; 10:7; 36:1; 140:3; Proverbs 1:16; Isaiah 59:7, 8).

Apart from Jesus Christ, there is no peace or spiritual power or capacity to overcome sin. When Christ is not reigning in your heart, the devil is, and the result is addiction to sin and misery. But when Christ is reigning within, you have the power of His Holy Spirit to resist sin and to overcome it. If you are an alcoholic, Christ is the answer. If you struggle with drug use, Christ is the answer. If you are addicted to sex, Christ is the answer. If you are bitter or proud or selfish or dishonest, Christ will give you the victory. Because He died for you, He is constantly available as the source of the power to overcome.

Some years ago, there appeared in the streets of Los Angeles an old man with a long flowing beard and a kindly face claiming to be Jesus. A crowd gathered round, and some were ready to believe, but just then, in a nearby street, a Salvation Army band began to play that old gospel song, "I shall know him, I shall know him. … By the print of the nails in his hands." Someone shouted, "Show us your hands, old man!" Needless to say, the imposter fled.

Our Savior suffered on the cross for our sins, and He will always bear the marks in His hands. The Bible says that He "Himself bore our sins in His own body on the tree, that we, having died to sins, might live for righteousness—by whose stripes you were healed. For you were like sheep going astray, but have now returned to the Shepherd and Overseer of your souls" (1 Peter 2:24, 25).

Paul continues his discussion in Romans, chapter 3, by underlining that "all the world" is "guilty before God" (Romans 3:19). Then he reminds us that the law can't save us. He writes: "By the deeds of the law no flesh will be justified in His sight, for by the law is the knowledge of sin" (Romans 3:20). The law of God has an important function; it points out our sin, and it points us to Christ. But the law cannot save us.

Paul reiterated the point in His epistle to the Galatians. To them he wrote that a person "is not justified by the works of the law but by faith in Jesus Christ … for by the works of the law no flesh shall be justified" (Galatians 2:16). In Romans 7, Paul explained the true function of the law. It does not save, but it does point out sin. Paul wrote: "I would not have known sin except through the law. For I would not have known covetousness unless the law had said, 'You shall not covet' " (Romans 7:7).

The apostle James clarifies the point. In James, chapter 1, verses 22–25, the law is likened to a mirror. Just as you look into a mirror to see the dirt on your face, so you look to the law to see how far you are out of harmony with God. And just as a mirror can't wash your face, so the law cannot change your heart. The washing, the changing, must come from Jesus Christ who gives us the Holy Spirit to transform our lives. Speaking to those who believe in Jesus, the Bible says: "You were washed … you were sanctified … you were justified in the name of the Lord Jesus and by the Spirit of our God (1 Corinthians 6:11). So the law points out our sin and points us to Christ, but Christ does the washing and the changing.

The answer to the sin problem is powerfully explained in Romans 3:21–31. Those 11 verses are among the most important verses in the Bible. Verses 21 and 22 read: "But now the righteousness of God apart from the law is revealed, being witnessed by the Law and the Prophets, even the righteousness of God which is through faith in Jesus Christ to all and on all who believe. For there is no difference."

Paul means by justification the gift of the righteousness of God.[4] When you receive that gift you have present salvation in Christ. Justification and salvation are one and the same thing. The righteousness of God is revealed to our hearts by the Holy Spirit. 1 Corinthians 2:10 tells us that "God has revealed" divine truth "to us through His Spirit." This is how the righteousness of God is revealed. It is revealed to our hearts by the Holy Spirit when we accept Jesus Christ as Savior and Lord. First Corinthians 2:12 informs us: "We have received, not the spirit of the world, but the Spirit who is from God, that we might know the things that have been freely given to us by God."

Throughout the Bible many passages indicate that God's righteousness is given to those who believe. For example, Job 29:14 reads: "I put on righteousness, and it clothed me; My justice was like a robe and a turban." It was the righteousness of God that he put on, and wearing it meant salvation. Isaiah testified to having the same experience. He wrote: "I will greatly rejoice in the Lord, my soul shall be joyful in my God; for He has clothed me with the garments of salvation, He has covered me with the robe of righteousness" (Isaiah 61:10).

The apostle John wrote: "He who does righteousness is righteous, just as He is righteous" (1 John 3:7). But how could we be righteous like God? The answer is that God takes up residence in our hearts by the Holy Spirit when we believe, and because the Holy Spirit is righteous, we have righteousness in our hearts. Paul wrote: "I have been crucified with Christ; it is no longer I who live, but Christ lives in me; and the life which I now live in the flesh I live by faith in the Son of God, who loved me and gave Himself for me" (Galatians 2:20). Christ is Holy, and Christ lives in the believer by the presence of the Holy Spirit. Jesus promised that the Father and the Son will come to the believer and make their home with him or her (John 14:23).

So the whole Bible supports Paul's belief that when we have faith in Jesus Christ, the righteousness of God is for us and upon us (Romans 3:22).

Then Paul adds: "For all have sinned and fall short of the glory of God" (Romans 3:23). That means that all have sinned in the past, and all are now falling short of the glory of God.[5] Our past sins are forgiven by Jesus Christ (Acts 13:38, 39). Yet we are still falling short of the glory of God because we are imperfect, fallen human beings; everything we do is tinged with human imperfection.

Even so, it is important to understand the Bible teaching that all sin is imperfection, but not all imperfection is sin. Everything we do is imperfect, but not everything we do is sin. Sin is turning away from the will of God. Sin is choosing to disobey God. Because my writing and speaking are tinged with human imperfection, it doesn't mean that my writing and speaking are sin. The Bible says that "whatever is not from faith is sin" (Romans 14:23). That means that if our works are done by faith in God, if they are motivated and guided by the Holy Spirit, even though they are tinged with human imperfection, they are not sin. Martin Luther put it biblically when he wrote: "Works that result from the Word and are done in faith are perfect in the eyes of God, no matter what the world thinks about them"[6]

Paul continues his discussion in Romans 3 by telling us in verse 24 that we are "justified freely by His grace through the redemption that is in Christ Jesus." That means that justification is the gift of God's grace. And it is vital to understand that the gift of grace is the gift of spiritual power. Over and over again in the Bible, God's grace is depicted as His power given to the person who believes in Jesus Christ.[7] For example, consider 1 Corinthians, chapter 1, verses 4 and 5: "I thank my God always concerning you for the grace of God which was given to you by Christ Jesus, that you were enriched in everything by Him in all utterance and all knowledge." And verse 7 adds: "So that you come short in no gift, eagerly waiting for the revelation of our Lord Jesus Christ." So grace enriches us spiritually; grace gives us knowledge, and grace prepares us spiritually to meet Jesus when He comes the second time.

Justification is the gift of grace. Justification involves three things: (1) the forgiveness of our sins (Acts 13:38, 39); (2) the righteousness of God counted for us in heaven and bestowed upon us (Romans 4)[8]; and (3) the righteousness of God bestowed upon us by the gift of the Holy Spirit (Titus 3:5–7).[9] This justification, which is a gift of God's grace, is what makes us right with God. Our sins are forgiven, God's righteousness is counted for us, and God's righteousness is bestowed upon us.

Romans 3:25 and 26 make the point that God gave His Son to die for our sins "to demonstrate at the present time His righteousness, that He might be righteous, and the one who declares and makes righteous the one who has faith in Jesus."[10]

Then Paul emphasizes that the believer can never boast about his works (Romans 3:27). Since righteousness is God's gift to the one who has faith, works of righteousness result from God working through us. Without Jesus such works would be impossible. Paul concludes that a person "is justified by faith apart from the deeds of the law" (Romans 3:28). But does that mean that the believer does not have to keep God's law? Verse 31 answers that question categorically: "Do we then make void the law through faith? Certainly not! On the contrary, we establish the law" (Romans 3:31). Romans 10:8 tells us that the law of God is written on the heart of the one who believes in Jesus. And Hebrews 8:10 informs us that God's law written on our hearts is the new covenant experience.

In summary we can say: (1) Justification is being made right with God; it results from the righteousness of God being counted for and bestowed upon the believer; (2) justification is by faith/grace alone; it is the free gift of God's grace to the one who believes; (3) justification results in obedience to the law of God.

Some years ago a boy quarreled with his father and left home. He said, "You'll never see me again!" Three tough years passed. He wanted to go home, but he was afraid. Would his father let him come back? He wrote to his mother, told her that he would be on a certain train as it passed the house. He asked her to hang something white in the yard if it was all right with his dad for him to come home.

The boy was nervous on the train. A minister noticed and asked what was wrong. The boy told him the whole story. They rode along together as the boy looked out the window. Suddenly he started up excitedly. "Look, sir, my house is just around the next bend, beyond the hill. Will you please look out the window for me to see if there is anything white hanging in the yard? I just can't stand to look!" Then the boy put his head in his hands.

The train lurched a bit as it made a slow curve, and the minister kept his eyes on the round of the hill. Then he forgot his dignity as he shouted, "Look, son, look!"

There was the little farmhouse under the trees. But you could hardly see the house for white. It seemed that those lonely parents had taken every white sheet in the house, everything they could find that was white, and had hung it out on the clothesline and on the trees!

The boy got off the train in the town, walked home, and there was an emotional reunion as mother, father, and son got their tears all mixed up together.

Our loving heavenly Father is calling you to come home. He opens his arms wide to receive you. All the love of heaven is extended to you if only you will come to Jesus and allow Him to come into your heart by the Holy Spirit. He will forgive all your sins and mistakes. He will count His perfect righteousness for you, and He will bestow His righteousness upon you by the gift of His Holy Spirit. Our loving heavenly Father is waiting to welcome you home. Come home, dear friend, come home right now!

Endnotes

1. The first two verses of Romans 3 underline the fact that the words or oracles (*logia*) of God were entrusted to the Jews. The next two verses make the point that the Jews' failure does not destroy God's faithfulness; He is perfectly righteous and just. God is *justified* (v. 4) in the sense that He is declared to be exactly what He is, perfectly righteous. (Compare 2 Timothy 4:8; 1 John 2:1; Revelation 16:5, 7; 19:2.) Romans 3:5–8 emphasize that, by contrast, our unrighteousness "recommends," "commends," "shows," "proves," "demonstrates" (*sunistemi*) the righteousness of God. But this does not justify our sin. We do not do evil so that good may result.
2. Romans 3:10 is clearly speaking of all humanity *before* belief in Christ. After justification, believers have the gift of Christ's righteousness (Compare Romans 6:18; 8:10; 9:30; 10:6–10; Isaiah 51:1, 7; 61:3, 10, 11).
3. My literal translation. The Greek of 1 John 2:29 reads: "ean eidete hoti dikaios estin, ginoskete hoti kai pas ho poion ten dikaiosunen ex autou gegennetai." "If you know that He is righteous, you know also that everyone who does righteousness has been born of Him." The born-again Christian does works that in God's sight are righteous. Compare 1 John 3:7: "Little children, let no one deceive you; he who does righteousness is righteous, just as He is righteous." In Romans 3:10–18, Paul is referring to people who are not justified, not born again. They are unrighteous, outside of Christ, having no desire for God or reverence for His ways. But the new birth changes lives; the righteousness of God is put to the account of believers and bestowed upon them by the presence and power of the Holy Spirit.
4. The gift of God's righteousness is what Paul means by justification (Romans 2:20, 21). Inspired Bible writers bear witness that God's righteousness is bestowed upon those who believe. (Compare Job 29:14; Psalm 37:30, 31; 132:9; Isaiah 32:15–17; 61:10, 11; 1 John 2:29; 3:7; Revelation 3:5; 19:7, 8.)
5. The first verb in Romans 3:23 is *hemarton*, which is in the aorist tense, or past tense. It may be translated "sinned," or "have sinned." The second verb in the text is in the present tense, *husterountai*. The present tense in New Testament Greek is very often a continuous tense. Hence this second verb may be translated, "are falling short," or "are continuously falling short." The point of the text is that we have all sinned in the past, and in the present we are still falling short of the glory of God. Even when we are

not sinning, we are falling short of the glory of God. We partially partake of God's glory now when we believe in Christ (Romans 2:7, 10; 9:4, 23), but we are seeking and anticipating the full glory of God bestowed upon us at the second coming of Jesus (Romans 5:2; 8:18). Because we remain fallen, imperfect human beings even after justification, because all our good works are tinged with human imperfection, we fall short of God's glory when we are not sinning. Only when we are ultimately glorified at Christ's return will we not fall short of God's glory.

6. *Luther's Works* (St. Louis, Mo: Concordia, 1961), vol. 3, p. 318.

7. Grace is the undeserved gift of God's power that transforms the life. (See 1 Corinthians 1:4–9; 15:10; 2 Corinthians 8:1, 2; 9:8, 14; Galatians 2:9; 2 Timothy 2:1; Hebrews 13:9; 2 Peter 3:18.)

8. See chapter 2, endnote 2.

9. See chapter 2, endnote 3. Compare Paul's discussion in Galatians 2 and 3. Galatians 2:16 ff. defines justification as God's saving act, which is available by faith/grace, not by our works. Then in Galatians 3:3, Paul reminds the Galatians that they began "in the Spirit." They began with justification (Galatians 2:16 ff.). Paul never separates the saving work of the Spirit from justification, as some try to do. Compare Galatians 3:5–9. The discussion is justification by the Spirit. Then in verse 14, Paul adds, "… that the blessing of Abraham might come upon the Gentiles in Christ Jesus, that we might receive the promise of the Spirit through faith." The blessing of Abraham was justification (Galatians 5:6; Romans 4). In justification, Abraham received the promise of the Spirit by faith. And we may have the same wonderful gift.

10. My translation. Romans 3:26 uses the noun "righteousness" (*dikaiosunes*), the adjective "righteous" (*dikaion*), and the participle of the verb "to make righteous and declare righteous" (*dikaiounta*). The lexical meaning of the verb "to justify" (*dikaioo*) is "to be acquitted, be pronounced and treated as righteous and thereby become *dikaios*, receive the gift of *dikaiosune*. … *dikaioo make free* or *pure*." (Arndt and Gingrich, *A Greek-English Lexicon of the New Testament*). Romans 3:26 translates: "… to show His *righteousness* at the present time, so that He might be *righteous* and the one who *makes and declares righteous* (or *righteouses*) those who believe in Jesus."

Chapter Six

What is Imputed Righteousness?

Romans 4

We continue our study by considering the teaching of Romans, chapter 4. This is Paul's discussion of imputed righteousness. The questions we need to ask Paul are: (1) What does he mean by imputed righteousness? Is this a purely legal concept, or is he talking about something that happens in our hearts? (2) How does Paul's message of Romans 4 relate to other passages in his writings that speak of righteousness by faith in Christ?

So far in our study of Romans, we have discovered that Paul defines justification as salvation. When we are justified by faith in Christ, God does three things for us: (1) Our past sins are forgiven; (2) the perfect righteousness of Christ is counted for us; (3) the righteousness of Christ is bestowed upon us by the gift of the Holy Spirit to our hearts.

A wealthy man coming home from abroad was distinctly annoyed when he was assessed a high import fee for a plain amber necklace he had purchased for a small amount in a Paris curio shop. In his annoyance, he determined to discover the reason for the high duty imposed on the necklace. He took the necklace to a competent jeweler in New York City. After a brief examination, the jeweler removed his eyepiece and approached the man. He said: "I'll give you $25,000 for the necklace."

The man was amazed. He pocketed the necklace and left. Sometime later he was in Chicago, and while there, decided to consult another authority on necklaces. He took his amber necklace to a prominent jeweler and asked him for an estimate of its value. This time the necklace was painstakingly scrutinized under the glass. The jeweler then turned to his client, and said: "I will give you $35,000 for that necklace."

The man couldn't conceal his curiosity any longer. He asked the jeweler what there was about that common-looking necklace that made it so valuable. The jeweler replied by handing him the eyepiece and asking him to look at the amber heads. As he did so, the astonished man read these words, "From Napoleon to Josephine." That necklace was the gift of a famous man to the woman he loved.

What value would you put on Christ's gift of His righteousness and salvation to us? Would you say it is worth $35,000, or perhaps even a million dollars? The fact is that Christ's gift to us, made possible by His death on the cross, is of inestimable value. It is the gift of the greatest Man who ever lived, and the gift of the God of the universe, because Jesus Christ is both. And it is His gift to those He loves. But this gift must be received. The Bible says that "those who receive the abundance of grace and the gift of righteousness will reign in life through the One, Jesus Christ (Romans 5:17). Christ's gift to us means we can have eternal life. And who would be so foolish as to turn down such a fabulous gift? Because of His love for you and me, Jesus Christ gave His life on Calvary's cross, and He now offers us the gift of His righteousness and the gift of eternal life. All He is asking is that we open our hearts and receive His gift.

That's the subject of Romans, chapter 4. In this chapter, Paul uses Abraham as the example of what happens to people when they receive Christ's gift of righteousness and salvation. Paul begins by asking: "What then shall we say that Abraham, our forefather according to the flesh, has found?" (Romans 4:1, NASB). The fact is that Abraham had found something wonderful, but it was not something he earned for himself; it was something God bestowed upon him because he had faith. So Paul adds: "If Abraham was justified by works, he has something of which to boast, but not before God. For what does the Scripture say?" (Romans 4:2, 3). Paul quotes Genesis 15:6, "Abraham believed God, and it was accounted to him for righteousness."[1]

Paul's point is that Abraham was not made right with God because of any works of his own. Abraham couldn't possibly earn God's favor. And nor can we. We are not justified, made right with God, because of our good works. We have sinned in the past, and nothing we could ever do could wipe out our guilt. Only faith in Jesus results in our being made free from guilt and in our being made right with God. Abraham understood that. That's why he believed God, and then God was able to give him the gift of His righteousness. When God "accounted" Abraham righteous, he legally counted him to be that which he simultaneously made him. God declared Abraham righteous and at the same moment gave him the gift of righteousness by the presence of the Holy Spirit in his heart.

That's what Paul explained to the Galatian Christians. He made it clear that "the blessing of Abraham" can "come upon the Gentiles in Christ Jesus, that we might receive the promise of the Spirit through faith" (Galatians 3:14). The blessing of Abraham was justification by faith. And Abraham received this blessing when God bestowed the Holy Spirit upon him. And we too may have this blessing when we receive the gift of the Holy Spirit through faith. So when God justified Abraham, when he made Abraham right with Himself, he declared him to be righteous and at the same moment made him righteous by bestowing the Holy Spirit upon him. And God does the same thing for you and me. You believe in Jesus and accept Him as your Savior and Lord, and God says, "I count the righteousness of Jesus for you. I declare you righteous in Christ, and I make you righteous by giving you the same blessing I gave to Abraham, the gift of the Holy Spirit." So the righteousness of Jesus is counted for you in heaven, and at the same moment the righteousness of Jesus is bestowed upon you by the gift of the Holy Spirit.

Now that's God's inestimable gift to us. That gift means that we are made right with God, and we have the assurance of eternal life.

The Swedish Nightingale, Jenny Lind, was a famous operatic singer. She was loved and appreciated wherever she sang. Money poured into her purse. Yet she left the stage when singing her best and never went back to it. She must have missed the fame and the applause of thousands. But she was content to live in privacy.

Once an English friend found her sitting by the seashore, with a Bible on her knee, looking out into the glory of the sunset. They talked, and the conversation led to the inevitable question. "Madam, how is it that you ever came to abandon the stage at the very height of your success?"

The famous woman quietly answered: "When every day it made me think less of this [laying a finger on the Bible] and nothing at all of that [pointing to the sunset], what else could I do?"

Do you get the point? Money and fame were of less importance to Jenny Lind than the fabulous value of God's gift of righteousness and salvation. And that's exactly how it should be. If something on earth, or some person on earth, takes you away from Jesus Christ and what He is offering you, the choice should be very simple. Nothing and no one should ever separate us from the Savior who loves us so much that He bestows Himself upon us by the Holy Spirit and gives us the assurance of eternal life!

Then Paul draws an interesting comparison. He writes: "Now to him who works, the wages are not counted as grace but as debt. But to him who does not work but believes on Him who justifies the ungodly, his faith is accounted for righteousness" (Romans 4:4, 5).

The first point in the comparison is a reference to the person who works for money. You have a job. You work for a salary. Your wages are counted, reckoned, or imputed to you as something that is owed to you. When you work for an employer, the employer is in your debt. He must pay you the wages that he has agreed to pay. That is what Paul means by wages as imputed, or reckoned, because they have been earned.

The second half of Paul's comparison refers to the believer in Christ whose "faith is accounted for righteousness." The believer does not and cannot work for Christ's righteousness. It can't be earned. It can only be received as a free gift. Wages earned are imputed, reckoned, or counted as something owed to you. But Christ's gift of righteousness is imputed, reckoned, or counted as a free gift. There is a legal accounting in both cases. But the legal accounting results in wages paid to the person who has worked for wages, while God's legal accounting results in the free gift of righteousness to the person who has faith in Jesus Christ. The counting, or imputation, results in an actual gift in both cases. The only difference is that in the first case the gift is earned, while in the second case the gift is free.

In fact, Paul uses the same Greek verb in Romans 4:4 that he uses in verse 5. The verb is *logizomai.* It may be translated, "counted," "reckoned," or "imputed." Paul's point is that the imputation of Christ's righteousness is a legal accounting of a tangible gift. God never declares you righteous without making you so. If God declared something that wasn't true, He would be a liar. If He declared us righteous without making us so, that would be legal fiction. God doesn't say, as some people think, that He declares you righteous in heaven, even though you remain unrighteous on earth. God doesn't say that now that He has declared you righteous, you can sin to your heart's content and you will be saved anyway. Something happens in heaven, and at the same moment something happens in your heart. The thing that happens in heaven is that God declares you righteous in Christ. The thing that happens in your heart is that God bestows the righteousness of Christ upon you by the gift of the Holy Spirit. Imputation of righteousness is a legal declaration of a tangible gift. And that gift of righteousness is the gift of spiritual power.

I can illustrate that by reference to an Old Testament passage. The passage is 2 Samuel, chapter 4, verse 2. The latter part of the verse says: "Beeroth is reckoned to Benjamin." Now the interesting point is that Beeroth was a town that was given to the tribe of Benjamin. The text in the Greek Old Testament uses the same verb that is used in Romans, chapter 4. Beeroth was reckoned, counted, imputed, to the tribe of Benjamin. When the Israelites were dividing up the land between the various tribes, they sat in a committee and decided that the town Beeroth would be imputed, or reckoned, to the tribe of Benjamin. That was a legal decision. But it was a legal decision that involved the actual gift of the town Beeroth to the tribe of Benjamin. So the legal decision was accompanied by an actual, tangible gift.

That is exactly how Paul is using the verb "impute" in Romans, chapter 4. You believe in Jesus; God then legally decides that Jesus' righteousness will be counted, or imputed, to you. That imputation means that God legally counts that which is an actual gift. Imputation is a legal accounting of an actual gift. God declares you righteous in Christ, and at the same moment makes you so by bestowing the righteousness of Jesus upon you by the gift of the Holy Spirit.

The story is told of a grandfather who found his grandson jumping up and down in his playpen, crying at the top of his voice. When Johnnie saw his grandfather, he reached up his little chubby hands and said, "Out, Gramp, out." The grandfather reached down to lift the little fellow out of his predicament; but as he did, the mother of the child stepped up and said, "No, Johnnie, you are being punished, so you must stay in." Johnny had been a naughty boy, and Mother insisted that he remain in his playpen for a while.

The grandfather was at a loss to know what to do. The child's tears and chubby hands reached deep into his heart, but the mother's firmness in correcting her son for misbehavior must not be taken lightly. Here was a problem of love versus law, but love found a way. The grandfather couldn't take the youngster out of the playpen, so he crawled in with him.

And that's what Jesus did. The only way He could save us was to become one of us. He crawled in with us, became a Man, and showed us how to live and how to die. And more than that, He bore our sins in His body on the cross (1 Peter 2:24). His sacrifice for us made it possible for Him to make us like Himself. Now He is able to bestow His righteousness, His purity upon us by bestowing the Holy Spirit upon us. That's what Romans, chapter 4, is talking about. It's telling us that, because of Jesus' suffering on the cross, we are both declared and made righteous when we accept Jesus as Savior and Lord.

This same wonderful experience, Paul reminds us, is for both Jews and Gentiles. All humanity is saved by Christ in the same way (Romans 4:6–12). And this salvation cannot be earned by law keeping. Romans 4:13, 14 reads: "For the promise that he would be the heir of the world was not to Abraham or to his seed through the law, but through the righteousness of faith. For if those who are of the law are heirs, faith is made void and the promise made of no effect."

Elsewhere Paul explains that the law of God has an important function. It is designed to point out our sin and point us to Christ. But it is not designed to save us from sin.[2] The law is the divine standard of righteousness, but the means by which we arrive at the standard is the free gift of God's grace, as verse 16 of Romans 4 points out: "Therefore it is of faith that it might be according to grace, so that the promise might be sure to all the seed, not only to those who are of the law, but also to those who are of the faith of Abraham, who is the father of us all."

Then Paul refers to Abraham's fathering Isaac when he was about one hundred years old. God had promised Abraham and Sarah that they would have a son in their old age. And they believed the promise. Romans 4:19–22 reads: "And not being weak in faith, he [Abraham] did not consider his own body, already dead (since he was about a hundred years old), and the deadness of Sarah's womb. He did not waver at the promise of God through unbelief, but was strengthened in faith, giving glory to God, and being fully convinced that what He had promised He was also able to perform. And therefore 'it was accounted to him for righteousness.' "

God had promised Abraham that this son born in his old age would be the ancestor of the Messiah. The Lord told him: "In you all the families of the earth shall be blessed" (Genesis 12:3). And this was the good news that the Messiah would come as one of Abraham's descendants, and that because of the work of the Messiah, the sins of the whole world would be atoned for.

Galatians 3:8 says: "And the Scripture, foreseeing that God would justify the nations by faith, preached the gospel to Abraham beforehand, saying, 'In you all the nations shall be blessed.' " So the promise of the coming Messiah as one of his descendants was the gospel to Abraham.

Abraham believed the gospel. He believed in the Messiah to come. Hence, he believed that God would give him a son in his old age who would be the ancestor of the coming Messiah. And because Abraham believed God's promises, the righteousness of God was given to him. That meant that Abraham was made right with God. His sins were forgiven, the righteousness of Christ was put to his account, and the righteousness of Christ was bestowed upon him by the gift of the Holy Spirit.

Then Paul adds the beautiful truth that we may have the same experience. He writes: "Now it was not written for his sake alone that it was imputed to him, but also for us. It shall be imputed to us who believe in him who raised up Jesus our Lord from the dead, who was delivered up because of our offenses, and was raised because of our justification" (Romans 4:23–25).

So when we believe the good news that Jesus Christ died for our sins, and when we believe that He was raised from the dead and became our heavenly High Priest and Mediator, we enjoy the same spiritual experience that God gave to Abraham. We can be saved from sin and made right with God just as surely as Abraham was made right with God.

All this depends on our willingness to accept and to exercise the faith of Jesus. Faith is God's gift to us when we respond to the convicting voice of the Holy Spirit. So when we cry out for God to deliver us from sin, and when we believe in Jesus as our Deliverer, the Lord comes into our hearts and gives us salvation. The Bible says: "This is the victory that has overcome the world—our faith" (1 John 5:4). Just as Abraham received God's gift of salvation by faith, so we may have that gift right now. But we must daily look to Jesus so that we can constantly receive His power and His presence in our lives. The secret of spiritual power and victory is to look always to Jesus. He is our Savior, our Lord, our ever-present Friend. He is the only one who can enable us to overcome our sinful obsessions and live as God wants us to live.

A ragged boy with a violin under his arm once roamed the streets of a great European city. Because he had no home or family, he wandered from place to place for food and shelter. This urchin had a strange gift for music. He had somehow come into possession of a violin, and he would stand on the street corners and play for the passing crowd. They were entranced by what they heard and would gather around to listen. When he had finished playing, they would toss some coins at his feet. In this way he made an honest but meager living.

In the same city was a famous musician. One day he happened to pass by the place where the ragged boy was playing. His attention was arrested by the unusual quality of the music. He lingered until the crowd had passed on and then said to the little violin player, "Son, to whom do you belong?"

"I don't belong to anybody," the boy answered.

"Well, where do you live?" was the next question.

"I don't have any place to live. I just sleep on the streets and wherever I can."

The man thought for a moment and then said, "How would you like to be my boy and come to live with me? I'll teach you all I know about how to play the violin."

The boy's eyes sparkled through the dirt and grime, and he said, "Mister, I'd love it!"

So the great musician took him to his own home. He had him cleaned up and dressed up, and the man became like a father to him. For several years he poured into the eager young mind and heart all that he knew about playing the violin.

Finally, the boy was ready for his first public recital, and the word went out that a great new musical prodigy was about to appear on the concert stage. On the night of the performance the hall was filled to capacity; even the balcony was packed.

At last the boy came out, put the violin beneath his chin, and began his concert. He played such music as the crowd had never heard before. At every pause there was deafening applause.

For some reason, however, the boy didn't seem to pay any attention to the ovation. He kept his eyes turned upward and played on and on. The audience was mystified by his strange manner. Finally one of the persons present said, "I don't understand why he is so insensible to all this thunderous applause. He keeps looking up all the time. I'm going to find out what is attracting his attention!"

Moving about in the concert hall, the observer found the answer. There in the topmost balcony was the old music master, peering over the banister toward his young pupil. He was nodding his head and smiling, as if to say, "You are doing well, my boy; play on!"

And the boy did play on, not seeming to care about the applause that came from the audience at the end of every piece. He kept his gaze upward. He was playing to please the master only.

That's the Bible message! We don't have to look to the crowd around us for approval; we must look to Jesus. He is our Master. He saves us, changes us, teaches us, molds us. He is the One we have to please. And by faith in Him and trust in His power, we can achieve as He wants us to achieve. Then whether or not the world around us applauds is irrelevant. "Turn your eyes upon Jesus. Look full in His wonderful face. And the things of earth will grow strangely dim in the light of His glory and grace."

Endnotes

1. Paul quotes Genesis 15:6 that reads, "And he believed in the Lord, and He accounted it to him for righteousness." The verb "accounted" is a translation of the Hebrew word *chashav.* In Paul's quotation of Genesis 15:6 in Romans 4:3 that verb is translated by the Greek verb *logizomai.* Both the Hebrew and Greek verbs have a range of meanings in the Hebrew and Greek Bibles. In short those words mean, "to impute," "to count," "to reckon."

   Did God impute to Abraham that which was not experientially so? Or was the imputation a declaration of the gift of righteousness that God simultaneously bestowed upon Abraham? In answer to those questions we must consider the uses of both *chashav* and *logizomai* throughout the Hebrew and Greek Bibles.

The verb "to impute" is sometimes used in the sense of regarding (considering, counting) a person to be something that he is not. In every instance in which the verb is so used, human error is involved. God is never said to impute something that is not so. Rachel and Leah complained that Laban regarded (counted, imputed) them as foreigners (Genesis 31:15). The imputation was a lie. Judah thought (counted) Tamar to be a professional harlot, even though she was not (Genesis 38:15). Eli thought (counted, imputed) Hannah drunk, but she was not (1 Samual 1:13). Job thought that God counted him as His enemy, but He did not (Job 13:24; 19:11).

The verb "to impute" in some instances refers to people being regarded as exactly what they are. Nehemiah's treasurers were "counted faithful" because they were (Nehemiah 13:13). Israel was not reckoned among the nations because it comprised the unique people of God (Numbers 23:9). The Emim were counted as giants because they were giants (Deuteronomy 2:11, 20). Job counted his comforters as stupid because they were (Job 18:3). Phinehas was counted as righteous because he was (Psalm 106:30, 31; compare Numbers 25:10–13).

The nonimputation of iniquity is forgiveness of sin (compare Psalm 32:1, 2 with Romans 4:6–8).

The verb "to impute" on occasions is used in the Old Testament to designate a tangible gift, or the specification of actual ownership. The tithe imputed to the priests was an actual gift of produce to them, one-tenth of which they paid as tithe and nine-tenths of which they and their families consumed (Numbers 18:27, 30). Joshua 13:3 mentions land "reckoned as Canaanite." The Lord had given it all to Israel but because of their failure to drive out the Philistines it was still in their hands. It was reckoned (imputed) to the people who were in actual possession of it. Second Samuel 4:2 records that the town Beeroth was "reckoned to Benjamin." In fact, the tribe of Benjamin owned that town because in the distribution of the property it had been given to them (compare Joshua 9:17; 18:21–25). The imputation was a tangible bestowal of property.

God did not count Abraham to be something that he was not. The imputation of righteousness to Abraham was the genuine bestowal of the righteousness of God upon him. It became his righteousness, not in the sense of a quality independent of a union with God, but in the sense of God's own indwelling in Abraham's life, so that his behavior became a genuine reflection of the righteousness of God. God declared Abraham to be what he simultaneously made him, righteous.

2. Romans 3:20; 5:20, 21; Galatians 3:24, 25.

Chapter Seven

Peace with God

Romans 5

Charlotte Deveny was eleven and her sister, Elizabeth, was thirteen. They had the privilege of going to a concert by the famous violinist Fritz Kreisler. He played some of his own compositions, melodies the girls knew, but they had never heard them played like this before. As they left the concert hall, their hearts were dancing to the beautiful tunes they had just heard.

Turning the corner of the building as they left, they ran into Charlotte's cello teacher, Ennio Bolognini. He asked how they had liked the concert, and they raved about it. Then he told them that he was having dinner with Mr. Kreisler, and they could come along if they would like. If they would like? There was nothing in the world they would like better! But there was a problem. Their mother expected them to come home right after the concert, and they were already late.

Elizabeth and Charlotte decided that if they had their teacher call and talk to their mother, she couldn't refuse. They rode over to Mario's, a nearby restaurant, and Mr. Kreisler soon arrived. Charlotte dialed home and put her teacher on the line. Soon the teacher came to the girls with the news that their mother said they were to come home immediately. They couldn't understand. They were sure she would let them stay.

Within the hour, they were home and rushed into the house. "Why didn't you let us stay, Mother?" they cried. "Why didn't you let us stay? We were going to have dinner with Fritz Kreisler."

"What? You were going to have dinner with Fritz Kreisler? Why didn't you tell me this yourself? Because of your teacher's accent, I couldn't understand a word he was saying, so I told him you girls should come home NOW!"

"But, Mother," they moaned, "we almost had dinner with Fritz Kreisler!"

It was almost, but not quite! And there are many times in life when we almost have wonderful experiences, but we miss out because of some mistake of our own or because some person or some set of events stands in our way.

It was like that for King Agrippa before whom the apostle Paul, as a prisoner, made his defense. Paul told the king how he found Christ, or better still, how Christ found him. Paul narrated: "As I journeyed to Damascus with authority and commission from the chief priests, at midday, O king, along the road I saw a light from heaven, brighter than the sun, shining around me and those who journeyed with me. And when we all had fallen to the ground, I heard a voice speaking to me and saying in the Hebrew language, 'Saul, Saul, why are you persecuting Me?' So I said, 'Who are You, Lord?' And He said, 'I am Jesus, whom you are persecuting. But rise and stand on your feet; for I have appeared to you for this purpose, to make you a minister and a witness both of the things which you have seen and of the things which I will yet reveal to you. I will deliver you from the Jewish people, as well as from the Gentiles, to whom I now send you, to open their eyes and to turn them from darkness to light, and from the power of Satan to God, that they may receive forgiveness of sins and an inheritance among those who are sanctified by faith in Me.'

"Therefore, King Agrippa, I was not disobedient to the heavenly vision, but declared first to those in Damascus and in Jerusalem, and throughout all the region of Judea, and then to the Gentiles, that they should repent, turn to God, and do works befitting repentance" (Acts 26:12–20).

While Paul spoke, King Agrippa was deeply moved and convicted. The Spirit of God was speaking to his heart, telling him that Paul was truly a man of God, and that Jesus of Nazareth was, indeed, the Messiah. The Spirit was telling him that he should be one of those to respond, confess his sins, repent, and surrender his life to Jesus Christ.

"Then King Agrippa said to Paul, 'You almost persuade me to become a Christian.' And Paul said, 'I would to God that not only you, but also all who hear me today, might become both almost and altogether such as I am, except for these chains.' " (Acts 26:28, 29).

You see, Agrippa was almost persuaded, almost, but lost.

"Almost persuaded now to believe;
Almost persuaded Christ to receive,
Seems now some soul to say,
'Go, Spirit, go Thy way,
Some more convenient day
On Thee I'll call.'

Almost persuaded; harvest is past;
Almost persuaded; doom comes at last!
'Almost' cannot avail;
'Almost' is but to fail!
Sad, sad the bitter wail,
'Almost — but lost!"

—P. P. Bliss.

Jesus is calling you to come to Him today. I appeal to you not to be almost a Christian, but to become a true, believing disciple of the Lord Jesus. There are wonderful advantages in this decision.

Romans, chapter 5, verses 1 and 2, encourages us: "Having been justified by faith, we have peace with God through our Lord Jesus Christ, through whom also we have access by faith into this grace in which we stand, and rejoice in hope of the glory of God."

Peace with God! Think of that! It's ours when we are justified by faith. That means that when we accept Jesus as our Savior and Lord, our past sins are forgiven, His perfect righteousness is put to our account, and His righteousness is bestowed upon us by the gift of the Holy Spirit. It means that Jesus becomes the Ruler of our lives, and His Spirit takes over the management of our minds and bodies. As long as we submit to His controlling power, we are able to think good, pure thoughts and to act in ways that are acceptable to God and a blessing to all with whom we come in contact. From being proud, selfish, obsessed people, we become humble, unselfish, forgiving, understanding servants of God and humans.

Paul adds, "And not only that, but we also glory in tribulations, knowing that tribulation produces perseverance; and perseverance, character; and character, hope. Now hope does not disappoint, because the love of God has been poured out in our hearts by the Holy Spirit who was given to us" (Romans 5:3–5).

The Bible doesn't teach that Christian believers won't have troubles and tribulations any longer. It teaches that now they relate to such trials with a new attitude, an attitude of trust in God and patient acceptance of His will for their lives. Now they know that God overrules the bad things that happen to them, things that Satan wants to use to destroy them, so that God miraculously brings good out of what the devil intends to be evil. "Tribulation produces perseverance; and perseverance, character; and character, hope." We hope for the love of God, and He gives it to us. And He does this by pouring the Holy Spirit into our hearts. Then we are truly sharers in the glory of Christ's character. His patience in trouble becomes ours. His love for enemies becomes ours. His power to overcome sin becomes ours. And His trust in God's will for the future becomes ours.

A missionary had worked with an old Indian chief, telling him about the Savior, who loved him and died for him. After thoroughly considering the claims of Jesus Christ upon his life, the old chief stated, "The Jesus road is good, but I have followed the old Indian road all my life, and I will follow it to the end."

But a year later he was seriously ill, and it was felt that he was not going to live. Sensing the seriousness of his condition, he called for the missionary to come to him and then asked, "Can

I turn to the Jesus road now? My road stops here. It has no path through the valley."

That's the wonderful thing about the "Jesus road." Proceeding straight through the valley of the shadow, it leads on to eternal life. When the whole future looks dark, there is light and life available through Jesus Christ.

And that light and life result from what Jesus Christ accomplished on Calvary's cross. Paul adds: "For when we were still without strength, in due time Christ died for the ungodly. For scarcely for a righteous man will one die; yet perhaps for a good man someone would even dare to die. But God demonstrates His own love toward us, in that while we were still sinners Christ died for us" (Romans 5:6–8).

Do you get the point? Christ didn't die only for good people who love Him. He died for those who have ignored and rejected him. In fact, He suffered the penalty for the sins of the whole world. That's exactly what the Bible teaches. "He is the atoning sacrifice for our sins, and not for ours only but also for the sins of the whole world" (1 John 2:2, NRSV). "In this is love, not that we loved God, but that He loved us and sent His Son to be the propitiation for our sins" (1 John 4:10). He "bore our sins in His own body on the tree, that we, having died to sins, might live for righteousness—by whose stripes you were healed. For you were like sheep going astray, but have now returned to the Shepherd and Overseer of your souls" (1 Peter 2:24, 25).

On Calvary's cross, Jesus Christ made provision for every human being to be forgiven and saved. Now we can come to Him in all our filthy rags of unrighteousness and truly be saved from sin. That's what Paul goes on to say in Romans, chapter 5. He tells us: "Having now been justified by His blood, we shall be saved from wrath through Him. For if when we were enemies we were reconciled to God through the death of His Son, much more, having been reconciled, we shall be saved by His life. And not only that, but we also rejoice in God through our Lord Jesus Christ, through whom we have now received the reconciliation" (Romans 5:9–11).

By accepting Jesus' sacrifice on the cross as being for us, we have salvation, reconciliation with God. And by depending on the living Savior, we have continuing spiritual life and spiritual growth. Not only does Jesus reconcile us to God when we believe, but He gives us the daily spiritual power we need to grow stronger and stronger spiritually. His gift of justification is what sanctifies us. He bestows Himself upon us in justification, and we have peace with God. Then His living presence in our hearts makes us holy people.

We can know God and Jesus Christ as our Savior and Lord. We can know Him as the One who changes our lives. We can have His power living in our minds and controlling our bodies. Then we can testify of His love to others who ask us about Him.

Will Durant tells of a little girl who came to her mother with the age-old question, "Mother, what is God like?" Mother hesitated. "You'd better ask Daddy." She did. "Daddy, what is God like?" He too hesitated. Later on in her childish possessions was found a slip of paper with this free verse on it:

> "I asked my mother what God was like. She did not know. Then I asked my father, who knows more than anyone else in the world, what God was like. He did not know. I think if I had lived as long as my mother or my father, I would know something about God."

The fact is, we can know enough of God's love to inform our children and to lead them to the Lord Jesus Christ.

In verses 12 through 21 of Romans, chapter 5, the Apostle Paul contrasts the results for us and for our world of Adam's sin, with the results for us and for our world of Jesus' death on the cross. Verse 12 reads: "Therefore, just as through one man sin entered the world, and death through sin, and thus death spread to all men, because all sinned."[1] Because of Adam's sin, his children were born sinful and in need of a Savior. Adam's sin earned for him and his children mortality. Adam and his posterity would have lived endlessly if they had never sinned. But when Adam fell into disobedience to God, he became a fallen, mortal human being who could only pass on to his children fallen natures and the certainty that eventually they would die.

Paul is not saying, as some interpreters would have us believe, that we were all born guilty of Adam's sin. He is saying that we all inherited fallen natures with propensities to sin. We have sinned because sin is natural to us. We have sinned because our fallen natures have controlled us. That's why Jesus said, "You must be born again" (John 3:3–7). We must have the Holy Spirit of God take over our lives so that our fallen natures no longer control us. Then we have salvation from sin.

All humans die because all humans have inherited fallen natures and mortality.[2] The Bible teaches that God "alone has immortality" (1 Timothy 6:16). The Bible teaches that believers in Jesus Christ will be given immortality at His second coming. 1 Corinthians 15:53 says that at Jesus' second coming, "this corruptible must put on incorruption, and this mortal must put on immortality." Then sin and death will be destroyed.

Unbelievers are sinners by nature. Believers have power from Christ not to sin. But both believers and unbelievers are subject to death. "The living know that they will die; but the dead know nothing" (Ecclesiastes 9:5). That's true for both those who believe in Christ and those who don't believe. The difference is that, for those who believe in Jesus, death is a temporary sleep from which they will be awakened at the second coming of Jesus when they will be given immortality. The Bible says: "The Lord Himself will descend from heaven with a shout, with the voice of an archangel, and with the trumpet of God. And the dead in Christ will rise first. Then we who are alive and remain shall be caught up together with them in the clouds to meet the Lord in the air. And thus we shall always be with the Lord" (1 Thessalonians 4:16, 17).

But "the rest of the dead" do "not live again until the thousand years" are "finished" (Revelation 20:5). The rest of the dead are those who die unbelievers in Christ. Unbelievers who are still living when Jesus comes will then be put to death. Then all unbelievers will be raised at the end of the millennium and put to death for eternity (Revelation 20:7–15).

There is wonderful hope for the future if you believe in Jesus Christ. That's one of the main reasons we can have peace with God. We are not afraid to die, because Jesus plans to raise us from the dead at His second advent and bestow eternal life and immortality upon us.

That's why Paul can confidently spell out the contrast between the results of Adam's fall and Christ's victory on the cross. Paul tells us in Romans 5:15: "The free gift is not like the offense." That means that Christ's gift is not like the results of Adam's fall. "For if by the one man's offense many died, much more the grace of God and the gift by the grace of the one Man, Jesus Christ, abounded to many." Adam earned death for all; Christ earned life for all. Unfortunately, not all accept the life. But the many who believe in Him have this wonderful gift.

Then Paul repeats himself for the sake of emphasis. Verse 16 tells us: "The gift is not like that which came through the one who sinned. For the judgment which came from one offense resulted in condemnation, but the free gift which came from many offenses resulted in justification." Adam earned condemnation for all humanity. Not that all are guilty of what Adam did. But all suffer the results of what he did. All are condemned to have fallen natures that are in need of a Savior.

I would illustrate it like this: Imagine a prostitute who has AIDS. She doesn't know she has it. She gets married and has a baby. More than likely the baby will be born with AIDS. The baby is not guilty of any sin the mother may have committed. But the baby is condemned to have the mother's disease.

Just so, we are not guilty of Adam's fall. But we are condemned to have a spiritual disease that we inherited. And that disease is a fallen nature that is subject to sin and death. Only the Savior could take away our sin, subject our fallen natures, and deliver us from death. By His death on the cross, Jesus has made justification available to all who are willing to believe. But justification, forgiveness for sin, the righteousness of Jesus counted for us, and the righteousness of Jesus bestowed upon us must be accepted. Jesus has provided eternal life for all, but we must accept it by faith if we are to enjoy it.

That's the teaching of Romans 5:17: "For if by the one man's offense death reigned through the one, much more those who *receive* abundance of grace and of the gift of righteousness will reign in life through the One, Jesus Christ." The operative word in that text is the word *receive.* Jesus wants us to receive by faith the gifts of righteousness and life that He is offering us.

The following verses must be interpreted in the light of the teaching of Romans 5:17. Verse 18 reads: "Therefore as through one man's offense judgment came to all men, resulting in condemnation, even so through one Man's righteous act the free gift came to all men, resulting in justification of life." Jesus earned justification for all, but remember, verse 17 tells us it must be accepted. Only those who accept it enjoy the gift.

Romans 5:19 reemphasizes the major point: "For as by one man's disobedience many were made sinners, so also by one Man's obedience many will be made righteous." All were made sinners by Adam's fall, because all inherited fallen natures. And the many who receive Christ's gift are made righteous.

Verses 20 and 21 contrast the power of sin and the power of God's grace. Sin abounds in our world. But God's grace is more powerful. God's grace is His loving provision of power to deliver us from sin. Sin results in death, but God's grace is His gift of righteousness and eternal life to those who believe. And these are the ones who have peace with God.

David Livingstone is recognized as one of the world's foremost explorers and Christian missionaries. For 30 years he traveled through Africa, making friends wherever he went. His example and his death were an inspiration, resulting in an army of explorers and missionaries to Africa. Because of his sufferings in opening up the vast continent of Africa to Christian influence, his words, "I never made a sacrifice" have made an indelible impression on men's hearts. Livingstone wrote:

> "People talk of the sacrifice I have made in spending so much of my life in Africa. Can that be called a sacrifice which is simply paid back as a small part of a great debt owing to our God, which we can never repay? Is that a sacrifice which brings its own best reward in healthful activity, the consciousness of doing good, peace of mind, and a bright hope of a glorious destiny hereafter? Away with such a word, such a view, and with such a thought! It was emphatically no sacrifice. Say rather it is a privilege. Anxiety, sickness, suffering or danger, now and then, with a foregoing of the common conveniences and charities of this life may make us pause and cause the spirit to waver and sink; but let this only be for a moment. All these are nothing when compared with the glory which shall hereafter be revealed in and for us. I never made a sacrifice. Of this we ought not to talk when we remember the great sacrifice which He made who left His Father's throne on high to give Himself for us."[3]

You don't make a sacrifice when you come to Jesus. The blessings you take on far outstrip the significance of the things you give up. Think of it! You believe in Jesus, and with no cost to you, He gives you forgiveness, power to overcome sin, the gift of eternal life, and the assurance that at His second advent you will be made immortal. Now accepting all that is no sacrifice! Jesus pleads with you today to come to Him and enjoy peace of mind. Jesus promises it. He says: "Peace I leave with you, My peace I give to you; not as the world gives do I give to you. Let not your heart be troubled, neither let it be afraid" (John 14:27).

Endnotes

1. Romans 5:12 has been variously translated. It may be translated as in the New King James Version: "Therefore, just as through one man sin entered the world, and death through sin, and thus death spread to all men, because all sinned." Some interpreters contend that the last phrase means "because all men sinned when Adam sinned." Others urge that it means that all men die because, like Adam, all men have sinned. Even

so, the force of the passage and the context is that sin and death result from Adam's fall, and that when Adam sinned, in some sense the whole world sinned.

Jerome's Latin Vulgate rendering of the passage is reflected in the Douay-Rheims version which has, "Wherefore as by one man sin entered into the world, and by sin death; and so death passed upon all men, in whom all have sinned." (*The Holy Bible Translated from the Latin Vulgate* [Douay-Rheims Version, Philadelphia: National Publishing Co., 1914], Romans 5:12.) The final phrase translates the Latin "in quo omnes peccaverunt." Augustine likewise rendered *eph' ho* by "in whom," or "in him." "By one man sin entered into the world, and death by sin, and so death passed upon all men for in him all have sinned." (Augustin, *On Marriage and Concupiscence*, 45 [vol. 5 of *Nicene and Post Nicene Fathers*, series I], p. 301; see also Augustin, *Against Two Letters of the Pelagians*, 7 [*NPNF* Series I, vol. 5], pp. 419, 420).

Augustine interpreted the text to mean that when Adam sinned all men sinned, so that all men are born guilty of Adam's sin. The contrast then, in Romans, chapter 5, is that when Christ died, all humanity died, and so all humanity was justified at the cross.

That interpretation is faulted by the fact that all humanity was not responsible for Adam's fall. We were not there, nor were we involved. All humanity suffers the *results* of Adam's fall. Every human being has been born with a fallen nature and with biases, propensities to sin. We were not born guilty of Adam's sin, despite Augustine's contention; we were born suffering the *consequences* of Adam's sin. In this sense, all humanity sinned when Adam sinned. We didn't commit the act; we suffer the results of Adam's act. Hence, the second half of the contrast is not that all humanity died when Christ died, but that Christ's death *makes available* to all humanity justification and life. All humanity were not justified at the cross. The cross makes justification *available* to all. Justification must be accepted (Romans 5:17). We were not there. We did not die; Christ died for us, and the result is that we can have deliverance from the demands of our fallen natures, deliverance from sin and eternal death. We can have the wonderful gifts of justification and eternal life.

2. Romans 5, verses 13 and 14, are designed to emphasize Paul's point that all sin and death are the result of Adam's fall. Before Sinai "sin was in the world, but sin is not imputed when there is no law." Sinners before Sinai were not judged by the written law; it didn't exist until Sinai. They were judged by the law made evident to their hearts by the Holy Spirit (see Romans 1:20; 2:11–16). The fact that they were sinners and judged as

such is testified to by the destruction of the world by a Flood (Genesis 7) and the destruction of Sodom and Gomorrah (Genesis 19).

Romans 5:14 reads: "Death reigned from Adam to Moses, even over those who had not sinned according to the likeness of the transgression of Adam, who is a type of Him who was to come." Adam sinned despite his perfect nature. His children sinned in response to the demands of their fallen natures. Their sin was not as serious as Adam's. But death reigned over them because they inherited mortality and sinful natures from Adam.

3. Paul Lee Tan (ed.), *Encyclopedia of 7,700 Illustrations* (Rockville, MD.: Assurances Publishers, 1979), p. 1178

Chapter Eight

From Death to Life

Romans 6

In the year 1864, a young Swiss banker named Henri Dunant was one of the most influential men in Europe. Ever since he had witnessed the bloody Battle of Solferino in 1859, and had worked for the wounded, Dunant had spent much of his fortune and most of his time publicizing his dream of a more humane world.

In 1864, delegates of nearly every country in Europe met at Geneva to sign a pact that would make his dream come true. This would establish a permanent international organization to care for the sick and wounded during war, and to alleviate human suffering everywhere.

But for Henri Dunant the cost had been great. Too much of his energy and money had gone into his crusade. His new humanitarian organization was thriving, but his business was failing. In 1867, he was declared bankrupt. Taking refuge in the slums of Paris, Dunant was soon forgotten. For years no one knew where he was. The newspapers announced that he was dead.

Then in 1895, almost 30 years later, a Swiss newspaperman visited a home for the aged in Heiden, an Alpine village. He interviewed an old man there—a man named Henri Dunant—and went away to write a story that made front-page news everywhere and brought immediate action.

Nations all over the world offered aid and honor to the old man. The Empress of Russia bestowed a life pension. The Swiss Diet awarded him a prize. Societies throughout the world appointed him to honorary membership. And in 1901, he shared in the first Nobel Peace Prize.

All because a Swiss newspaperman discovered a poverty-stricken old man and wrote these words to introduce his story: "The founder of the Red Cross is alive and in need!"

Much more significantly, the Founder of the Christian Church is alive and well, and very much in need of your love and service. That's what Romans, chapter 6, is all about. Because of Jesus' suffering and death on the cross, we can all have forgiveness for sin, the power not to go on sinning, and the power to reflect the love of Jesus Christ. In fact, when we believe in Jesus, we have the gift of eternal life now.

That's what Paul explains to us in Romans, chapter 6. He begins by asking: "Shall we continue in sin that grace may abound?" (Romans 6:1). The answer is obvious. "Certainly not! How shall we who died to sin live any longer in it?" (v. 2). We died to sin when we were justified by faith. We died to sin when our past sins were forgiven, the righteousness of Jesus Christ was counted for us, and the righteousness of Jesus was bestowed upon us by the gift of the Holy Spirit. All that is included in justification. And when we received that gift from Christ, we were delivered from our old life of habitual sinning. The result is that we have "peace with God" (Romans 5:1) and the reign of grace in our hearts (Romans 5:21). We are free from condemnation and free from fear of death. Christ and the Father have come and taken up their abode in our lives through the presence of the Holy Spirit (John 14:17–23).

Justification is death to sin. Who would want to replace such a thrilling experience of renewal with a reversion to a life of sin? God's grace is His loving salvation, and that is always greater than sin. But we certainly don't imagine that we can demonstrate the immensity of grace by persisting in sin. "How can we who died to sin live any longer in it" (Romans 6:2)?

Paul illustrates our death to sin by pointing out the true significance of Christian baptism. He writes: "Do you not know that as many of us as were baptized into Christ Jesus were baptized into His death? Therefore we were buried with Him through baptism into death, that just as Christ was raised from the dead by the glory of the Father, even so we also should walk in newness of life. For if we have been united together in the likeness of His death, certainly we also shall be in the likeness of his resurrection (Romans 6:3–5).

As Christ died bearing our guilt, was buried, and rose to fullness of life, so we die to sin, are buried in baptism, and come forth to new life with Christ. Baptism by immersion is the only form of baptism that accurately represents this experience. Jesus was baptized by immersion. When John the Baptist had baptized Jesus, the Bible says, Jesus "came up immediately from the water" (Matthew 3:16). Jesus went down into the water of the Jordan River, was dipped under the water by John, and then came up out of the water. He was baptized by immersion.

The reason John was baptizing in the Jordan River, according to John 3:23, was precisely because "there was much water there." John wouldn't have needed much water if he had only been sprinkling water on people or merely pouring water over their heads. The simple fact is that he was baptizing by immersion.

That's why in Romans, chapter 6, Paul likens baptism to the death, burial, and resurrection of Christ. As Jesus died, so we die to sin when we accept Him as Savior and Lord. As Jesus was buried, so the believer who has died to sin is buried in the waters of baptism. And as Jesus rose from the dead, so the believer rises from the waters of baptism to live the new life that Christ has given. Only baptism by immersion correctly illustrates the death, burial, and resurrection of Jesus Christ.

Paul's major point is that the Christian believer has died to sin. He explains that "our old man," that is, our old self, our old manner of life, "was crucified with Him, that the body of sin might be done away with, that we should no longer be slaves to sin. For he who has died has been freed from sin" (Romans 6:6, 7).

In the writings of Paul the "old man" is defined as the former manner of life, the old life of habitual sinning.[1] In Ephesians 4:22–24, Paul instructs "that you put off, *concerning* your former conduct, the old man which grows corrupt according to the deceitful lusts, and be renewed in the spirit of your mind, and that you put on the new man which was created according to God, in righteousness and true holiness."

The "old man," or "old self," does not go on dying in Paul's teaching. His death is not progressive; it's a single event. The death of the "old man" (Ephesians 4:22) was an event that for the believer occurred in the past. It is not a gradual process. Nor does Paul anywhere say anything about the "old man" rearing his ugly head and having to be put to sleep again. Paul presents the ideal situation that the "old man" of sin should die once and never be resurrected. He is dead and buried and that is that! The old life of habitual sinning is resurrected only if the individual rejects Christ and turns again to the habits and practices of his former life.

Paul wrote to the Ephesians: "That you put off, concerning your former conduct [or manner of life], the old man" (Ephesians 4:22). The former manner of life is the old man. Therefore, Paul defines the "old man" as the old life of habitual sinning. He was not instructing the Ephesians to put the old life of sin to death. They had already experienced this in the new birth. Paul was instructing them to "put off *concerning* the former manner of life." He wanted them to stop committing sins that were characteristic of their former lives of habitual sinning. Colossians 3:3 translates literally: "For you died, and your life has been hidden with Christ in God." You see, "the old man" was dead, but it was still necessary for the Christians constantly to guard themselves from sin. Colossians 3:9 reads: "Do not lie to one another, since you have put off the old man with his deeds." Lying was characteristic of their old life of habitual sinning; hence, by Christ's grace they were to be strictly honest and pure. The new man is the new life of habitual victory in Christ. Therefore Paul reminds us: You "have put on the new man who is renewed in knowledge according to the image of Him who created him" (Colossians 3:10).

The Greek of Romans 6:7 translates literally: "For he who died has been justified from sin."[2] So justification is identified as death to sin. As we have seen in previous chapters, justification is forgiveness for the past, the righteousness of Jesus legally put to our account, and the righteousness of Jesus bestowed upon us by the gift of the Holy Spirit. So when we are justified we are made right with God because we have died to sin. The power of Christ drives the sin away and fills us with the presence of His Spirit.

In August 1893, a Mississippi jury found Will Purvis, a twenty-one-year-old farmer, guilty of killing a neighbor after a petty quarrel. Throughout the trial he had protested his innocence, yet was unable to produce evidence to clear himself. He was sentenced to hang.

On February 7, 1894, Purvis was led to the scaffold. A crowd had gathered, and many of the grimly silent people still had faith in his innocence. With sad eyes they watched the guards slip the black hood over his head and adjust the noose. Then the trap was sprung. Suddenly a shout went up from the crowd of spectators. The noose had not held. Purvis had fallen to the ground unhurt!

The sheriff ordered the guards to lead Purvis back for a second attempt. But the crowd had just seen a miracle. For them, that was final proof of the farmer's innocence. They demanded that he be spared until a higher authority could decide his fate.

Three appeals to the State Supreme Court were rejected, and another hanging date was set—December 12, 1895. But a week before the second execution date, a mob broke into the jail and freed him. For a year, relatives gave him shelter; then a new governor commuted his sentence to life imprisonment, and Will Purvis gave himself up.

In 1898, in response to petitions signed by thousands of Mississippians, the governor granted Purvis a full pardon. Will was now a free man. But the question remained, who was the murderer? The answer came in 1920 when a man named Joe Beard made a full deathbed confession.

The Bible says that despite our old lives of sin, when we come to Jesus, we are free from condemnation; we are innocent in Christ. Romans, chapter 8, verse 1, reads: "There is therefore now no condemnation to those who are in Christ Jesus." By accepting

Jesus, we have died to sin, and by His power, we can now be free from the sins that were characteristic of our old way of life.

The apostle Paul reemphasizes that point in Romans 6:8–13. He writes: "Now if we died with Christ, we believe that we shall also live with Him, knowing that Christ, having been raised from the dead, dies no more. Death no longer has dominion over Him. For the death that He died, He died to sin once for all; but the life that He lives, He lives to God. Likewise you also, reckon yourselves to be dead indeed to sin, but alive to God in Christ Jesus our Lord. Therefore do not let sin reign in your mortal body, that you should obey it in its lusts. And do not present your members [that is, your mind and body] as instruments of unrighteousness to sin, but present yourselves to God as being alive from the dead, and your members as instruments of righteousness to God" (Romans 6:8–13).

That's just another way of saying that, since our old lives of habitual sinning are dead, we should not commit sins that are characteristic of that old manner of life. Then Paul adds: "For sin shall not have dominion over you, for you are not under the law but under grace" (Romans 6:14). That text is not saying that the law need no longer be kept. The book of Romans and many other passages of Scripture teach that God's holy law of Ten Commandments is still the standard of righteousness. For example, Romans 3:31 says: "Do we then make void the law through faith? Certainly not! On the contrary, we establish the law." Romans 7:7 tells us that we would not know sin "except through the law." Paul says: "I would not have known covetousness unless the law had said, 'You shall not covet.' " And Romans 8:3, 4 tells us that Christ died so "that the righteous requirement of the law might be fulfilled in us who do not walk according to the flesh but according to the Spirit."

Then what does Romans 6:14 mean? "For sin shall not have dominion over you, for you are not under the law but under grace." Paul's points is that, because Christ's grace (His powerful divine presence) is reigning in your heart, you can overcome all sin. Sin can't have dominion over you when Christ is reigning in your heart by the presence of the Holy Spirit. The person "under the law" is the one who attempts to overcome in his or her own strength. That person is attempting to use law keeping as a means of salvation. Earlier in Romans, as well as in Galatians and other epistles, Paul rules out law keeping as a means of salvation. The law points out our sin, but it does not save us. If we try to use the law as the means of salvation, we will fall into sin, and then we will be under the condemnation of the law.

But now God's grace has freed us from the mistake of using the law as the means of salvation, and God's grace has freed us from the condemnation of the law.

Then Paul refers to the person who is not serving Christ as a slave to sin, and the person who is serving Christ as a slave of righteousness. He rejoices that the Roman Christians had become willing slaves of righteousness. Paul says: "God be thanked that though you were slaves of sin, yet you obeyed from the heart that form of doctrine to which you were delivered. And having been set free from sin, you became slaves of righteousness" (Romans 6:17, 18).

Now the interesting point is that, whether you like it or not, you will be one or the other. Either you will be a slave to sin or a willing slave of righteousness. There is no middle ground. Either you are serving sin, living for self, satisfying your own sinful passions and desires, or you are submitting to the love of Jesus Christ and receiving power from Him to do what is right. You are either a willing slave of sin or a willing slave of righteousness. And the gift of righteousness is what Paul means by justification.

When you are justified, Jesus comes to live in your life by the presence of the Holy Spirit. Justification is Christ bestowed. And this gift results in your being a holy person. That's what Paul emphasizes in Romans 6:19: "Just as you presented your members [that is your mind and body] as slaves of uncleanness, and of lawlessness leading to more lawlessness, so now present your members as slaves of righteousness for holiness."

Holiness is sanctification.[3] The gift of Christ to our hearts by the Holy Spirit is what makes us holy or sanctified people. Justification is Christ bestowed; sanctification is Christ possessed. You have the possession because you have received the bestowal. If someone puts one thousand dollars in your bank account, you now have spending power. The putting of the money in your account represents justification. Now you have the power to live for Christ and to do the things He asks you to do, and that's sanctification.

Paul comments further: "For when you were slaves of sin, you were free in regard to righteousness" (Romans 6:20). How true that is! Before we found Jesus as the Source of our power, we were slaves to sin. We often knew we were doing wrong, but we didn't have the power to do otherwise. Then we found Jesus, or better still, Jesus found us, and He gave us the power of the Holy Spirit. Then the change came. Now we have the power to do works that in the sight of God are righteous.

When we were serving sin, we were doing things of which we are now ashamed. Paul reminds us of that. "What fruit did you have then in the things of which you are now ashamed? For the end of those things is death. But now having been set free from sin, and having become slaves of God, you have your fruit to holiness, and the end, everlasting life" (Romans 6:21, 22). Once again we are reminded that justification sets us free from sin, and the result is holiness of life, or sanctification.

"For the wages of sin is death, but the gift of God is eternal life in Christ Jesus our Lord" (Romans 6:23). The wages of sin, the result of sin, is eternal death; not eternal life in hell, but eternal death. Death is a state of nonexistence. If you choose to identify yourself with sin, you will die with it, and you will die for eternity. But if you identify yourself with Christ you will live with Him for eternity. Sin and death go hand in hand. And Christ and eternal life go hand in hand. Jesus wants each of us to submit to His rulership, simply because, as our Creator, He knows that it is for our greatest happiness to live in accord with the principles of His government. And the basis of His government is love.

History records the contrasting statements of those who faced death apart from Christ and those who faced death knowing Christ. Napoleon Bonaparte, the famous or infamous military strategist of France, said while waiting for death: "I die before my time, and my body will be given back to the earth. Such is the fate of him who has been called the great Napoleon. What an abyss between my deep misery and the eternal kingdom of Christ!"

Voltaire, the noted French infidel, said to his doctor: "I am abandoned by God and man! I will give you half of what I am worth if you will give me six months' life. Then I shall go to hell, and you will go with me."

Thomas Hobbes, a skeptic who corrupted some of England's great men, sighed: "If I had the whole world, I would give it to live one day. I shall be glad to find a hole to creep out of the world at. I am about to take a leap into the dark!"

M. F. Rich, an atheist, cried: "I would rather lie on a stove and broil for a million years than go into eternity with the eternal horrors that hang over my soul! I have given my immortality for gold, and its weight sinks me into an endless, hopeless, helpless hell."

Sir Thomas Scott, on his deathbed, said: "Until this moment I thought there was neither a God nor a hell. Now I know and feel that there are both, and I am doomed to perdition by the just judgment of the Almighty."

By contrast, when facing death, Dwight L. Moody, the great evangelist, exclaimed: "I see earth receding; heaven is opening. God is calling."

John Wesley, eighteenth-century English preacher and religious leader, said with confidence, "The best of all is, God is with us."

Mrs. Catherine Booth, wife of the Salvation Army general, said joyfully, "The waters are rising, but so am I. I am not going under, but over. Do not be concerned about dying; go on living well. The dying will be right."

Mrs. Ann Hasseltine Judson, missionary to Burma and wife of Adoniram Judson, faced death with these words: "Oh, the happy day will soon come when we shall meet all our friends who are now scattered—meet to part no more in our heavenly Father's house."

What a difference in these famous last words! Do you know why? The Bible has the answer. "He who believes in the Son has everlasting life; and he who does not believe the Son shall not see life, but the wrath of God abides on him" (John 3:36).

A personal faith in Jesus Christ made—and still makes—the difference! The modern outlook is, "It doesn't matter what you believe so long as you're sincere. The important thing is to believe something!"

But that doesn't work in real life, nor in real death. Napoleon, Voltaire, Hobbes, Rich, and Scott all believed in *something*—but it didn't help them! The others believed in *Someone*—Jesus Christ—and this personal belief brought personal peace, even in the hour of death. The soul who can claim, "The Lord is my shepherd," is the only one who can truthfully conclude, "Yea, though I walk through the valley of the shadow of death, I will fear no evil: for You [God] are with me" (Psalm 23:1, 4).

The Bible says: "Believe on the Lord Jesus Christ, and you will be saved" (Acts 16:31). Will you believe Christ? Will you receive Him as your personal Savior—today?

If you will, you can say with the apostle Paul: "For to me, to live is Christ, and to die is gain" (Philippians 1:21).

Endnotes

1. The "old man" is not the fallen nature. When we accept Jesus as Savior and Lord, the old life of habitual sinning dies, but we still retain fallen natures. That's why Paul wrote: "I discipline my body and bring it into subjection, lest, when I have preached to others, I myself should become disqualified." Paul retained a fallen nature that had to be subjected daily by the power of Christ. Paul wrote to the Galatians: "Walk in the Spirit, and you shall not fulfill the lust of the flesh. For the flesh lusts against the Spirit, and the Spirit against the flesh; and these are contrary to one another, so that you do not do the things that you wish. But if you are led by the Spirit, you are not under the law" (Galatians 5:16–18). The born-again Christian experiences the constant conflict of "flesh" and "Spirit." The Holy Spirit

in the believer's life wars against the sinful desires that are characteristic of the fallen nature. The old life of habitual sinning has gone, but the struggle against sin is continual. If we are led and controlled by the Holy Spirit, we are not under the law in two senses: (1) we are not under the law as the means of salvation; only Christ is the means of salvation, and (2) we are not under the condemnation of the law, because, by the power of the Spirit, we are obeying the law (See Romans 8:3, 4, 9, 10).

2. The Greek of Romans 6:7 reads: *ho gar apothanon dedikaiotai apo tes hamartias.* It translates literally: "For he who has died has been justified from sin." Hence, justification is the death of the "old man," the old life of habitual sinning. When Jesus changes a life by the power of the Holy Spirit, that is justification (Titus 3:5–7). The death of the old man, or old life, is the same experience that Jesus referred to as the new birth (John 3). The point is that Paul and Jesus were speaking of the same experience, even though they were using different imagery.
3. Romans 6:19 says that believers in Jesus are "slaves of righteousness for holiness." The word translated "holiness" also means "sanctification" (*hagiasmon*). Those who believe in Jesus accept justification. They become willing slaves of righteousness. The righteousness of God is given to them by the presence of the Holy Spirit (Romans 8:9, 10). This gift of righteousness is what makes them holy, or sanctified. There is a causal relationship between justification and sanctification. Justification causes sanctification, or holiness. Justification is Christ bestowed; sanctification is Christ possessed. You have the possession because you have received the bestowal. Justification and sanctification are inseparable. You cannot have one without the other. Of course, the gift of righteousness that makes you holy is to be a continuous daily gift so that sanctification is holiness now as well as continuous growth in holiness.

Chapter Nine

Jesus, the Only Answer

Romans 7

Catherine hurried through the dirty streets of London's east end on her way to Gateshead Methodist Chapel to hear her husband preach. Ragged children played in the alleyways while mangy dogs pawed through the garbage. Just ahead of her, a shabbily clad woman sat on the steps of a ramshackle tenement house, a jug in her hand.

Poor, poor woman, Catherine thought. If only she'd go over to the chapel to hear my husband speak, I'm sure her life would be changed by the power of God.

A voice said to her, "Speak to that woman."

Startled, Catherine looked around to see who might have spoken. There was no one except children and dogs going about their play. Was it her imagination? Or had the Lord spoken? The thought sent chills down her spine.

"No, Lord, I'm afraid," Catherine reasoned. "Besides, she wouldn't listen. She's probably drunk."

"Speak to the woman."

"But, Lord, I'll be late for the meeting," Catherine argued.

"Wouldn't you be doing God more service by inviting her to the chapel than going there yourself?" God seemed to say to her.

Catherine took a deep breath. "All right, Lord, if you say so, I'll try."

Smiling at the woman, Catherine shyly asked, "Would you like to come to the chapel with me?"

The woman sighed and shook her head. "Can't. Got to stay home with my husband. He's drunk." She nodded her head toward the door.

"May I talk to him?" Catherine surprised herself with this question. "Maybe I can help him."

"No use," the woman mumbled. "He's so drunk he'd never hear a word you'd say."

"Please," Catherine persisted. "Let me try. I don't mind that he's drunk, and I'm not afraid."

The woman got up then and led her into the small, dark apartment to where her husband slumped in a chair, a jug on the floor beside him. He didn't seem to notice their presence.

"Lord, what shall I say?" Catherine sent a quick prayer to God for guidance.

She said, "God loves you!" She spoke with authority. "Listen to me! He loves you so much that He sent Jesus to die on the cross for your sins! He cares about you."

The man turned his eyes toward her and listened intently, as though trying to grasp the truth that God really loved him. Encouraged, Catherine took out her Bible and opened it to Luke 15. Beginning at verse 11, she read the story of the prodigal son.

As she read about the father running to meet his son, tears welled up in the man's bloodshot eyes and trickled down his dirty cheeks.

"God loves you like that father loved his son," Catherine spoke gently. "Now, I want to pray for you."

After the prayer, Catherine promised to come back for a visit to share more of God's love. The man nodded, wiping the tears from his eyes. Catherine did return, and before long, this man, along with ten other alcoholics, began studying the Bible with her. All eleven quit drinking and found a new life in Christ Jesus.

That brief encounter with God's Word was the turning point not only in the drunkard's life but in Catherine's as well. Awakened to the power of personal contact, she pledged herself to spend two evenings every week visiting systematically from house to house, sharing God's message of love. It strengthened her belief that God can use women as well as men to do His work. It impressed upon her the power of God to change the worst of sinners.

After that encounter in London's east end in 1860, Catherine Mumford Booth threw all of her energies into working with her husband, William Booth, for the afflicted, the forgotten, and the downtrodden of society. Together, they founded the Salvation Army. She is known as the "mother of the Salvation Army."

From her first public testimony in 1860 until her death in 1891, she was known as a dynamic, fervent, and forceful speaker. Catherine once said that she felt more at home on the platform than she did in the kitchen. She was a sought-after temperance lecturer, and large crowds turned out to hear her speak at open-air meetings as well as in churches and public halls. On the twenty-fifth anniversary of the Salvation Army, thousands gathered to hear her speak.

Catherine worked not only for alcoholics but for prostitutes also, establishing London's first rescue home for young girls caught in prostitution. She lobbied with government leaders and helped secure the passing of the Criminal Law Amendment Act that was designed to protect teenage girls from prostitution.

According to Norman Murdock, "No man of her era exceeded her in popularity or spiritual results, including her husband."

When Catherine Booth died, fifty thousand people filed past her casket as she lay in state for five days in London's Congress Hall.[1]

The story of that great woman's ministry graphically illustrates the power of the Christian gospel. And that's the message of Romans, chapter 7. The Apostle Paul begins the chapter by contrasting the old life of sin with the new life of spiritual victory in Christ. He illustrates this contrast by referring to a woman whose husband dies. Then, legally, she is free to marry another man.

Paul makes the application. He writes: "You also have become dead to the law through the body of Christ, that you may be married to another, even to Him who was raised from the dead, that we should bear fruit to God" (Romans 7:4). Dead to the law doesn't mean that the law doesn't have to be obeyed. It means free from the condemnation of the law because Jesus Christ is now the means by which we can overcome sin. Our old life of habitual sinning has died. Now we are married to Jesus Christ. He is the second husband in Paul's illustration. He is the One who makes it possible for us to live for God.

Paul proceeds to point out: "When we were in the flesh, the passions of sins which were aroused by the law were at work in our members to bear fruit to death. But now we have been delivered from the law, having died to what we were held by, so that we should serve in newness of the Spirit and not in the oldness of the letter" (Romans 7:5, 6).[2]

Paul's point is that we were unaware of the sinfulness of our lives until the law revealed it. Then sin fought for the supremacy over our newly discovered convictions. Our "old man" of sin, our old life of habitual sinning, died when we found Christ. He released us from (1) the effort to earn salvation by our own law keeping; He delivered us from legalism, and (2) Christ delivered us from the condemnation of the law.

The written will of God is still the standard of righteousness. Romans 3:31 reads: "Do we then make void the law through faith? Certainly not! On the contrary, we establish the law." The law is now written on our hearts. Hebrews 8:10 contains God's promise to believers: "I will put My laws in their mind and write them on their hearts; and I will be their God, and they shall be My people."

Only as Christ reigns in our lives can we obey God's law. We can't save ourselves by our unaided efforts to keep the law. As surrendered believers in Christ, we serve in newness of Spirit because the Holy Spirit is now in charge of our minds.

Paul goes on to explain in more detail that there is nothing wrong with the law. He asks: "Is the law sin? Certainly not! On the contrary, I would not have known sin except through the law. For I would not have known covetousness unless the law had said, 'You shall not covet' " (Romans 7:7). You see, the function of the law is to point out our sin and to point us to Christ. But the function of the law is not to save us from sin. A mirror points out the dirt on your face, but it doesn't wash your face. The law reveals that you and I are sinners. But only Christ can cleanse us from sin.[3]

Paul says that before the law spoke to him, he wasn't aware that he was a sinner (Romans 7:8). He was alive without the law. "But when the commandment came, sin revived, and I died" (Romans 7:9). That means that the law revealed his sin, and the law condemned him to death. Then he knew that he needed a Savior. "Therefore the law is holy, and the commandment holy and just and good" (Romans 7:12).

Then Paul asks, "Is the law responsible for my death?" He answers "Certainly not! But sin, that it might appear sin, was producing death in me through what is good, so that sin through the commandment might become exceedingly sinful. For we know that the law is spiritual, but I am carnal, sold under sin" (Romans 7:13, 14).

I am the sinful one. There's nothing wrong with the law. The law does what it is supposed to do. It tells me I am a sinner. Sin is the reason for my spiritual death, not the law. But when I respond to the law's conviction that I need a Savior, then I look up to Christ and cry out for Him to deliver me from sin.

That's why the Bible is so important. It tells us of our need of Jesus Christ, and it tells us how to find Him so that we can be delivered from sin.

The true story is told of an Aymara Indian man in Bolivia who was a heavy drinker. One night his aim was to get drunk and then to return home, his usual habit. But on his way home he fell from his horse and lay there on the trail all night in a drunken stupor. His horse remained standing beside him. When the man woke up early the next morning, he noticed a black object sticking out of the dust. Wiping away the dust, he found it was a Bible and wondered who could have left it there. He began reading the Bible immediately and felt God speaking to him. He returned home and told his wife what had happened. "I am giving my life to Christ!" he said. He had never heard the gospel preached, but he continued to read the Bible out loud. Some time later his wife also accepted Christ. Together they decided to contact a mission, the address of which they found on the inside cover of the Bible. They traveled 120 miles to meet one of the missionaries. Later, the couple confirmed their new found faith by being baptized. It still remains a mystery how that Bible came to be at the side of the trail.

In Romans, chapter 7, Paul spells out the struggle we all have to depend on Christ and not on ourselves in the battle with sin. Paul says: "I do not understand my own actions. For I do not do what I want, but I do the very thing I hate" (Romans 7:15, NRSV).[4] Now that's true of the person who knows what is right, but who has not accepted Christ, and it is also true of the person who has given his or her life to Christ but who temporarily has stopped depending on Him. Every born-again Christian knows that at times we do things that we hate to do, because we know those things are wrong. And non-Christians who know the difference between right and wrong, sometimes do things that they hate to do because they know those things are wrong. This is a universal human problem. Apart from the power of Christ at any stage of our spiritual development, we are sure to fall into sin. When we focus on ourselves instead of on Jesus, when we focus on our human problems instead of trusting in the Lord, or when we cherish desires for evil, and allow those desires to lead us away from Christ, we do things that we hate to do, simply because we don't have the power in and of ourselves to overcome.

Paul explains why we fall into sin. He says: "I know that nothing good dwells within me, that is, in my flesh. I can will what is right, but I cannot do it" (Romans 7:18, NRSV). You see, we have fallen natures. When Christ comes into our lives, He controls our natures so that our fallen propensities cannot overcome us. But unless we are totally dependent upon Christ, we can choose to do right, but cannot put our choice into action. In other words, we are powerless to do the good things that we want to do, simply because the power of Satan and the power of our fallen natures are stronger than our human wills. That's why Paul says, "I can will what is right, but I cannot do it."

He adds: "I do not do the good I want, but the evil I do not want is what I do" (Romans 7:19, NRSV). Sin within urges me to do things that I really don't want to do (v. 20). "So I find it to be a law that when I want to do what is good, evil lies close at hand. For I delight in the law of God in my inmost self, but I see in my members another law at war with the law of my mind, making me captive to the law of sin that dwells in my members" (Romans 7:21–23).[5]

Even the born-again Christian has that problem. Paul himself wrote to the Corinthian Christians: "I discipline my body and bring it into subjection lest, when I have preached to others, I myself should become disqualified" (1 Corinthians 9:27). Romans, chapter 7, is simply confronting us with the paradox that one part of us wants to serve God while another part wants to serve sin. Our minds are convinced that certain things are right and good, and we want to do those things. But we have that fallen nature pushing us to disobey God and to do what we know is wrong. And we despise ourselves for our weakness.

What is the answer to that terrible conflict in our natures? How can we overcome the desire to sin and do the things we really want to do? Paul cries out in despair, as you and I do, "Wretched man that I am! Who will rescue me from this body of death? Thanks be to God through Jesus Christ our Lord!" (Romans 7:25, NRSV).

The answer Paul gives is the only one that works. You can use all the psychological techniques you know, but they are not enough to keep you from sinning. You can exercise your mind and body, you can eat the right foods, get plenty of sleep, drink lots of water, and take time for recreation. All of that helps. But, in the final analysis, none of that will keep you from falling into your besetting sin. Human effort to overcome is bound to fail, unless that effort is supplemented by the power of Christ. That's the message of the book of Romans. Our works, however noble in intent, can never save us from sin. The conflict in our minds can never be resolved until we submit our lives and our wills to Jesus Christ.

Now let's look at the solution from a practical point of view. What should we do so that Christ's power will be manifest in our lives? What practical things can we do to ensure that when we are tempted to commit some sin, we will have the strength to overcome the temptation? First, we must begin every day by submitting our lives to the care and keeping of God. That means getting out of bed and reading a portion of His Word. There is great blessing and strength involved in studying the Bible. We should spend time with the Word of God every morning. Then we must bow in prayer and ask the Lord to give us the power to live for Him today. Submit your life to Him in the morning and ask Him to guide you in every aspect of your day's activities. Ask Him to keep you focused on what is good and to shelter you from evil.

Then during the day, when you are tempted to say or do what you know is wrong, you can immediately shoot up a prayer to the Lord to give you the power you need to do the right thing.

As soon as we are conscious of the urge to sin, we need to pray three prayers: (1) "Lord, I'm helpless. I like this sin" (You wouldn't be tempted if you didn't like it). (2) "Lord, give me the power to overcome this thing that I know is wrong." And (3), "Thank You, Lord, for hearing my prayer and giving me the power to overcome. Thank you for the victory."

That third prayer is absolutely essential. Even before you see the result, thank God for it. That's faith. Faith is praise; praise is faith. Praising God for the victory is an act of faith. And "this is the victory that conquers the world, our faith. Who is it that conquers the world but the one who believes that Jesus is the Son of God?" (1 John 5:4, 5, NRSV). The prayer of faith is the means of victory. But remember, Jesus is the One who gives the victory. You don't earn it. Your will doesn't produce it, even though your will is involved. Jesus is the only One who can take charge of your mind and give you the power not to sin.

H.M.S. Richards, Senior, who for years was the *Voice of Prophecy* radio speaker, was interviewed once by a radio host who asked him, "How would you summarize the gospel?" His answer consisted of two words: "Jesus only." And that is the bottom line of the Christian faith. When Jesus becomes the most important Person in our lives; when our focus is on Him every day; when we rely totally on Him for the power to reflect His love; when we rely totally on Him for the power to overcome sin and do the things that He wants us to do, and the good things we want to do, then we have victory. Jesus is our "righteousness and sanctification and redemption" (1 Corinthians 1:30).

We come to know Jesus better and better as we spend time with His Word every day. Then He is able to speak to us. That's what the Bible is for. It is God's voice speaking to our minds and hearts and showing us how to live and how to act in every situation. God's Word is about Jesus Christ; we come to know Him through His Word.

The tears still come to evangelist Raul Camerero when he remembers the chance encounter that changed his life. It happened while he was on a bus in Cordoba, Argentina, on his way to a party. Raul recalls: "At the precise moment when the driver was closing the door, an arm holding out a small booklet reached into the vehicle, and I hurriedly grabbed the booklet. I was able to see only the woman's hand, because she quickly withdrew her arm to keep it from being caught in the door. I stuffed the booklet into my jacket pocket and forgot about it."

Back then, Raul was an unhappy young man. Although he was reared in a Christian home, there were many things about his faith he didn't understand. Not even his regular attendance in church seemed to satisfy the longing for contentment and happiness in his heart.

Hoping to fill that void elsewhere, Raul immersed himself in boxing, soccer, and other popular Argentinean sports. He also became a regular at parties thrown by his friends. But even those things did not bring him the happiness he sought.

Then came the hand in the bus and the mysterious booklet that Raul had so hastily shoved into his pocket.

About an hour later, while still riding the bus, he tells us: "I remembered the booklet and took it out to see what it was about. I recognized it as the Gospel of Matthew, because on visits to my aunt I had read a Bible given to her by a Bible Society worker." Raul began by reading the subtitles on the first few pages, until he came to the Beatitudes. He says: "Then I started to read slowly, and my whole body shuddered when I meditated upon the words."

At that moment the young man seemed to lose all sense of time and space. He forgot all about the bus and even the people sitting next to him. He says: "The words of the Gospel came alive. I felt Jesus begin to teach and tell me, 'Happy are those who know they are spiritually poor; the kingdom of heaven belongs to them!' "

He came to the words: "Happy are the pure in heart; they will see God." Anxiety overcame him and tears rolled down his cheeks. He says: "I called out in desperation, 'Lord, I will never see your face unless you cleanse my life.' At that moment I felt the affectionate hug of a father embracing a prodigal son." Raul soon afterward joined a church and, along with his wife, was baptized. He became an evangelist, and now rejoices in telling others the good news about Jesus Christ.

However weak you may feel you are, there is infinite power available through Jesus Christ. He loves you infinitely, and He will lift your spirits above the mundane things of this old world of sin, and give you a life of service and fulfillment, along with the wonderful assurance of eternal life.

Endnotes

1. Adapted from Ron and Dorothy Watts, *Powerful Passages* (Pacific Press: Boise, Idaho, 1996), pp. 95–99.
2. Romans 7:1–6 records Paul's illustration and his application. The married woman represents us. The first husband is the "old man" of sin (compare Romans 6:6). The second husband is Christ. We were unaware of the sinfulness of our lives until the law revealed it. Then sin fought for the supremacy over our newly discovered convictions. "Now we have

been delivered from the law, having died to that we were held by, so that we should serve in newness of the Spirit and not in oldness of letter." Our "old man" of sin died when we found Christ. This released us from (1) the effort to earn salvation by our own law keeping (legalism); (2) the condemnation of the law. The "oldness of letter" refers to legalism from which we have been delivered (see Romans 2:29; 2 Corinthians 3:6). The written will of God (the law) is still the standard of righteousness (Romans 3:31; 7:7, 12, 14; 1 John 2:4; Revelation 12:17; 14:12). But only as Christ reigns in our lives can we obey it. We serve in newness of Spirit when the Holy Spirit is in charge of our minds (see Romans 8:1–11).

3. The law is not responsible for our sin problem. The law functions to point out our sin. This is its correct function (see Romans 3:20; 5:20; Galatians 3:19, 24; 1 Timothy 1:9). The law to which Paul refers in Romans 7:7 is the Ten Commandments. This is the law he quotes.
4. The question is, to what stage of life does this passage refer, to the state of the unjustified person or to the condition of the justified, born-again Christian? The answer is clearly that it refers to *the individual who has accepted the law of God but is unable to obey it.* This is true of the unjustified person who knows God's will but who has not surrendered to Christ. It is also true of the justified person who has temporarily taken his eyes off Christ and is not maintaining a relationship with Him.
5. Romans 7:21–23: Evil is in our natures in the sense that, because we are fallen, we retain propensities to sin, even after justification. Only one who has accepted the law of God as right and true could say, "I delight in the law of God in my inmost self" (v. 22, NRSV). The war going on (v. 23) is between the fallen nature and the "law of my mind." The person alluded to is convinced that God's will is right and should be performed, but, at the moment of temptation, this person has not surrendered to Christ as the Source of the power to overcome.

Chapter Ten

The New Life in Christ

Romans 8

A little boy wanted to meet God. He knew it was a long trip to where God lived, so he packed his suitcase with Twinkies and a six-pack of root beer, and he started his journey. When he had gone about three blocks from his home, he met an old man. He was sitting in the park just staring at some pigeons. The boy sat down next to him and opened his suitcase. He was about to take a drink of his root beer when he noticed that the old man looked hungry. So he offered him a Twinkie.

The old man gratefully accepted it and smiled at the boy. His smile was so pleasant that the boy wanted to see it again, so he offered him a root beer. Again he smiled at him. The boy was delighted! They sat there all afternoon eating and smiling, but they never said a word.

As it grew dark, the boy realized how tired he was, and he got up to leave. But before he had gone more than a few steps, he turned around, ran back to the old man, and gave him a hug. The old man gave him his biggest smile ever.

When the boy opened the door to his own house a short time later, his mother was surprised by the look of joy on his face. She asked him, "What did you do today that made you so happy?"

He replied, "I had lunch with God." But before his mother could respond, he added, "You know what? He's got the most beautiful smile I've ever seen!"

Meanwhile, the old man, also radiant with joy, returned to his home. His son was stunned by the look of peace on his face, and he asked, "Dad, what did you do today that made you so happy?"

He replied, "I ate Twinkies in the park with God." However, before his son responded, he added, "You know, he's much younger than I expected."

Too often we underestimate the power of a touch, a smile, a kind word, a listening ear, an honest compliment, or the smallest act of caring, all of which have the potential to turn a life around. People come into our lives for a reason, a season, or a lifetime. We have the privilege of accepting them, and cherishing them with love and caring.

St. Francis of Assisi said to his followers: "Preach the gospel. Use words if you have to." Bess Cochrane, in *Without Halos*, tells of how radiant Mandy was when she went to church. The minister said to her, "You have found happiness, haven't you, Mandy?" To which she replied, "No, suh! I ain't found it. I'se made it."

You see, when Jesus Christ comes into your heart by the presence of His Holy Spirit, your most urgent wish is to give joy and happiness to other people. And that's what Romans, chapter 8, is all about. It is one of the most important chapters in the Bible. It speaks to our need for the power of the Holy Spirit in our lives so that we can live for God and others, instead of selfishly living for ourselves.

The chapter begins by telling us that "there is therefore now no condemnation for those who are in Christ Jesus" (Romans 8:1). There is no condemnation for believers in Jesus Christ because their sins have been forgiven. And that's what Paul means by justification. The previous chapters have told us that if we believe in Jesus, we will be justified from sin. That means that our past sins are forgiven, that Jesus' perfect righteousness is put to our account, and that His righteousness is bestowed upon us by the Holy Spirit. So it's the Holy Spirit who sets us free from sin and selfishness and bestows upon us the character of Jesus.

Romans 8:2 reads: "For the law of the Spirit of life in Christ Jesus has made me free from the law of sin and death." That simply means that the Holy Spirit, whom Jesus gives to us when we believe, sets us free from the power of sin and death. It means that Christ's power manifested in our lives by the presence of the Holy Spirit delivers us from evil. We now have a power beyond ourselves to overcome our sinful desires and obsessions. And we are set free from death in the sense that we are given the gift of eternal life (John 3:36; 5:24; 1 John 5:11–13). Certainly we will die at the end of life, but we will live for eternity with Jesus when He comes the second time to raise the believing dead, whom He will take to be with Him in the heavenly kingdom.

The "law of sin and death" (Romans 8:2) is not referring to the Ten Commandments. It is referring to the law that sin always results in death. Paul has already said that in Romans 6:23: "For the wages of sin is death, but the gift of God is eternal life in Christ Jesus our Lord."

Then when we are set free from the power of sin and the fear of death, we have the power to obey God's law of Ten Commandments. That's the message of the next two verses, Romans 8:3, 4: "For what the law could not do in that it was weak through the flesh, God did by sending His own Son in the likeness of sinful flesh, on account of sin: He condemned sin in the flesh, that the righteous requirement of the law might be fulfilled in us who do not walk according to the flesh but according to the Spirit."

What a wonderful passage that is! The law of God is the standard of righteousness. The law points out our sin and points us to Christ. But the law cannot save us. Then how can we ever reach God's standard of obedience to His law? The answer is that Christ died "so that the just requirement of the law might be fulfilled in us, who walk not according to the flesh but according to the Spirit" (Romans 8:4, NRSV). The law's requirement is God's requirement for us. God wants us to obey His law of Ten Commandments. These commandments are not suggestions; they are commands. But on our own, in our own strength, we don't have the power to obey this law. That's where Christ comes in. He died for our sins on the cross, and because of His sacrifice, He is able to offer us the power to obey His law. That power comes to us from the Holy Spirit, whom Jesus imparts to us when we believe in Him.

Then in Romans 8:5–10, Paul proceeds to contrast the life apart from Christ with the life in fellowship with Christ. He spells out the contrast in all of its stark reality: "For those who live according to the flesh set their minds on the things of the flesh, but those who live according to the Spirit set their minds on the things of the Spirit" (Romans 8:5, NRSV). You see, those living according to the flesh are those who don't believe in Jesus Christ. They are ruled by their sinful desires. By the "flesh" in this context, the Bible means the life of sin apart from Christ.

By contrast, the Holy Spirit living within us and controlling our minds gives us victory over sin. We now have power from above not to yield to our sinful desires and power to reflect the love of Jesus. Now we can realize our true potential as sons and daughters of God, because the Spirit of Jesus Christ is in charge of our minds.

Paul goes on to say: "To set the mind on the flesh is death, but to set the mind on the Spirit is life and peace. For this reason the mind that is set on the flesh is hostile to God; it does not submit to God's law—indeed it cannot, and those who are in the flesh cannot please God" (Romans 8:6, 7, NRSV). Those in the flesh are those who have not accepted Jesus Christ as Savior and Lord. These persons have chosen to live in sin, satisfying their own selfish, sinful desires. They are headed for eternal death, because "the wages of sin is death" (Romans 6:23). Not only will they die at the end of this life, but ultimately they will be put to death for eternity (Revelation 20). At the end of the millennium, they will be raised from the dead and judged. Then God will put them to death for eternity. The Bible calls that the second death. It is mentioned in Revelation, chapter 20, verses 14 and 15. And the Bible says: "Anyone whose name was not found written in the Book of Life was cast into the lake of fire" (Revelation 20:15).

By contrast, those who are "not in the flesh," but "in the Spirit," are those who believe in Jesus Christ. They have accepted His sacrifice on the cross as being for them. They believe that He has died for their sins, and they have given Him charge of their lives. He is their God and King. They can please God because they have His power to reflect His loving character and to obey His law.

That's what Paul talks about in Romans 8:9, 10 (NRSV): "But you are not in the flesh; you are in the Spirit, since the Spirit of God dwells in you."[1] That means that you are not lost; you are not unjustified, not outside of Christ. You are in the Spirit; you are justified; your sins have been forgiven; the righteousness of Jesus is both counted for you and bestowed upon you. The Holy Spirit is in charge of your mind and body.

Then the text adds: "Anyone who does not have the Spirit of Christ does not belong to him" (Romans 8:9, NRSV). So if the Spirit of God is not in charge of your mind and body, you can't claim to be a Christian. You are then outside of Christ; living apart from Him; you are "in the flesh" and headed for eternal death.

But the contrast is wonderful! Romans 8:10 (NRSV): "But if Christ is in you, though the body is dead because of sin, the Spirit is life because of righteousness." That means that when Christ is dwelling in your life by the presence of the Holy Spirit, although you are still a fallen human being and every day brings you one day closer to the grave, yet the Holy Spirit is now your life, and His presence in your heart is righteousness in your heart. Righteousness is the qualification for heaven. Jesus said that the righteous go "into eternal life" (Matthew 25:46).

The whole point of the book of Romans is that you don't make yourself righteous. You are not righteous because you do good works. You do good works meaningfully because you have accepted Christ's righteousness. And His righteousness is given to you by the gift of the Holy Spirit. Christ in your heart is the Holy Spirit in your heart and is righteousness in your heart. When you have His divine presence, you have righteousness, and you have the gift of eternal life. That's what the next verse says: "If the Spirit of him who raised Jesus from the dead dwells in you, he who raised Christ from the dead will give life to your mortal bodies also through his Spirit that dwells in you" (Romans 8:11). By

His Spirit, Christ gives new life to our mortal bodies now. When He is in charge of our minds and bodies, we have new spiritual and physical vitality. And it's also true that when Jesus comes the second time, He will give us new bodies and bestow immortality upon us, because His Spirit is in charge of our lives.

Philippians 3:20, 21 promises us: "Our citizenship is in heaven, from which we also eagerly wait for the Savior, the Lord Jesus Christ, who will transform our lowly body that it may be conformed to His glorious body." So our mortal bodies are to be transformed and made like Christ's immortal body. And that's the emphasis in 1 Corinthians 15:53 that explains: "This corruptible must put on incorruption, and this mortal must put on immortality." This happens at the second coming of Jesus that Paul calls "the last trump" (1 Corinthians 15:52).

The message of the first eleven verses of Romans, chapter 8, is that there are two ways open to us. One way is the way of the flesh, the way of sin that leads to death. The other is the way of life and peace, the way of Jesus Christ, that leads to an eternity of joy in His heavenly kingdom.

On the Great Continental Divide some fifty miles from Denver, Colorado, the celebrated Moffat Tunnel was bored through James Peak, rising 13,000 feet above sea level. Rain falling on the eastern slope of James Peak enters the south fork of Boulder Creek, and makes its way to the Atlantic Ocean by way of the Gulf of Mexico, where giant hurricanes whirl and dance and destroy. Rain falling on the western slope of James Peak enters Fraser Creek, and makes it way to that vast ocean that Balboa, the discoverer, named the Pacific, the ocean of peace.

So it is with each one of us. We stand at the great divide. Two ways lie in view. To the left is the way of sin and death. To the right is the way that leads to righteousness, peace, and paradise.[2]

> "There are two ways for trav'lers, only two ways;
> One's a hill pathway of battle and praise;
> The other leads downward, tho' flow'ry it seem,
> Its joy is a phantom, its love is a dream."
>
> —F. E. Belden

That's why Paul adds the words of Romans 8:12–17 (NRSV): "So then, brothers and sisters, we are debtors, not to the flesh, to live according to the flesh—for if you live according to the flesh, you will die; but if by the Spirit you put to death the deeds of the body, you will live. For all who are led by the Spirit of God are children of God. For you did not receive the spirit of slavery to fall back into fear, but you have received a spirit of adoption. When we cry, 'Abba! Father!' it is that very Spirit bearing witness with our spirit that we are children of God, and if children, then heirs, heirs of God and joint heirs with Christ—if, in fact, we suffer with him so that we may also be glorified with him."

And suffering there will be! But suffering for Christ's sake is a joy by contrast with the misery of suffering because the evil one has control of our lives. The remainder of Romans 8 addresses the issue of suffering and how the Christian believer must relate to it. Verse 18 is a thrilling promise: "I consider that the sufferings of this present time are not worthy to be compared with the glory which shall be revealed in us." At the moment, Paul tells us, because of sin and death, the whole creation groans in misery, waiting to "be set free from its bondage to decay" (v. 21, NRSV). And "we ourselves, who have the first fruits of the Spirit, groan inwardly while we wait for adoption, the redemption of our bodies" (Romans 8:23, NRSV). Also, the Holy Spirit "Himself makes intercession for us with groanings which cannot be uttered" (Romans 8:26). The Holy Spirit assists us in expressing our longings to God. Jesus Christ is the one Mediator between God and humanity (1 Timothy 2:5; 1 John 2:1), but the Holy Spirit, who dwells in our hearts and guides our thoughts, expresses our longings for us with divine eloquence surpassing anything of which we could be capable.

But despite the suffering for nature and for ourselves, resulting in the pleadings of the Holy Spirit, "all things work together for good to those who love God, to those who are called according to his purpose" (Romans 8:28). Now that doesn't mean that after you have given your life to Christ you won't have any more suffering, heartache, sickness, tragedy, or death. It means that all things good and bad work together for our good. God overrules the evil that Satan and wicked people do to us, and by a divine miracle He brings good out of what the evil one intended to use to destroy us. For the believer who loves Jesus, God counteracts the suffering and the tragedy to bring blessing out of circumstances that would otherwise ruin us.

The best illustration of that is the life story of Joseph. He was sold into Egyptian slavery by his wicked brothers. The devil led those selfish, jealous brothers to commit that terrible crime. God had nothing to do with it. But years later, Joseph's brothers went down into Egypt to buy grain for their families because there was a famine in Canaan. In those intervening years, Joseph had been a slave and a prisoner. But God blessed him and promoted him to become the governor of Egypt, second in authority and power only to Pharaoh himself. When Joseph finally made himself known to his brothers, he made a very remarkable statement. He said: "Do not therefore be grieved nor angry with yourselves because you sold me here; for God sent me before you to preserve life. … So now it was not you who sent me here, but God" (Genesis 45:5, 8).

God had nothing to do with the sin of those wicked brothers. God didn't tempt them to sell their brother into slavery. Satan was responsible for that. But God overruled; He counteracted the wicked act of those brothers. God brought good out of the act that Satan and wicked men had intended to use to destroy Joseph.

And that's what God does for those who love Him and who accept Jesus Christ as Savior and Lord. God doesn't cause their sufferings, sickness, and tragedy. Satan causes these things. But God counteracts them; He overrules them to bring great blessing out of what would otherwise destroy us.

Take, for example, the notorious September 11 attack on the World Trade Center. That was a wicked act produced by evil men who were led and controlled by Satan. There was death and tragedy for many, and many families in New York were devastated by the loss of loved ones. But God is able to overrule and counteract even such a wicked crime. The country has become much more united since then. Thousands of people have reached out after God, realizing that they need His love and protection. Afghanistan has been opened up for the Christian gospel. Women and girls in that country can now be real people, receiving a good education, and living normal lives. The power of evil has been, and is being, counteracted, as God intervenes to bring good things and blessings out of what evil men and Satan had intended would destroy America and destroy thousands of innocent people.

But you say people died in this tragedy. That's true. But Paul goes on to explain that nothing, not even death, can separate the believer from Jesus Christ. We don't have to fear death when our lives are surrendered to the Lord Jesus Christ. The latter verses of Romans, chapter 8, are a paean of praise:

> "If God be for us, who can be against us? He that spared not his own Son, but delivered him up for us all, how shall he not with him also freely give us all things? Who shall lay any thing to the charge of God's elect? It is God that justifieth. Who is he that condemneth? It is Christ that died, yea rather, that is risen again, who is even at the right hand of God, who also maketh intercession for us. Who shall separate us from the love of Christ? shall tribulation, or distress, or persecution, or famine, or nakedness, or peril, or sword? … Nay, in all these things we are more than conquerors through him that loved us. For I am persuaded, that neither death, nor life, nor angels, nor principalities, nor powers, nor things present, nor things to come, nor height, nor depth, nor any other creature, shall be able to separate us from the love of God, which is in Christ Jesus our Lord" (Romans 8:31–39, KJV).

When Lincoln was in the White House he had a son they called Tad, a lively fellow who never regarded anyone as a stranger. One day among the many who waited in the reception room to see the President personally there sat a sad and troubled soldier. Tad made friends with him. When he heard the soldier's story and saw how anxious he was to see Mr. Lincoln and how fearful he was that there would be no time, Tad said, "Don't worry, I'll see that you get in."

The lad disappeared, and the hours wore on. Finally the President's secretary stepped out and announced, "Mr. Lincoln is very sorry, but he can see no one else today." The soldier's heart sank as he turned to leave. Then in a sudden desperation he faced the secretary and said, "Tad told me he would see that I got an audience with the President today." The secretary eyed the soldier and read upon his face a simple sincerity. She replied, "If Tad said you could see Mr. Lincoln today, you shall see him. He never turns Tad down."

My friend, that's the kind of relationship that exists between Jesus and the heavenly Father. The Bible says that Jesus is our heavenly Mediator. He takes our sorrows and our joys and He presents our case before the Father's throne. And the Father never turns Him down. You can come confidently to God through the mediation of Jesus Christ, and you can know that you are always heard and understood.

That's why the Bible explains: "It is Christ Jesus, who died, yes, who was raised, who is at the right hand of God, who indeed intercedes for us" (Romans 8:34, NRSV). That's why nothing can separate us from the love of Christ. Hardship, tragedy, death, you name it—none of this can destroy our relationship with Jesus Christ. And Christ and the Father are so bound together as our one God, that we can know for sure that God is on our side.

So don't be discouraged when things go wrong. Just remember to be daily surrendered to Jesus and to His will for your life, and all things good and bad will be used by God to bring blessings to you and to others with whom you come in contact.

As the blind poet, George Matheson, put it:

"Of Joy that seekest me through pain,
I cannot close my heart to Thee;
I trace the rainbow through the rain,
And feel the promise is not vain
That morn shall tearless be."

Endnotes

1. Christ in you (Romans 8:10) is the same experience as the Spirit in you (v. 9), and the Spirit in you is righteousness in you. Compare Jesus' statements in John 14:15–18. Jesus urged that we keep His commandments (John 14:15). Then He offered the power to obey, the presence of the Holy Spirit. Jesus said, "I will pray the Father, and He will give you another Helper, that He may abide with you forever, even the Spirit of truth, whom the world cannot receive, because it neither sees Him nor knows Him; but you know Him for He dwells with you and will be in you. I will not leave you orphans; I will come to you."

   The manner in which the Spirit dwells in us cannot be explained psychologically or biologically; we must accept His presence by faith. Some have made a huge point of the idea that if we believe that the Holy Spirit really dwells in us, we are giving credence to pantheism. Nothing could be farther from the truth! Pantheism involves a denial of God's personality and identifies God and nature. Pantheism teaches that God is in every living thing—plants, trees, animals, as well as humankind. The Bible teaching of Christ in the believer by the Holy Spirit is designed to emphasize that God is in control of the believer's mind and body, but this teaching accepts the personality of God and denies pantheism. Again and again the Bible speaks of the indwelling Holy Spirit. Jesus said it: "He dwells with you and will be in you" (... *hoti par humin menei kai en humin estai*) (John 14:17). Jesus underlined the point in verse 23: "If anyone loves Me, he will keep My word; and My Father will love him, and We will come to him and make Our home with him." Jesus was speaking of a close spiritual fellowship between the believer, Himself, and His Father. So close is this spiritual fellowship that Jesus could speak of it as an indwelling.

   Elsewhere in Scripture, the fact of Christ's dwelling in our hearts by the Holy Spirit is emphasized. For example, Colossians 1:27 speaks of "Christ in you the hope of glory." The same truth is underlined in Revelation 3:20: "Behold, I stand at the door and knock. If anyone hears My voice and opens the door, I will come in to him and dine with him, and he with me." Certainly it is metaphoric language, but nevertheless, language that strongly suggests Christ's control over our minds and bodies. The believer is willingly infilled with the divine power of Christ, manifested by the abiding presence of the Holy Spirit in His life.

2. Adapted from Arthur E. Lickey, *God Speaks to Modern Man* (Washington, D.C.: Review and Herald, 1952), pp. 89, 90.

CHAPTER ELEVEN

DID GOD PREDETERMINE OUR SALVATION?

This question is especially relevant because millions of contemporary Christians hold the once-saved-always-saved belief, based on the doctrine of double predestination. This doctrine teaches that in the eternal ages before the creation of our world God decreed that certain ones will be saved and others lost. Those predestined to be saved are the elect to whom God gives His irresistible grace. Once they have responded to this grace, which they inevitably will, they cannot fall away from a right legal relationship with God and be lost. Those who were predestined to be lost cannot respond to God's grace and be saved.

Writers who believe predestinarian teaching make statements like the following by Randolph O. Yeager: "The argument in Romans is devastating in its attack upon the notion that salvation can be earned by works produced by man. It also shows that while no amount of good works can bring the sinner into right relationships with God, once the sinner has that right relationship, by grace through faith, no amount of evil can separate Him from God, nor terminate his standing as God's child. However low, miserable and degrading our state may be, children of God never suffer any diminution of our standing."[1]

This simply means that elect believers remain legally saved even if they should fall into the most degrading sins. Of course every Christian believer wishes to have a settled assurance of salvation. The Bible teaches that if we believe in Christ we enjoy the beginnings of eternal life now (John 3:36; 1 John 5:11–13). But it does not follow from this that disobedience to God's laws does not change a person's salvation standing. It does not follow that no matter what professed believers do they still remain saved. Some Christians seem to have a sense of security that nothing can dispel. They regard obedience to laws as legalism. They declare that if the so-called elect want to turn away from Christ, they cannot. And temporary defection from a life of faith will inevitably be reversed. They think a once-saved person will most certainly be an inheritor of the eternal kingdom of Christ.

We can see at a glance that such a doctrine could produce very lax Christians who do whatever they wish and still cling to the so-called certainty of eternal security. Does the Bible teach that God requires obedience to His law? Certainly the Bible denies that we are saved by obedience (Romans 3:20–22; Galatians 2:16). But does the Lord expect the saved soul to obey Him? Does He plan to save us *in* our sins or *from* our sins? And can a saved soul turn away from obeying God and be lost? Can a once-saved person choose to reject salvation? These are the questions that this chapter considers.

An amusing story tells of a group of theologians who were discussing predestination and free will. The argument grew so heated that sides were drawn and the group broke up into two fiercely prejudiced factions. But one theologian, not knowing to which camp he belonged, stood for a moment trying to decide. At last he made up his mind to join in with the predestination crowd.

When he tried to push his way in they asked, "Who sent you here?"

"Nobody sent me," he replied, "I came of my own free will."

"Free will!" they shouted at him. "You can't come in here of your own free will. You belong with the other group."

So he turned and went toward the free will group. When he tried to join them someone asked, "When did you decide to join us?"

"I didn't decide," he said. "I was sent here."

"Sent here!" They were horrified. "You can't join us unless you choose to by your own free will." And so he was excluded from both companies.

The question is, what does the Bible teach?

First, God does not will all that He foresees. If God willed all that He foresaw would happen, as many theologians have taught, ultimately He would be responsible for all the evil in our world. It is true that He foresaw everything that would occur. He declares "the end from the beginning, and from ancient times things that are not yet done" (Isaiah 46:10). But He did not will or cause humanity's sin, suffering, and misery.

Even though God has always foreseen the destruction of the wicked at the end of the world (2 Thessalonians 1:7–10; Revelation 21:27), it has never been His will that they should be lost. Peter wrote that God is "not willing that any should perish but that all should come to repentance" (2 Peter 3:9). Because our world is finally to be destroyed by fire, Peter urges all to lead lives of "holy conduct and godliness" (v. 11). So concerned was Peter that the believers to whom he was writing should be saved at the Second Advent, he urged that they beware of falling away into sin and of being lost at last (v. 17). Only God could foresee who would be true till the end and who would fall away, but He did not will that anyone should be lost. The point is that God's foreknowledge is not equivalent to His will for humankind.

Paul emphasized the same message. God's design is that all humanity should be saved. He "desires all men to be saved and to come to the knowledge of the truth" (1 Timothy 2:4). The Lord knows that, because not all will choose Christ as Savior and Lord, not all will be saved. Only those who "*receive* abundance of grace and of the gift of righteousness" will have "life through the One, Jesus Christ" (Romans 5:17). But God wishes that all would receive, and He does all that an infinitely loving God can do to make it so.

The Bible says: "The grace of God that brings salvation has appeared to all men" (Titus 2:11). God's grace has not been made available only to certain ones whom He has predestined to salvation; it is readily available to all. As Jesus so beautifully explained it, "God so loved the world" that He planned for "the world" to be saved through Christ (John 3:16, 17). His grace and love were not reserved for a select class, while the rest were left untouched and unmoved. God has no favorites in respect to salvation. All people are His children, and He wishes to save them all.

Ezekiel 33:11–16 teaches that if a righteous person turns away from the Lord and lives in sin again, he or she will be lost. But the repenting sinner will be saved. God most certainly did not will that some would be lost because He foresaw that it would be so. Despite God's foreknowledge of the ultimate damnation of the wicked, He moves upon their hearts with earnest entreaties. In fact, He foresaw and rejoiced that some wicked people would respond to His pleas and finally be saved.

Isn't it a terrible insult to the Deity to argue, as the predestinarians do, that all God foresees is His will for humanity? Did God will that Adam would fall into sin, that pre-Flood humankind would live in moral degradation and ultimately be destroyed, that the inhabitants of Sodom and Gomorrah would become so debased that He would have to rain fire and brimstone upon them, that people would reject Christ's love and subject Him to merciless torture, and that the history of our world would be filled with the record of hatred, violence, disease, and death? To credit all that to the will of God is preposterous in the extreme! Such a doctrine drives people away from Christ because they cannot believe that a loving God would will such evil.

What God foresees will happen in the future is often not His will at all, but the will of Satan and of those who reject Christ.

Second, the Bible teaches that Christ died for all humankind, not only for the elect. The predestinarians often teach that Christ died only for those whom He had decreed to save. He bore their guilt on the cross, but did not bear the guilt of those whom He had decreed to damn. This is quite contrary to Bible teaching.

The Bible says: "He [Christ] Himself is the propitiation for our sins, and not for ours only but also for the sins of the whole world" (1 John 2:2). The Bible also teaches that because "One died for all, then all died. And He died for all, that those who live should live no longer for themselves, but for Him who died for them and rose again" (2 Corinthians 5:14, 15). In other words, Christ died for all, hoping that all would accept Him and be saved from sin. In this sense, "God was in Christ reconciling the world to himself" (2 Corinthians 5:19). The apostle Paul announced that Christ's sacrifice made justification available for all humanity (Romans 5:18), so that everyone willing to receive can have life (v. 17). Christ offers Himself as the Savior of the whole world. John wrote: "We have seen and testify that the Father has sent His Son as Savior of the world" (1 John 4:14). Jesus died to save the world (John 12:47).[2]

The story is told of an Indian and a white man brought under deep conviction of sin by the same sermon. The Indian was immediately led to rejoice in pardoning mercy. The white man was for a long time in distress, almost to despair. But he was at last brought to a sweet sense that his sin was forgiven. Some time later, meeting his Indian brother, he said to him: "How is it that I should be so long under conviction, when you found peace at once?"

"Oh, brother," replied the Indian, "me tell you! There come along a rich prince; He propose to give you a new coat; you look pretty good. Your old one will do a little longer. He then offer me a new coat. I look at my old blanket! I say, this good for nothing. Brother, you try to keep your own righteousness, you won't give it up; but I poor Indian, had none, so I glad at once to receive the righteousness of God—the Lord Jesus Christ."

And that's the way it is. Because Christ died for all, all may choose to receive the righteousness of Christ and be saved.

Third, God's predestination is based on His foreknowledge of human choice. The Bible teaches that God first foresaw how people would decide; then He predestined to salvation those whom He knew would accept Christ. God didn't impose arbitrary decrees upon humanity. He didn't decide that some would be saved and others lost, irrespective of their personal choice. And

He did not make it impossible for some to reject His grace and just as impossible for others to accept His grace.

The Bible teaches that those who were predestined to salvation were those whom God foreknew. "For whom he foreknew, he also predestined to be conformed to the image of his son" (Romans 8:29). The statement obviously means that God's foreknowledge that certain ones would choose Christ came first. Then He predestined them to salvation because He foresaw that they would choose to serve Him. Because in the ages before creation of our world God foresaw that certain ones would submit to Christ's loving authority, He predetermined that He would save them from sin, give them the new-birth experience, and invest them with the glory of Christ's character (v. 30). They are saved not because God arbitrarily decided ahead of time that they should be saved, but because they choose Christ as Savior and Lord. God foresaw that they would choose Christ, and on this basis, He was able to have a plan for their lives that is fulfilled as long as they are in submission to His will.

Peter reiterated Paul's teaching. He introduced his first epistle by writing: "Peter, an apostle of Jesus Christ to the pilgrims of the Dispersion … elect according to the foreknowledge of God the Father, in sanctification of the Spirit, for obedience and sprinkling of the blood of Jesus Christ" (1 Peter 1:1, 2). You see, the "elect" [chosen] pilgrims were chosen "according to the foreknowledge of God the Father." God did not choose these believers because He foresaw their good works. Faith is not a work. God foresaw that they would respond in heart to the drawing, convicting ministry of the Holy Spirit. On the basis of His foreknowledge, God chose them for holiness, spiritual cleansing, and obedience to Jesus Christ.[3]

Fourth, God gives everyone the power to choose Christ. The predestinarians argue that the only ones who can choose Christ are the elect to whom God has given irresistible grace. In the final analysis, they are saved because God chose them, not because they choose Him. The rest of humanity have no ability to choose Christ and salvation.

But the Bible does not teach that. The Bible calls for God's people to choose Him and put away their sins, implying that they have the power of choice. Joshua's command to Israel, "Choose for yourselves this day whom you will serve" (Joshua 24:15) would have been quite irrelevant if they had lacked the power of choice. The people chose God, He came into their lives, and they then had the power to obey. Of course, God's grace, in the form of divine conviction, engendered their choice in the first place. But His grace was available to all because all the people were invited to choose.

The book of Proverbs reminds us that failing to "choose the fear [reverence] of the Lord" results in rejection by God. If we turn away from God, rejecting His counsel and leading in our lives, we cannot expect Him to answer in time of need (Proverbs 1:28–30). But if we choose Him and walk in His way, we will be blessed. The wise man added, "But whoever listens to me will dwell safely, and will be secure without fear of evil" (v. 33). Such a promise would be meaningless if the predestinarians were correct in maintaining that human beings have no ability to choose God.

Isaiah completely shatters the idea that only the elect have been called by God. The Lord spoke through Isaiah to His apostate people: "I will destine you to the sword, and all of you shall bow down to the slaughter; because, when I called, you did not answer, when I spoke, you did not listen, but you did what was evil in my sight, and chose what I did not delight in" (Isaiah 65:12, NRSV). God's grace led Him to call these people, but they chose evil rather than God's will. His grace was by no means irresistible! They resisted God's call, and He rejected them.

The Lord has taught us through the apostle Paul that "the righteousness of God which is through faith in Jesus Christ" is "to all and on all who believe" (Romans 3:22). We are not left in doubt about how many are offered the gift, for Paul adds, "there is no difference, for all have sinned and fall short of the glory of God" (vs. 22, 23). The "all" who have sinned are offered without distinction the gift of Christ's righteousness if they will believe and submit to His love. The passage means nothing unless all sinners have the ability to choose to believe in Christ.

Jesus said that after His death He would "draw all peoples" to Himself (John 12:32). Jesus also said, "No one can come to Me unless the Father who sent Me draws him" (John 6:44). But He draws all to Himself! That being so, all have the ability to come to Him by their own choice. That's why Jesus' very comforting invitation to burdened souls is given to all humanity. He said: "Come to Me, all you who labor and are heavy laden, and I will give you rest" (Matthew 11:28).

John the Baptist testified "that all through him might believe" (John 1:7). Jesus is "the true light, which enlightens everyone" (v. 9, NRSV). Those who respond to the light are given "power to become children of God" (John 1:12, NRSV). Isaiah had presented the same truth. He extended God's loving invitation to all. "Look to Me, and be saved, all the ends of the earth" (Isaiah 45:22)!

It is not Christ's will that only an elect group of arbitrarily chosen people should believe in Him. He wants the whole world to believe, for He says, "Whoever desires, let him take the water of life freely" (Revelation 22:17). Jesus prayed: ". . . that the world may believe that you sent me" (John 17:21). His prayer implies that the whole world has the ability to believe.

Finally, once saved believers can fall away and be lost. The warning is all through the Bible that it is possible for believers to apostatize and be lost. This is why we are constantly admonished to watch, pray, study the Word, and daily surrender to Christ's loving will. The apostle Paul wrote: "I keep under my body, and bring it into subjection: lest that by any means, when I have preached to others, I myself should be a castaway" (1 Corinthians 9:27, KJV). What is a castaway? The Greek word is *adokimos*, which means "not standing the test," "unqualified," "worthless," "base." Paul knew that it was a very real possibility that if he did not keep his fallen nature under the control of the

Holy Spirit by daily yielding his will to Christ's loving authority, he would become worthless, unqualified, a castaway.

Hebrews, chapter 6:4–6, teaches that people who "have once been enlightened, and have tasted the heavenly gift, and have shared in the Holy Spirit, have tasted the goodness of the word of God and the powers of the age to come" (NRSV) can fall away and be lost. Unless they cease crucifying Christ by lives of sin, they cannot be renewed unto repentance and be saved. Once-saved people can be lost in sin, and backsliders can be saved only if they repent by accepting Jesus as Lord of their lives.

Hebrews 10:23–38 makes a similar point. We are instructed to cling to our faith "without wavering" (v. 23), because if we waver and choose to live in sin again, there is nothing more the Lord can do for us. "For if we willfully persist in sin after having received the knowledge of the truth, there no longer remains a sacrifice for sins, but a fearful prospect of judgment, and fury of fire that will consume the adversaries" (vs. 26, 27, NRSV). Toward the end of the chapter comes the very clear statement from God: "My righteous one will live by faith. My soul takes no pleasure in anyone who shrinks back" (v. 38, NRSV). Such people who revert to a life of sin "are lost" (v. 39, NRSV); they "draw back to perdition." You see, it is very possible for a once-saved soul to fall away and be lost by rejecting Christ's repeated overtures of love.

Peter, who knew what falling is all about, warned believers of the danger of lapsing into lives of sin. He wrote: "For if, after they have escaped the pollutions of the world through the knowledge of the Lord and Savior Jesus Christ, they are again entangled in them and overcome, the latter end is worse for them than the beginning" (2 Peter 2:20).[4]

The Bible urges us to accept Jesus Christ as Savior and Lord, and the Bible teaches that all people, irrespective of who they are, have the privilege of choosing Him as their Lord and King.

The preacher George W. Truett told the story of his preaching one night to a large crowd. At the end of the sermon, he gave an invitation for people who wanted to give their lives to Christ to come forward and occupy the three front pews in the church. Many came forward quietly and thoughtfully. Among them was a girl who was about fourteen or fifteen years old. She kept looking back as she came forward. Then she turned around and went back down the aisle and sat beside her father. She put her arms about her father's neck, and a person sitting just behind them heard her say: "Papa, you and I told mother we would meet her in the better world, when she left us last year, and I want to keep the promise. I want us to settle it, Papa. I went forward that they might pray for me. But I thought you would come too. I want us to settle it tonight. Oh, Papa, I want us to keep our promise to Mother, but I could not stay down there without you. Since Mother died, and we have been together, I have never left you except when I had to, Papa. I cannot now go without you. I want you to surrender to Christ tonight, but I cannot go without you, and I have come back to ask you if you won't surrender to Christ."

The big, strong, trembling man—and it turned out that he was one of the judges of the high court of his state—said: "Little girl, Papa will go with you. You are right." Together they went and knelt and prayed together.[5]

My friend, you and I have the privilege of making the same decision. So much hangs on our willingness to choose Christ as our Lord and Savior. We can have eternal life. We can have unending blessings in Christ's kingdom. We can be with our loved ones for eternity. We don't have to die in our sins. Now is the time to decide for Christ. Our old world is coming to an end, and Jesus will soon appear the second time. He wants us to be ready to meet Him, and the way to be ready is to enter into fellowship with Him every day, allowing Him to guide our lives, and receiving His constant gift of power to serve Him faithfully. Won't you come to Jesus today?

Endnotes

1. Randolph O. Yeager, *The Renaissance New Testament,* 18 vols. (Gretna, Louisiana: Pelican, 1983), vol. 11, p. 200.
2. John the Baptist hailed Jesus as "the Lamb of God who takes away the sin of the world!"; not merely the sins of the elect. Christ died for the sins of the whole world, even for those who reject Him. The book of Revelation teaches that sinners who repent can be saved. People are lost because they don't repent, not because they were not arbitrarily chosen for salvation (Revelation 2:21; 9:20, 21; 16:9, 11). Jesus referred to Himself as "the living bread which came down from heaven. If *anyone* eats of this bread, he will live forever" (John 6:51).
3. Romans 11:2 tells us: "God has not cast away his people whom he foreknew." The ones God foreknew were like the seven thousand in the time of Elijah who had not bowed the knee to Baal (v. 4). They were the "remnant according to the election of grace" (v. 5), who had received God's blessing (v. 7). But the greater part of Israel was rejected by God because of unbelief (v. 20). They would be accepted again, as the Christian Gentiles were accepted, if they would believe in Christ (v. 23). The remnant of Israel who were accepted by the Lord were those who had retained their faith. God foresaw their faith.

   Ephesians 1:4, 5, are verses often quoted by predestinarians: "He chose us in Him before the foundation of the world … having predestined us to adoption as sons by Jesus Christ to Himself, according to the good pleasure of his will."

   Note verses 11, 12: Christians were "predestined according to the purpose of Him who works all things according to the counsel of His will, that we *who first trusted in Christ* should be to the praise of his glory." The Ephesians "believed" in him and "were sealed with the Holy Spirit of promise (v. 13). Compare verse 19: It speaks of "the exceeding greatness of his power toward us who believe." Ephesians 2:8 teaches that we are saved by grace through faith. 1 Peter 1:20 (NASB): Christ was "*foreknown* [*proegnosmenou*] before the foundation of the world." (Compare 1 Corinthians 2:2, 7, 8; Revelation 13:8.) But Jesus could have failed (Hebrews 4:15). He overcame as our Example (1 Peter 2:21). He overcame in the same way we must overcome (Revelation 3:21). We are instructed to "walk just as he walked" (1 John 2:6). Christ was "foreknown before the foundation of the world" in the sense that God foresaw that He would not choose to sin.

4. Many other passages of Scripture teach that once-saved believers can fall away and be lost. See 2 Peter 3:17; Luke 8:13; 12:46; Matthew 18:23–35; Ezekiel 33:13, 18; 1 Timothy 4:1; 5:12; Revelation 2:4, 5; 1 Samuel 10:6, 9; 31:4.

5. Adapted from Paul Lee Tan, *Encyclopedia of 7,700 Illustrations* (Rockville MD.: Assurance, 1979), pp. 1206, 1207.

Chapter Twelve

God's Foreknowledge of Our Faith

Romans 9

Marcel Sternberger was a Hungarian immigrant who lived in Long Island, New York. He always took the 9:09 Long Island Railroad train from his suburban home to Woodside, where he caught a subway train into New York. On the morning of January 10, 1948, he caught the 9:09 as usual. But on the way, he suddenly decided to visit Laszlo Victor, a Hungarian friend who lived in Brooklyn and who was ill. He could have waited to see his friend after office hours, but he thought his friend could stand a little cheering up.

So at Ozone Park, Sternberger changed to the subway for Brooklyn, went to his friend's house, and stayed until mid-afternoon. He then boarded a Manhattan-bound subway for his Fifth Avenue office. The car was crowded, but just as he entered, a man sitting by the door suddenly jumped up to leave, and Sternberger took the seat.

Sternberger was a photographer, and he was struck by the features of the man sitting to his left. He was a man probably in his late thirties, and his eyes seemed to have a hurt expression. He was reading a Hungarian-language newspaper, and since Sternberger was Hungarian, that got his attention. After a few minutes the two men got into conversation. The man's name was Paskin. He had been a law student when the war broke out, but he had been put into a labor battalion and sent to the Ukraine. Later he was captured by the Russians and put to work burying the German dead. After the war he walked hundreds of miles, until he reached his home in Debrecen, a large city in eastern Hungary.

Then he told Sternberger the rest of the story. His old home was now occupied by strangers. But he learned that the Nazis had taken his wife to Auschwitz. Paskin gave up all hope, and he left for Paris where he managed to emigrate to the United States in October 1947, just three months before Sternberger met him on the train.

Then Sternberger remembered a young woman whom he had met recently who was also from Debrecen. She had been sent to Auschwitz. From there she had been transferred to work in a German munitions factory. Her relatives had been killed in the gas chambers. Later she was liberated by the Americans and brought to the U.S. in the first boatload of displaced persons in 1946. Sternberger had her address and phone number.

Then casually he asked the man riding the train with him, "Is your first name Bela?" The man turned pale. "Yes!" he said, "How did you know?"

Sternberger asked, "Was your wife's name Marya?" "Yes! Yes!" he said.

They got off the train at the next stop and went to a phone booth. They called Marya, and after a time she answered. Sternberger asked her the address of her house in Debrecen, and it matched exactly the address Paskin had given him. Then he handed the receiver to Paskin, and with great emotion he spoke to his wife for the first time in years. Sternberger put Paskin into a taxicab and directed the driver to Marya's address, and there was an indescribably joyous reunion of husband and wife.

Was it chance that Sternberger suddenly decided to visit his sick friend and hence take a subway line into the city that he had never ridden before? Was it chance that caused the man sitting by Paskin to leave just as Sternberger entered the car, so that he could have the seat? Was it chance that caused Bela Paskin to be sitting beside Sternberger, reading a Hungarian newspaper? Was it chance or did God arrange this series of events?

Romans 8:28 says that "all things work together for good to those who love God, to those who are the called according to His purpose." That doesn't mean that God causes all things. It means that God overrules; He providentially intervenes; He counteracts the work of Satan to bring good out of what the evil one would use to destroy us.

Then the next two verses say: "For whom He foreknew, he also predestined to be conformed to the image of His Son, that He might be the firstborn among many brethren. Moreover whom He predestined, these He also called; whom He called, these He also justified; and whom He justified, these He also glorified" (Romans 8:29, 30).

Put in simple language, this means that God foresaw the faith of those who accept Jesus Christ as Savior and Lord. And on the basis of His foreknowledge of their choice, He was able to work out a plan for their lives. God was able to arrange wonderful blessings for Joseph, even though his wicked brothers had sold him into Egypt. And God was able to counteract the bad things that had happened to Bela Paskin and his wife, Marya, and to bring them happily together again. God doesn't predetermine that certain ones will believe or that others will not believe in Christ. He foresees our belief, and because of His foreknowledge of our choice, He is able to put into action a wonderful plan for our lives.

In the preceding chapter, we studied what the Bible teaches about predestination. We discovered five points that the Bible teaches: (1) God does not will all that He foresees; (2) Christ died for all humankind, not only for the elect; (3) God's predestination is based on His foreknowledge of human choice; (4) God gives everyone the power to choose Christ; and (5) once-saved believers can fall away and be lost.

Now we come to Romans, chapter 9, which is often misapplied by predestinarians to prove that in the eternal ages before Creation, God arbitrarily decreed that some will be saved and others lost and that they have no choice in the matter. If the chapter were teaching that idea, it would be contradicting the clear message on predestination elsewhere in Scripture.

The bottom line in Romans, chapter 9, is contained in the last four verses: "What shall we say then? That Gentiles, who did not pursue righteousness, have attained to righteousness, even the righteousness of faith; but Israel, pursuing the law of righteousness, has not attained to the law of righteousness. Why? Because they did not seek it by faith, but as it were, by the works of the law. For they stumbled at that stumbling stone. As it is written: 'Behold, I lay in Zion a stumbling stone and rock of offense, and whoever believes on Him will not be put to shame.'" (Romans 9:30–33).

Paul's point is that God's gift of righteousness is given only to those who have faith in Jesus Christ. The Israelites of his day tried to earn righteousness by their obedience to the law, and they failed. But the Gentiles who had faith in Jesus Christ were given His free gift of righteousness. The fact is that God accepts for salvation only those who have faith in Jesus.

Now it's important to realize that faith is not a human work. Faith is not a work that earns the gift of righteousness. Faith is God's gift to those who respond in heart to the conviction of the Holy Spirit. Even so, faith is our response, our choice. We can choose to believe in Jesus or we can choose not to believe. We can choose to respond in heart to the conviction of the Holy Spirit or we can reject His conviction.

God foresees who will accept Jesus and who will not. And on the basis of His foreknowledge, He then has a plan for the lives of those whom He foresees will accept Jesus. God's predestination is His plan for the lives of those whom He foresees will have faith in His Son, Jesus Christ. God doesn't foreordain that some will believe and others will not believe. He foresees human choice; He foresees our faith response. And when He foresees that you will accept Jesus as your Lord and Savior, then He is able to make all things that happen to you, the good and the bad, part of His great plan for saving you from sin. God is able to counteract Satan's evil acts for those who have faith in Jesus Christ. He was able to overrule Satan's designs and bring Bela Paskin and his wife back together again.

That's the message of Romans, chapter 9. In verses 6 and 7, Paul writes: "For they are not all Israel who are of Israel, nor are they all children because they are the seed of Abraham; but, 'In Isaac your seed shall be called.' "

Not all Israelites truly belong to Israel, He says. Why? Because many did not believe in Jesus Christ. Paul adds, "In Isaac your seed shall be called." What does that mean? You see, Isaac was a miracle child. Abraham and Sarah believed God's promise, and they had a child in their old age. Isaac, the miracle child, is a symbol of the life of faith! Just as Abraham and Sarah believed in God, so we can believe in Jesus Christ. And when we do, we are then part of spiritual Israel.

Romans 9:8 spells out the application: "Those who are the children of the flesh, these are not the children of God; but the children of the promise are counted as the seed." In other words, those who have faith in Jesus Christ are the children of the promise, and these are the ones whom God accepts as the true children of Abraham.

Then Paul gives a second illustration in verses 10–13 (NRSV): "Nor is that all; something similar happened to Rebecca when she had conceived children by one husband, our ancestor Isaac. Even before they had been born or had done anything good or bad (so that God's purpose of election might continue, not by works but by his call) she was told, 'The elder shall serve the younger.' As it is written, 'I have loved Jacob, but I have hated Esau.' "

God foresaw that Jacob would respond in faith to His call and that Esau would not. Faith is not a human work; it is God's gift. Jacob accepted it; Esau did not. God offered salvation to both men. The passage doesn't teach that God's pre-election of Jacob was independent of Jacob's choice of grace; it teaches that God's predestination was independent of Jacob's good works (v. 11). Faith is not a work that saves us; it is an engendered response to God's grace. God chose Jacob ahead of time because he foresaw that Jacob would have faith. He rejected Esau ahead of time because He foresaw that Esau would not have faith. God didn't hate Esau in the modern sense of the term. The Greek word for "hate" is *miseo*. In this context, it means "to love less," or "to put to one side." Because God is love (1 John 4:8) He is incapable of hating in the human sense of the term. God knew ahead of time that the works of both Jacob and Esau would be bad. Both men were sinners. But God knew ahead of time that Jacob would have faith and would repent of his sins. On that basis, God had a predetermined plan for Jacob's life. He knew that Jacob would surrender to Him, and He worked things out so that His plan for Jacob's life would be fulfilled.

A tired, careless youth working on the deck of a Pittsburgh-bound boat in the Ohio and Pennsylvania Canal lost his hold on a grimy rope one drizzly night and tumbled into the icy water. It was an impenetrably black night, but by great good luck the rope's end dangled over the side within reach of the young man who floundered about. He grasped it and hauled himself aboard. His escape was miraculous.

"Why was I spared?" he asked himself. "I have been saved to do some real good with my life," he decided. And so James A. Garfield began the career that led him to the White House.

God had a plan for Garfield's life, and so God overruled his accident to enable His plan to work out. God overrules evil; He counteracts it, so that His plan for those who believe in Jesus will be fulfilled.

Romans 9:14–16 (NRSV) reiterates Paul's point: "What then are we to say? Is there injustice on God's part? By no means! For he says to Moses, 'I will have mercy on whom I have mercy, and I will have compassion on whom I have compassion.' So it depends not on human will or exertion, but on God who shows mercy."

The point is that God shows mercy to those whom He foresees will have faith in Jesus Christ. He chooses those whom He knows ahead of time will choose Jesus. This choice is not a human work; it is a heart response to the call of God's Holy Spirit. God doesn't force people to choose Christ. His grace is not irresistible. It can be rejected. But those who don't reject God's grace have the wonderful joy of having His plan for their lives fulfilled.

That doesn't mean that they can't suffer any more. The devil sees to it that God's believing people sometimes suffer terribly.

But our loving God overrules the suffering to bring blessing out of what the devil would use to destroy us.

It reminds me of the story of a woman who boarded a bus and obeyed the driver's command to step to the rear. There were no empty seats, so she took her place with those who were standing. Suddenly a young man tapped her on the shoulder and offered her a seat. She thanked him and sat down. The bus rolled on, and a little later, when the seat to her left was vacant, the young man who had been so kind sat down. As he did, a woman to the right leaned across and said to the young man, "I'm glad to see you've found a seat at last. You've been constantly up and down, giving your seat to someone."

The young man very casually replied, "Oh, I don't like to see women stand. You see, my legs can't get tired; they are both artificial."

And that is the attitude of suffering believers in Jesus Christ. They accept their lot in life, knowing that, in some way that may not be revealed in this life, God will overrule the suffering to bring joy and salvation to them and to other people.

Paul continues in Romans 9 by referring to Pharaoh. "For the Scripture says to Pharaoh, 'Even for this same purpose I have raised you up, that I might show My power in you, and that My name might be declared in all the earth.' Therefore He has mercy on whom he wills, and whom He wills He hardens." (Romans 9:17, 18).

Pharaoh chose to reject God. He refused to believe God and to accept His loving authority. Some passages say that God hardened Pharaoh's heart (For example, see Exodus 4:21; 7:3). But other passages say that Pharaoh hardened his own heart (See, for example, Exodus 8:32; 9:34). The paradox is explained by two simple facts: (1) In Scripture, God is often said to cause that which He allows, even though the real cause is the devil; and (2) God's loving appeals will soften one heart and increasingly harden another, because one will choose to accept them and another will not. Appeals rejected result in deepening alienation from the Lord. Just as the same sun hardens clay but melts wax, so God's love hardens those who reject Him and softens those who respond to Him in love.

There is no suggestion in the passage that Pharaoh was predestined to be lost, that he had no choice but to react negatively to God's appeals. God wills to have mercy on believers, and wills to reject unbelievers. Pharaoh had a choice. He could have accepted God's will, but he chose not to. He made himself an enemy of God, and he suffered the terrible consequences.

In Romans 9:22, Paul speaks of "the vessels of wrath prepared for destruction." The objects, or vessels, of wrath are those who choose not to believe. In the next verse, Paul speaks of "the vessels of mercy, which He had prepared beforehand for glory, even us whom he called, not of the Jews only, but also of the Gentiles" (Romans 9:23, 24). The objects, or vessels, of God's mercy are those who choose to believe in Jesus Christ for the gift of righteousness. They are not people whom God has arbitrarily chosen for salvation while He chooses to damn the rest of the world. God's foreknowledge of our choice of Jesus Christ led Him to regard us as the objects of His mercy.

In Romans 9:27, Paul quotes Isaiah: "Though the number of the children of Israel be as the sand of the sea, the remnant will be saved." The remnant who are saved are those who believe in Jesus Christ, whether they are Jews or Gentiles. Romans 11:23 (NRSV) says: "And even those of Israel, if they do not persist in unbelief, will be grafted in, for God has the power to graft them in again." That's the whole point of Romans 9. If people will believe, they will be part of God's remnant that will be saved. If they will not believe, they will be rejected.

Then comes Paul's bottom-line argument to which we referred earlier (Romans 9:30–33). The Gentiles did not try to earn righteousness by their own obedience to the law. By faith, they accepted Jesus' gift of righteousness. But the Israelites tried to earn righteousness by works of law. The result was that, not only did they not become righteous, but they were rejected by God.

Romans, chapter 9, must be interpreted in the light of the overall teaching of Scripture on the question of human choice and divine predestination. The message throughout the Bible is that God hoped all would accept His love. But in sorrow He predestined to salvation only those who He foresaw would accept Him. He has given light and the power to choose to every human soul. People are not lost who accept Christ and allow His Spirit to reign in their hearts.

Have you chosen Christ as Lord of your life? There is forgiveness, power to become like Jesus, and eternal life with Christ available for you if you receive Him as Savior and Lord.

A group of businessmen went to a remote mountain retreat for a weekend of leadership training. Expecting graphs, statistics, and pep talks, they were "blown away" when their boss asked them to trade their notebooks for shovels.

"I want you to dig a ditch 2 feet wide and 10 inches deep around the perimeter of my cabin," he said. And with those words, he disappeared inside the cabin.

At first nobody said anything. But soon their silence turned into questioning. Then they started arguing about 9 inches being close enough to 10, and complaining about having risen to the top of the corporate ladder, only to be forced to do manual labor.

Finally, Bill, a newcomer to the group, turned to the others and said, "Who cares why he told us to do it, let's just do it!"

With those words, the cabin door opened, and the boss reappeared. "Gentlemen," he said, as he grabbed Bill's hand, "I'd like you to meet your new vice president."

There are three things we can learn from that story: (1) When God doesn't explain something, it's because you don't need the details. (2) When God doesn't speak, it's because He's working things out. (3) When God tests you on one level, it's because He's getting ready to take you to the next. So don't question His wisdom. God's purposes for your life will be fulfilled if you believe in Him and obey Him.

Little four-year-old Ashley surprised her mother, Kathleen Treanor, by asking the disturbing question: "Mommy, would you be sad if I died?"

Her mother replied, "Of course I would, Ashley. I'd miss you terribly."

The little one replied. "But don't be sad, Mommy. Someday we'll be in heaven. God will watch over you."

Then the conversation changed to happier subjects.

A few days later, Kathleen brought Ashley to Grandma LaRue's house. Grandma was a wonderful sitter, whose home overflowed with love, comfort, and joy. Without a doubt, crafts and homemade cookies would soon be on the way.

After tenderly kissing Ashley goodbye, Kathleen jumped in her car and hurried off to work. She was sitting at her desk when she heard a huge blast that rocked Oklahoma City. A co-worker flipped on the television, and there they saw the results of the terrible explosion at the Murrah Federal Building. Kathleen could hardly believe her eyes. *Not in my hometown*, she thought. *Not here!*

Within moments, her sister called with the unimaginable news, unraveling the last shred of Kathleen's protective shroud of peace. Luther and LaRue Treanor had taken Ashley to their appointment with the Social Security office, which was inside the Murrah building. Her little four-year-old, Ashley, was in that devastated structure, the one she was watching on the news! In a few days, Kathleen's mother and father, along with Ashley, were found among the dead.

Kathleen slipped into a deep, dark depression, not able to comprehend how evil minds could change the destiny of so many innocent souls. But months later Kathleen remembered Ashley's words just before the explosion, "Don't be sad if I die. Someday we'll be in heaven. God will watch over you." Suddenly, Kathleen realized she was being prepared for a mission far beyond her understanding. She began a healing ministry to other suffering people. After September 11, she went to New York and ministered to many grieving individuals, giving them new faith and new hope for the future.

No one knows what the future holds. But God does. And for those who put their trust in Him, His merciful overruling

Providence provides healing in this life and the blessed hope of a joyous eternity with Him. Trust Him, my friend; He loves you.

Chapter Thirteen

How to be Saved

Romans 10

When the Second World War flamed across the Pacific after Pearl Harbor, all American, British, and Australian personnel were hastily evacuated from their mission stations, and properties were left in the hands of native converts, many of whom were only a few years removed from cannibalism. When the Japanese swept down upon New Georgia in the Solomon Islands, three ships operated by the Seventh-day Adventist Church at Marova Lagoon were turned over to the British Army. The mission properties were left in the care of Kata Ragoso, a mission-educated son of a chieftain.

Under the command of a British major, the three small schooners slipped in and out of the waters of Guadalcanal and other islands, laying mines and harassing the enemy. Finally the tiny fleet gathered in Marova Lagoon to wait for orders to flee to Australia. In a few days, a native paddled alongside one of the ships and shouted in pidgin English: "Jap man 'e come! 'Im 'e come plenty big fella ship! You go one time quick!"

Two of the ships got under way, but the engines of one ship, the *Portal*, wouldn't start. So the British crew of the *Portal* dumped two drums of gasoline into her cabin and tossed in a lighted torch as they abandoned ship. Flames quickly engulfed the cabin and were sweeping along the deck as the other two ships sailed off with the British sailors.

On the beach, Ragoso and a dozen natives sadly watched the burning of the mission vessel that had brought them a new way of life. They loved this small ship. Ragoso said to his friends in pidgin English: "She boat belong God fella. He maybe no let burn if we make pray." And pray they did—in simple, childlike faith. Then it happened. As though a giant snuffer had been suddenly lowered over the *Portal*, the flames died down and went out.

The excited islanders paddled out to the smoking schooner. Nothing much seemed damaged but the cabin paint and the rigging. After a quick inspection, Ragoso and his friends worked the small ship into a hidden inlet and up a small stream. There they anchored her among a dense growth that formed an umbrella over the stream. The masts were lowered and lashed along the deck. Palm branches were cut and positioned to hide the craft.

But Ragoso wanted to be sure that even if the Japanese did find the schooner, they could never use it. He and several other natives went to work on the engine. Early next morning, Japanese forces steamed into the lagoon. The islanders found themselves under the iron rule of tyrannical conquerors, but not a single one betrayed the hiding place of the *Portal.*

Three years went by. Then came a day in 1945 when the war came to an end, and Pastor Norman Ferris, a missionary from Australia, returned to Marova Lagoon. Great was the rejoicing, and when the excitement had subsided, several natives ran to the beach and jumped into a canoe. Ragoso explained proudly, "They go bring 'im boat *Portal*." Pastor Ferris responded, "But the *Portal* has been destroyed. The government wrote and told us."

Ragoso chuckled, "Government 'im 'e no savi. 'Im 'e boat belong God fella. 'E no burn."

In a few minutes the *Portal* slipped alongside the dock and Pastor Ferris went aboard. "This is wonderful," he exclaimed. "But Ragoso, she has been stripped of her engine. The Japanese must have found her."

Ragoso chuckled again. "We got," he said.

Ragoso fingered a chain hanging from his neck. On it were a half dozen small washers and nuts. He said, "Ragoso 'e wear engine for necklace. See? Other boy 'e plenty got, too. You wait. We bring."

In they came from up and down the coast, each bringing a precious part for the engine. Some had hung them in trees;

others, like Ragoso, had worn them around their necks. Within a week the engine was reassembled. But would it run? While hundreds of islanders watched, Pastor Ferris pressed the starter. The old engine sputtered, coughed, and roared into life.

The *Portal* ran for years after that and became the queen of the mission fleet. Ragoso often repeated, "*Portal* 'im 'e God fella's boat. 'E no burn."[1]

Now that's faith. Those humble natives trusted in God, and He rewarded their faith. And that's how the Bible explains we are to be saved. We trust in God, we believe in Jesus Christ and accept Him as our Savior and Lord, and we are His for eternity. We won't burn in the fires of the last great day. We will be taken to be with Jesus for eternity.

That's the message of Romans, chapter 10. The apostle Paul explained that many of the Israelites of his day could not be saved because they trusted in their own righteousness instead of accepting the righteousness of God. He grieved over his countrymen. He wrote: "Brethren, my heart's desire and prayer to God for Israel is that they may be saved. For I bear them witness that they have a zeal for God, but not according to knowledge. For they being ignorant of God's righteousness, and seeking to establish their own righteousness, have not submitted to the righteousness of God" (Romans 10:1–3).

Those verses continue the lament that begins with verse 30 of the previous chapter, Romans 9. Paul pointed out that the Gentiles received the gift of Christ's righteousness because they sought it by faith. But the Israelites did not receive the gift of Christ's righteousness because they tried to earn it by their own works of law. They didn't have faith in Christ, and so they could not be saved and could not be given the righteousness of God.

Chapter 10 continues the same theme. Righteousness and salvation cannot be earned by human merit. It can only be received as a free gift from God to those who have faith in Jesus Christ. That's the meaning of Romans, chapter 10, verse 4. The verse translates literally from the Greek text: "For Christ is the end of the law for righteousness to all those who believe." That simply means that when you believe in Christ, He comes into your heart and brings to an end your attempt to earn salvation and righteousness by your own works.[2]

Romans 10:4 is not saying that Christ brings the law to an end. He has never abolished His law, and He never will. Again and again, the Bible teaches that God's law can be obeyed by faith in Christ. Romans 3:31 reads: "Do we then make void the law through faith? Certainly not! On the contrary, we establish the law." Romans 7:7 tells us: "What shall we say then? Is the law sin? Certainly not! On the contrary, I would not have known sin except through the law. For I would not have known covetousness unless the law had said, 'You shall not covet.' "

So the law still functions as the standard of God's righteousness. The law points out our sin and points us to Jesus Christ. Romans, chapter 8, verses 3 and 4, tells us: "For what the law could not do in that it was weak through the flesh, God did by sending His own Son in the likeness of sinful flesh, on account of sin: He condemned sin in the flesh."

Romans 10:4 is not telling us that the law has been done away with. It is telling us that Christ is the end of the attempt to earn righteousness by works of law for those who believe in Jesus Christ. When we accept Him, He is the means by which we receive the gift of righteousness by faith, and that gift empowers us to obey His law.

Then in the next few verses, Paul continues to contrast the attempt to earn righteousness with the acceptance of Christ's gift of righteousness by those who have faith. Romans 10:5 reads: "Moses writes about the righteousness which is of the law, 'The man who does those things shall live by them.' " Paul is quoting Leviticus 18:5 that says: "You shall therefore keep My statutes and My judgments, which if a man does, he shall live by them: I am the Lord."

This is not teaching righteousness by works.[3] In the context of the Old Testament, the passage means that faithfulness to God's covenant makes it possible for believers to obey God's law.

The covenant is an agreement with God based on love for Him. Obedience to the law that results from the covenant relationship with God, which is loving fellowship with God, is the means of life. Through Moses, the Lord spoke to the children of Israel at Sinai: "Now therefore, if you will indeed obey My voice and keep My covenant, then you shall be a special treasure to Me above all people; for all the earth is Mine" (Exodus 19:5).

God's covenant offered at Sinai was the same covenant that He offered to Abraham in Genesis, chapter 17 (see Galatians 3:15–18), and the very basis of it was, and is, righteousness and salvation by faith in the Messiah to come. We enter into loving fellowship with God when we believe (Deuteronomy 6:4–6). He writes His law on our minds by giving us the Holy Spirit (Hebrews 8:10–12; John 14:15–18). This involves the gift of Christ's righteousness to our hearts (Romans 8:9, 10). Circumcision, the sign of the covenant between Abraham and God (Genesis 17), symbolized the bestowal oı Christ's righteousness upon those who believe (Romans 4:11).

When Moses wrote that "the person who does these things will live by them," he meant that the person who has faith in God and obeys His law by faith is the person who shall live. But it is also true that if a person never sinned but always obeyed God's law, that person would have life. No human being has been able to do that. And that's why Paul goes on to explain righteousness by faith.

Paul writes: "The righteousness that comes from faith speaks in this way" (Romans 10:6). Then he proceeds to quote Deuteronomy 30, verses 11–14: "Do not say in your heart, Who will ascend into heaven?" And Paul adds, "that is, to bring Christ down from above." Then he continues to quote, "… or, 'Who will descend into the abyss?' " And Paul adds, "that is, to bring Christ up from the dead." Paul asks, "But what does it say?" In other words, what does righteousness by faith teach? Paul answers by quoting Deuteronomy 30:14: "The word is near you, even in your mouth and in your heart." Paul adds: "that is, the word of faith which we preach" (Romans 10:8).

Now that's a mighty important revelation! It means that the New Testament message of righteousness and salvation by faith is identical to the Old Testament message. Paul taught exactly what Moses taught. When you believe in Christ, the law of God is written on your heart. You don't obey the law of God *to be saved.* You obey the law of God *because you are saved.* You obey the law that God writes on your heart when you believe in Jesus Christ.

That's what God's everlasting covenant is all about. Hebrews 8:10–13 quotes Jeremiah 31:31–34. The New Testament quotes the Old Testament on the question of righteousness and salvation by faith. The Lord says: "This is the covenant that I will make with the house of Israel: After those days … I will put My laws in their mind and write them on their hearts; and I will be their God, and they shall be my people" (Hebrews 8:10).

Think of that! God's law is written on our hearts! That's what is involved in the everlasting covenant experience. We believe in Jesus Christ, and His Holy Spirit comes into our hearts and writes His will on our minds. We serve Christ not to earn merit and earn righteousness. We serve Him because we love Him and because He gives us His merit and His righteousness.

We trust Him in every situation of life, even when things go wrong. As Romans 8:28 reminds us, He overrules the bad things to bring blessing to us, and through us, to others.

Pedro was a little boy who lived in a small farm house in Spain. Pedro loved Jesus very much, and his mother and father always took him to church whenever they could afford to make the trip. One morning when Pedro got up his father called him and said, "Son, you'll have to be quite careful today. Your mother is very ill. The doctor says she will have to be kept quiet for a few days." So all day long, whenever Pedro thought of it, he asked God to heal his mother quickly.

The next day Pedro and his father went into a room to have their morning worship. Pedro's father began to read from his Bible: "God is our refuge and strength, a very present help in trouble." Then he was rudely interrupted by a loud banging on the door. They opened the door, and someone shouted, "The soldiers are coming! They are burning all the houses and killing the people! Don't stop for anything, but flee quickly!" Then they were gone to the next house to warn the people.

Poor Pedro thought his heart would break. He knew they couldn't go and leave his sick mother behind. Then his father read some more of the passage where he had left off: "Therefore we will not fear, though the earth should change, and though the mountains shake in the heart of the sea. ... The Lord of hosts is with us; the God of Jacob is our refuge" (Psalm 46:1, 2, 11, NRSV). Then they got down on their knees and asked God to protect them from all harm and danger.

They looked out the window to see what would happen. They saw the soldiers coming nearer, and they watched the flames of the burning houses. It seemed as if nothing could save them. They had to rest entirely on God. Suddenly it began to get dark, and the wind began to blow. Before long the rain was coming down very hard. The soldiers began to think of getting to the next town for shelter. So they left, and didn't come near Pedro's house. He had learned that "God is our refuge and strength, a very present help in trouble."

In a few more days Pedro's mother was able to be about again, and she found Pedro a much changed little boy. Now he trusted in Jesus more than he had ever trusted before.

The Bible says: "If you confess with your mouth the Lord Jesus and believe in your heart that God has raised him from the dead, you will be saved. For with the heart one believes to righteousness, and with the mouth confession is made to salvation" (Romans 10:9, 10). Accepting Jesus as Savior and Lord is the means of salvation. We must accept not only that Jesus died for our sins but that He rose from the dead. That's why Paul says that if we believe in our hearts that God raised Him from the dead, we will be saved.

First Corinthians, chapter 15, emphasizes the importance of believing that Jesus rose from the dead. Paul writes: "If Christ has not been raised, your faith is futile, and you are still in your sins. ... But in fact Christ has been raised from the dead, the first fruits of those who have died. For since death came through a human being, the resurrection of the dead has also come through a human being; for as all die in Adam, so all will be made alive in Christ. But each in his own order: Christ the first fruits, then at his coming those who belong to Christ." (1 Corinthians 15:17–23, NRSV).

Because Christ rose from the dead, those who die believing in Him will be raised at His second advent. When we believe that in our hearts and confess it openly by the things we say and the way we live, we have salvation. Christ gives us the gift of His righteousness, and this gift is justification.

The Bible says that " 'Whoever believes on Him will not be put to shame.' For there is no distinction between Jew and Greek, for the same Lord over all is rich to all who call upon Him" (Romans 10:11, 12). Then Paul goes on to say that people can only believe if they hear the gospel, and they can hear the gospel only if someone is sent to proclaim the gospel (Romans 10:13–16). "So then faith comes by hearing, and hearing by the word of God" (Romans 10:17). That's why all Christians should be in the business of making Christ known to the people around them. Because Christ died for all, all should have the opportunity to hear the gospel call. Jesus wants to be the Savior of our neighbors and friends, and He urges us to invite them to come to Him and believe.

Paul reminds us that in his day the good news of salvation through Christ went to the whole known world. Romans, chapter 10, verse 18, reads: "But I say, have they not heard? Yes indeed: 'Their sound has gone out to all the earth, and their words to the ends of the world.' "[4] Christ's apostles obeyed His command to present the gospel in Jerusalem, Judea, Samaria, and to the ends of the earth (Acts 1:8). And Christ urges us to be involved today in presenting the gospel to the world. Jesus promised that when this "gospel of the kingdom will be preached in all the world as a witness to all the nations ... then the end will come" (Matthew 24:14).

The good news of salvation through Christ must go to every nation on earth. The Muslim nations also must have an opportunity to hear the gospel message. We are just as responsible to them as we are to every other group on earth. We are seeing some signs that the good news of salvation through Jesus Christ is being taken to Muslim countries. And we must pray and work to make Jesus known everywhere.

Paul spoke to the Israelites of his day:[5] "Did Israel not understand? First Moses says, 'I will make you jealous of those who are not a nation; with a foolish nation I will make you angry' " (Romans 10:19, NRSV). In other words, the national chauvinism of the Israelites was not to stand in the way of the Christians who were instructed to proclaim the gospel to the Gentiles. Paul quotes Isaiah, who wrote the words of God Himself: "I have been found by those who did not seek me; I have shown myself to those who did not ask for me" (Romans 10:20, NRSV). The Gentile nations of earth have heard and are hearing the good news of salvation through Christ. They did not seek for Him, but when they have heard the gospel, many in those nations have responded. And they are responding today.

If you don't think Christ cares enough about you to work for your salvation, you are wrong. By His Spirit he speaks to your heart, and He won't let go as long as there is hope that you will come to Him and give Him your life.

Some years ago on a hot summer day in South Florida, a little boy decided to go for a swim in the old swimming hole behind his house. In a hurry to dive into the cool water, he ran out the back door, leaving behind shoes, socks, and shirt as he went. He jumped into the water, not realizing that as he swam toward the middle of the lake, an alligator was swimming toward the shore. His mother in the house was looking out the window and saw the two as they got closer and closer together. Frantically she ran toward the water, yelling to her son as loudly as she could. Hearing her voice, the little boy became alarmed and made a U-turn to swim to his mother.

But it was too late. Just as he reached her, the alligator reached him. From the dock, the mother grabbed her little boy by the arms just as the alligator snatched his legs. That began an incredible tug-of-war between the two. The alligator was much stronger than the mother, but the mother was much too passionate to let go.

A farmer happened to drive by, heard her screams, raced from his truck with his gun, took aim, and shot the alligator.

Remarkably, after weeks and weeks in the hospital, the little boy survived. His legs were extremely scarred by the vicious attack of the alligator, and on his arms were deep scratches where his mother's fingernails dug into his flesh in her effort to hang on to the son she loved.

The newspaper reporter who interviewed the boy after the trauma asked if he would show him his scars. The boy lifted his pant legs. And then, with obvious pride, he said to the reporter, "But look at my arms. I have great scars on my arms too. I have them because my mom wouldn't let go."

We have scars too, not from an alligator, but from our painful struggles with sin. Satan is the evil alligator who gets his teeth into us and refuses to let go. But our Lord Jesus Christ loves us so much that He pulls us to Himself, and He won't let go either as long as there is some hope of saving us. In the midst of your struggles, God is there, holding on to you, and not allowing you to be destroyed.

Trust Him today, trust Him every day. Remember the words of the Bible: "If you confess with your lips that Jesus is Lord and believe in your heart that God raised him from the dead, you will be saved" (Romans 10:9, NRSV).

Endnotes

1. Adapted from Reuben Hare, *Fuzzy-Wuzzy Tales* (Washington, D.C.: Review and Herald, 1950), pp. 60–68.
2. Romans 10:4 translates literally from the Greek: "For Christ is the end of the law for [unto, as a means of] righteousness to all those who believe." The text is not saying that the law is abolished. Compare

Romans 3:31; 7:7; 8:3, 4; James 2:10–12; 1 John 2:4; Revelation 12:17; 14:12. Note the context of Romans 10:4 (9:30–10:4). The contrast is between righteousness by faith and righteousness by works. Paul's point is that exercising faith in Christ is the end of the attempt to earn salvation and righteousness by our own works.

3. In Romans 10:5, Paul quotes Leviticus 18:5. This text is not teaching righteousness by works. In the context of the Old Testament, the passage means that faithfulness to God's covenant makes it possible for believers to obey God's law. Obedience to the law that results from the covenant relationship is the means of life. Compare Ezekiel 16:60; 20:11; 36:26, 27. Maintaining the covenant relationship is basic to obedience to God's laws: Exodus 19:5, 6. This is the same covenant relationship that God gave to Abraham (Genesis 17). The essence of the covenant relationship with God is love for God, fellowship with Him, resulting in obedience to His law (see Deuteronomy 6:4–6). Taken out of its Old Testament context, Leviticus 18:5 may mean that perfect obedience to the law of God is the means of life. But no human being is capable of such perfect obedience apart from a covenant relationship with God. Only when we enjoy loving fellowship with God do we desire to obey His law, only then do we have the power from above to keep His law. Hence, Paul goes on to emphasize the essence of the covenant relationship, the fact that the law of God must be written on our hearts.
4. Paul is quoting Psalm 19:4.
5. Romans 10:19 quotes Deuteronomy 32:21; Romans 10:20 quotes Isaiah 65:1; Romans 10:21 quotes Isaiah 65:2.

CHAPTER FOURTEEN
GOD'S CHOSEN PEOPLE TODAY
ROMANS 11

Who are God's chosen people today? The short answer is that His chosen people are those who have faith in Jesus Christ as Savior and Lord. They are people saved by grace who, because of their faith in Jesus, devote themselves to the service of God and who, by the power He imparts to them, obey His commandments. They don't obey to be saved; they obey because they are saved. These people come from all nationalities, all ethnic groups, and from every walk of life. They include blacks and whites, Asians and Caucasians, the rich and the poor, the educated and the uneducated. Whoever you are, you may be one of God's chosen people if you believe in Jesus Christ and, because of your belief, and by virtue of the power God gives, you obey His commandments.

While Cameron Townsend was a third-year student at Occidental College in Los Angeles, he volunteered to go to Guatemala as a Bible salesman. But in 1917, World War I was raging in Europe. The United States was expected to join the war shortly, and Townsend thought it his patriotic duty to forego missionary service and serve his country. But a young woman missionary who was on furlough said to him: "You cowards! Going to war where a million other men will go, and leaving us women to do the Lord's work alone! You are needed in Central America to sell Bibles to people who walk in darkness."

These words gave Cameron Townsend second thoughts. To his surprise the captain of the National Guard unit agreed to release him. He said: "You'll do a lot more good selling Bibles in Central America than you would shooting enemy soldiers in France."

So Townsend went to Guatemala as a missionary. He was assigned a territory for Bible sales that was largely rural. But the two hundred thousand Indians who lived there couldn't read, and they didn't understand Spanish. They had no use for the Spanish Bibles he tried to sell them. They complained: "If your God is so smart, why hasn't He learned our language?"

That question challenged Townsend. He decided to learn their language, reduce it to writing, and translate the Scriptures into their language. He found the language highly confusing. But he learned it and translated the Gospel of Mark for the Indians. They were delighted. They said, "Now God speaks our language!"

After spending thirteen years with that Indian tribe, Townsend decided that God was calling him to do something about the need of hundreds of other tribes that didn't have the Scriptures in their own language. He resigned his work in the Central American Mission and founded the Wycliffe Bible Translators and Summer Institute of Linguistics. He did this without the backing of any denomination or any major missionary organization. And for the next fifty years, Cameron Townsend gave his life to making the Bible available to people in their own languages.

By 1985, three years after his death, the Wycliffe Bible Translators had 6,000 workers working on Bible translations in 1,000 language groups.

What inspired Townsend to make such a significant contribution to fulfilling Christ's command that we take the gospel to the whole world? When he was a boy, every weekday his father read three chapters from the Bible and five on Sunday. Every day after breakfast, he gathered his family for morning devotions. And every day his father ended his prayers with a petition for the fulfillment of Isaiah 11:9: "May the knowledge of the Lord cover the earth as the waters cover the sea."

The Wycliffe Bible Translators, founded by Cameron Townsend, developed into the largest Protestant missionary organization in the twentieth century. From Latin America,

Wycliffe Translators expanded into Africa, Asia, the Pacific Islands, and later into Russia.

In 1963, the government of Peru awarded Cameron Townsend its Order of Distinguished Service for his help in reducing illiteracy in the country. In 1966, the United States House of Representatives and Senate named September 30 as Bible Translation Day. At a personal meeting with the president in the Oval Office in 1970, Townsend was able to announce, "Mr. President, we've just entered our five-hundredth language."

By 1989, Wycliffe Translators had completed more than seven hundred translations of the New Testament. Approximately thirty new translations are completed every year. More then one thousand new translations are in the process of being prepared.

Billy Graham called Townsend "the greatest missionary of our time." But Townsend said, "The greatest missionary is the Bible in the mother tongue. It never needs a furlough, is never considered a foreigner."[1]

It was faith in the Lord Jesus Christ that led Cameron Townsend to do the great work he did. He believed, he served, he obeyed Christ's great commission. And that's what it means to be one of God's chosen people today.

Romans, chapter 11, speaks about this. The apostle Paul asks: "Has God rejected his people? By no means! I myself am an Israelite, a descendant of Abraham, a member of the tribe of Benjamin. God has not rejected his people whom he foreknew" (Romans 11:1, 2, NRSV). The ones God foreknew were the ones whom He foresaw would have faith in Jesus Christ. Paul has already told us in Romans 9, verses 30 to 32, what was wrong with the Israelites. The Gentiles accepted Christ by faith, but the Israelites tried to earn righteousness and salvation by their own works. The result was tragedy.

When Jesus was being tried before the Roman governor, Pilate, the Israelites shouted: "His blood be on us and on our children" (Matthew 27:25)! Jesus had predicted: "The kingdom of God will be taken away from you and given to a people that produces the fruits of the kingdom" (Matthew 21:43, NRSV).

He told the Israelites who had rejected Him: "Your house is left to you desolate" (Matthew 23:38).

Now, the New Testament tells us, the literal nation Israel has been replaced as God's chosen people by spiritual Israel, consisting of believing Jews and Gentiles. Thus the Christian Church has taken the place of the Israelite nation as God's chosen people. Galatians 3:7 (NRSV) announces: "Those who believe are the descendants of Abraham." Galatians 3:27–29 (NRSV) makes the point clearly: "As many of you as were baptized into Christ have clothed yourselves with Christ. There is no longer Jew or Greek, there is no longer slave or free, there is no longer male and female; for all of you are one in Christ Jesus. And if you belong to Christ, then you are Abraham's offspring, heirs according to the promise."

Paul says the same thing in Romans, chapter 9, verses 6–8 (NRSV): "It is not as though the word of God had failed. For not all Israelites truly belong to Israel, and not all of Abraham's children are his true descendants. ... This means that it is not the children of the flesh who are the children of God, but the children of the promise are counted as descendants."

In Romans 9, verse 24 (NRSV), Paul emphasizes that God's people include "us whom he has called, not from the Jews only but also from the Gentiles."

The point is that God's chosen people today comprise all those who believe in Jesus Christ as Savior and Lord, whether they happen to be Jews or Gentiles. These are the ones spoken of in Romans 11:5–7 (NRSV). Paul writes: "So too at the present time there is a remnant, chosen by grace. But if it is by grace, it is no longer on the basis of works, otherwise grace would no longer be grace. What then? Israel failed to obtain what it was seeking. The elect obtained it, but the rest were hardened."

They were hardened by the same love of God as saves those who choose to believe. The same hot sun will melt wax and harden clay. The same love of God will soften the heart of the person who chooses to respond and harden the heart of the one who chooses not to respond. And those who choose to respond to God's love are included among God's remnant people today.

Audrey was a young woman who was confused. She didn't believe the Christian faith, but neither could she accept atheism. While studying secular philosophy in France, she had given up her belief in the Bible, but she had nothing to fill the vacuum that remained. "I guess I'm an agnostic," Audrey reasoned. "I'm not sure there is a God, but then again, I'm not sure there isn't." Life had no meaning for her. She thought, *If it is true that there is no life beyond this one on earth, then what does it matter how I live now?*

Then one night Audrey locked herself in her bedroom determined to discover what she believed. In the darkness, she went to the window and threw it open. Looking up to the heavens she cried out: "God, if there be a God, if You will give me some philosophy that makes reasonable sense to me, I will commit myself to follow it."

She paced the floor, mulling over the philosophies she had studied in college. Then the words of Jesus came to her mind: "Whosoever liveth and believeth in me shall never die. Believest thou this" (John 11:26, KJV)? *Of course not!* Audrey thought. *I've already settled that question. Bible stories don't make sense. I can't believe those miracle stories—the virgin birth, Jonah and the whale, and Noah and the Flood. The Bible is not reasonable.*

But she couldn't get the words out of her mind: "Whosoever liveth and believeth in me shall never die. Believest thou this?" She later wrote: "Suddenly God's mysterious revelation was given to me. I could not reason out the mystery of the incarnation, but God caused me to know that this was a fact. I knelt in tears of joy and worshiped him as Savior and Lord."

Audrey Wetherell Johnson served with the China Inland Mission as a teacher for fourteen years until forced to leave China in 1950 due to the political situation. In 1958, she founded the Bible Study Fellowship, now located in San Antonio, Texas, an international organization that promotes disciplined personal Bible study. She inspired thousands to accept the authority of God's Word for their lives.[2]

That's what faith in Jesus does. God's Holy Spirit convinces a person that Jesus is, indeed, the Savior of the world, that He died for our sins, and that He lives today as our risen Savior. Faith transcends human reason, because faith is given to us by God's Holy Spirit. When you believe, you become a child of God, and you then belong to God's remnant people.

Paul said it. He wrote: "There is a remnant, chosen by grace" (Romans 11:5, NRSV). That means that God chooses those who respond to the conviction of the Holy Spirit by choosing to believe in Jesus. The New Testament elsewhere gives us the characteristics of this remnant church. Revelation, chapter 12, verse 17, tells us that the dragon, Satan, is angry with the woman, the last-day church, "those who keep the commandments of God and have the testimony of Jesus Christ." In other words, when by faith we keep all God's commandments and have faith in the testimony of God's chosen prophets, we belong to God's chosen people today.

Keeping the commandments is only possible by faith in Jesus Christ. First John 5:3–5 (NRSV) announces: "For the love of God is this, that we obey his commandments. And his commandments are not burdensome, for whatever is born of God conquers the world. And this is the victory that conquers the world, our faith. Who is it that conquers the world but the one who believes that Jesus is the Son of God?"

The passage is telling us that conquering the world means keeping the commandments of God. And we obey His commandments by faith in Jesus Christ. When we believe, Jesus gives us the power to keep His commandments.

Keeping His commandments means keeping all of them, including the fourth commandment, the Sabbath command. Jesus obeyed the fourth commandment. He observed the Sabbath day as a day of worship (Luke 4:16). He commanded His followers to observe the Sabbath after His death (Matthew 24:20). There is nothing in the New Testament telling us that the day was changed from the seventh to the first day of the week. The seventh-day Sabbath today is the same day that Jesus and His apostles kept, and we keep it by faith. We are not saved because we keep the Sabbath; we keep the Sabbath because we are saved. Those who belong to God's remnant, chosen by grace, will obey all His commandments and observe the seventh-day Sabbath.

Moreover, Revelation 12:17 tells us that God's remnant have the testimony of Jesus. What is that? Revelation 19:10 says that the testimony of Jesus is the "spirit of prophecy." In other words, God's remnant will have among them the spirit of prophecy. They will acknowledge God's prophets and follow the counsels of the Holy Spirit given to the prophets.

Romans, chapter 11, makes it very clear that Israelites who choose to believe in Jesus Christ as Savior and Lord are just as much part of God's remnant as the Gentiles who believe. Speaking of the Israelites, Paul wrote: "Through their stumbling salvation has come to the Gentiles, so as to make Israel jealous. Now if their stumbling means riches for the world, and if their defeat means riches for Gentiles, how much more will their full inclusion mean!" (Romans 11:11, 12, NRSV).

Then Paul likens the unbelieving Israelites to branches that were broken off the olive tree. And he speaks of the believing Gentiles as new branches that "were grafted in their place to share the rich root of the olive tree" (Romans 11:17, NRSV). But the believing Gentiles must never be lifted up with pride, imagining that they are somehow spiritually superior. Paul warned: "Do not boast over the branches. If you do boast, remember that it is not you that support the root, but the root that supports you" (Romans 11:18, NRSV). The Judeo-Christian message given by the prophets is for both Jews and Gentiles. And when anyone chooses to believe in Jesus, the entire message of the Bible is for them.

Paul tells us that the Israelites were "broken off" from God's olive tree "because of their unbelief, but you stand only through faith" (Romans 11:20, NRSV). Then he adds: "And even those of Israel, if they do not persist in unbelief, will be grafted in, for God has the power to graft them in again. For if you have been cut from what is by nature a wild olive tree and grafted, contrary to nature, into a cultivated olive tree, how much more will these natural branches be grafted back into their own olive tree" (Romans 11:23, 24, NRSV).

Paul says: "A hardening has come upon part of Israel, until the full number of the Gentiles has come in. And so all Israel will be saved" (Romans 11:25, 26, NRSV). In the context of Scripture teaching, that means that those of Israel who don't choose to believe are hardened by their faithlessness, and they will not be part of God's remnant church. But those who do choose to believe, like the believing Gentiles, will be part of God's remnant church. "All Israel" that will be saved (Romans 11:26) refers to the full number of the believing Gentiles and the full number of the believing Israelites who comprise spiritual Israel. This is the Christian church around the world, composed of all nationalities. Whoever choose to accept Jesus Christ as Savior and Lord, whether Jews or Gentiles, Americans, Japanese, Spanish, British, Germans, Australians—in fact, all nationalities—comprise spiritual Israel, and these are the ones who will be saved.

Paul adds: "And so all Israel will be saved; as it is written, 'Out of Zion will come the Deliverer; he will banish ungodliness from Jacob. And this is the covenant with them, when I take away their sins' " (Romans 11:26, 27, NRSV).[3]

God's covenant with believers ensures that their sins are forgiven and His law of love is written on their hearts. Hebrews, chapter 8, verses 10–12 (NRSV), describes this covenant. God says: "This is the covenant that I will make with the house of Israel after those days, says the Lord: I will put my laws in their minds, and write them on their hearts, and I will be their God, and they shall be my people. And they shall not teach one another or say to each other, 'Know the Lord,' for they shall all know me, from the least of them to the greatest. For I will be merciful toward their iniquities, and I will remember their sins no more."

That's exactly what God says to us in Romans 11:27 (NRSV): "This is the covenant with them, when I take away their sins." Now that means two things. It means that God forgives our past sins and mistakes. And it also means that God gives us the power to obey His law that He writes on our hearts and minds when He gives us the Holy Spirit.

Remember 1 John 5:4: "This is the victory that has overcome the world—our faith." And remember Romans 3:31: "Do we then make void the law through faith? Certainly not! On the contrary, we establish the law." And Hebrews 8 tells us that the law of God is upheld or established because it is written on our hearts.

That means that God's remnant people, His last-day church, consists of those who, believing in Jesus Christ, receive His power to obey Him in everything and who believe all that His Word teaches.

Throughout history many people have died for this faith in Jesus Christ. During the short five-year reign of Mary Tudor in England, 300 persons were put to death for their belief that they could come directly to God through Jesus without the mediation of saints and priests. Thus Queen Mary has been remembered for 400 years as "Bloody Mary."

Most of those martyrs were simple working people who had learned to read the Bible and follow its precepts. But some were scholars and church leaders. In September 1553, Bishops Thomas Cranmer, Nicholas Ridley, and Hugh Latimer were brought from the Queen's prison in the Tower of London to Oxford, where they were examined for their so-called heresies. They were excommunicated and condemned to death.

Hugh Latimer was now a frail eighty years of age with a failing memory. But he refused to recant and stood firm for his faith. The Martyrs Memorial in the university city of Oxford hallows the spot where Hugh Latimer and Nicholas Ridley were burned at the stake on October 6, 1555.

Before they were burned to death, they knelt together and prayed. Then they were fastened by chains to an iron post, and a bag of gunpowder was hung around each of their necks. The fires were then lighted. Latimer encouraged Ridley by saying: "Be of good comfort, Master Ridley, and play the man. We shall this day light such a candle, by God's grace, in England, as I trust shall never be put out!" Both men were burned to death.

In his early years, Latimer had been a priest of the established church. Then he met a man named Thomas Bilney. Bilney confessed to Latimer that his life had been changed by the teachings of the Word of God. He quoted for him 1 Timothy 1:15: "Christ Jesus came into the world to save sinners, of whom I am chief." Bilney experienced forgiveness and peace directly from Jesus Christ, and He introduced Latimer to the same experience. Latimer became a great preacher of the Bible truth of righteousness and salvation by faith in Jesus Christ. His sermons attracted large crowds and were appreciated by the common people for their directness and simplicity. He preached in the open air to as many as 6,000 people at a time. And when called to answer for His faith in Christ, he gave His life rather than reject the Lord who had saved him.[4]

That is what it means to be one of God's chosen people today. It means to accept and serve Jesus Christ as Savior and Lord whatever the circumstances of our lives, whatever the opposition. Praise God! "Christ Jesus came into the world to save sinners."

Endnotes

1. Adapted from Ron and Dorothy Watts, *Powerful Passages* (Boise, Idaho: Pacific Press, 1996), pp. 42–46.
2. *Ibid*, pp. 125–127.
3. Romans 11:26, 27 quote Isaiah 59:20, 21; 27:9.
4. Adapted from Watts, *Ibid.*, pp. 166–170.

Chapter Fifteen

The Results of Knowing Jesus

Romans 12

In *Decision* magazine, October 2001, Raul Ries tells the story of his life. Raul grew up in Mexico City. Throughout his childhood, his father abused him, his mother, and his grandmother. Raul's father was an alcoholic, and he often forced him to go with him to bars where he got into drunken brawls. By the time he was eight or nine years old, Raul was full of hatred.

As a teenager Raul took his anger out on others. The family moved to Los Angeles, where Raul learned martial arts. By his senior year in high school he had been in and out of jail. At a party he saw his girlfriend with another guy, and he beat him almost to death. Raul was arrested and given the choice of military or jail. It was 1966, and he chose to go to Vietnam. There he was assigned to a reconnaissance team. They would surround the Viet Cong villages, kill all the men first and then kill the women and children. Eventually Raul was shipped back to the U.S., where he was sent to Oakland Naval Hospital and enrolled in the psychiatric program.

In 1968 he was given an honorable discharge. He married Sharon Farrel and began family life. Before long he was fighting in bars and cheating on Sharon. He was just as abusive to his wife as his father had been to him. In 1972, after four years of abuse, Sharon decided to leave him. By now they had two sons, and Sharon didn't want them to grow up abusers.

Raul came home one evening and found suitcases in the hallway. He flew into a rage, pulled his rifle from the closet and loaded it with 18 rounds. He planned to kill his wife and boys as soon as they arrived home from church. He began punching holes in the walls, shattering picture frames, and knocking over shelves. He hit the television set with the rifle butt, but instead of breaking it, he hit a button and turned the TV on. There appeared on the TV a pastor talking about Jesus and His life. Raul was furious. He tried to shoot the television, but couldn't pull the trigger. He kept listening to the man talk about the love of God. He seemed to be speaking directly to Raul, and he realized that what the preacher said was his last chance and his only hope for life.

Raul began to cry uncontrollably. He knelt and prayed, "God, if you're real, and if you are a God who is able to save people, I want you to come into my life tonight." Then he felt his anger melt away, and a new peace came into his heart. He wiped the tears from his face, put away his rifle, and drove to the church to find Sharon and tell her what had happened. When he arrived the pastor was giving an altar call. Raul couldn't find Sharon, so he went to the altar where someone prayed with him. Then he drove home. As he walked closer to the house, he could hear Sharon crying.

He called out, "Sharon, open the door." She had put the chain across the door, but opened it a crack and asked, "What do you want?" He told her, "I accepted Jesus Christ tonight." She shut the door in his face; she didn't believe him. Finally he convinced her to let him in the house, but it took months for her to believe that he had truly changed. Then she forgave him for the pain he had caused her and their boys.

Raul began to attend church in Costa Mesa and to read the Bible. In the fall of 1972, he began visiting schools telling the story of his conversion. Soon he was visiting eight schools a week. Raul was ordained to the ministry in 1975, and since then he has founded a large church that supports several ministries. God forgave his sins, took away his anger, and mended his broken marriage. Now he has the privilege of reaching out to others, helping them with problems like the ones he used to have.

Romans, chapter 12, tells us how Raul's life was changed, and how our lives can be changed. Speaking for God, the apostle Paul said: "I beseech you therefore, brethren, by the mercies of God, that you present your bodies a living sacrifice, holy, acceptable to God, which is your reasonable service. And do not be conformed to this world, but be transformed by the renewing of your mind, that you may prove what is that good and acceptable and perfect will of God" (Romans 12:1, 2).

Because God is so wonderfully forgiving and merciful to those who respond to His call, it is most reasonable to make a total surrender of our lives to Him. The Greek word translated "reasonable" also means "spiritual."[1] And there is nothing more reasonable and spiritual than to give your life to Jesus Christ. He will then give you the power to overcome the evil habits that have been destroying your peace of mind and destroying your ability to relate meaningfully with other people.

Romans 12:1 says that the reasonable person who comes to Jesus is made "holy, acceptable unto God." You see, when Jesus comes into your mind by the presence of His Holy Spirit, you have the power to control your passions, your appetites, and your emotions. You have the power to be a new person, controlled by love instead of by hate and bitterness.

Earlier in the letter to the Romans, Paul writes: "God be thanked that though you were slaves of sin, yet you obeyed from the heart that form of doctrine to which you were delivered. And having been set free from sin, you became slaves of righteousness" (Romans 6:17, 18). When we come to Jesus and give Him our hearts, we become willing slaves of righteousness. Jesus gives us His righteousness, and we have the power to live transformed lives. That's the experience that Raul had when He responded to Jesus' love.

Romans 12, verse 2, tells us that believers in Jesus are transformed[2] by the renewing of their minds. This is the work of the Holy Spirit; He changes our minds. He takes away the impurity, the anger, the bitterness, the evil desires, and gives us purity, peace, and the ability to love instead of hate. That's the message that comes through also in Romans, chapter 8. We are told that "those who live according to the flesh set their minds on the things of the flesh, but those who live according to the Spirit, the things of the Spirit. For to be carnally minded is death, but to be spiritually minded is life and peace. Because the carnal mind is enmity against God; for it is not subject to the law of God, nor indeed can be. So then, those who are in the flesh cannot please God. But you are not in the flesh but in the Spirit, if indeed the Spirit of God dwells in you. Now if anyone does not have the Spirit of Christ, he is not His. And if Christ is in you, the body is dead because of sin, but the Spirit is life because of righteousness" (Romans 8:5–10).

That passage is simply saying that serving sin results in death. But serving Jesus Christ, by allowing Him to control our lives, results in life and peace, because His righteousness is given to us by His Holy Spirit. Paul wrote the same message to the Christian believers in Corinth. He wrote: "Now we have received, not the spirit of the world, but the Spirit who is from God, that we might know the things that have been freely given to us by God" (1 Corinthians 2:12). Then Paul adds in verse 16, "We have the mind of Christ."

In each of our lives there is a terrible battle going on for control of our minds. The devil and his demons try to destroy us by tempting us to think evil thoughts. They inject thoughts of hate, of evil passion, of greed, and selfishness. But when we come to Jesus, His Spirit takes over the control of our minds, and we have the power to think loving, pure, unselfish thoughts. Our minds are transformed. They are renewed. We have the mind of Christ, because we have given Him control of our minds. The power Christ supplies makes possible thought and action that are good, pleasing to God, and perfect in His sight.

Paul wrote to the Corinthians: "Let us cleanse ourselves from all filthiness of the flesh and spirit, perfecting holiness in the fear of God" (2 Corinthians 7:1). We cleanse ourselves from every defilement by coming to Jesus and allowing Him to cleanse us. Then He gives us His holiness, transforms our minds, and makes us new people. Then we are, as the Bible says, "blameless and innocent, children of God without blemish in the midst of a crooked and perverse generation, in which you shine like stars in the world" (Philippians 2:15, NRSV).

The Bible teaches that all our thoughts can be under the control of God. We don't have to think evil thoughts. We don't have to retain unholy desires and passions. The Bible says that "the weapons of our warfare are not merely human, but they have divine power to destroy strongholds. We destroy arguments and every proud obstacle raised up against the knowledge of God, and we take every thought captive to obey Christ" (2 Corinthians 10:4, 5, NRSV).

That means that by the power Jesus gives us, all our thoughts can be under the control of God. We can have pure minds. We can achieve our true mental potential. We can think, and speak, and act in ways that are productive and meaningful, in ways that are a blessing to our families and to all those with whom we come in contact.

Some years ago Robert Parr wrote the story in the *Australasian Record* of a physician named Axel Munthe. He was a Swede who had a great love for the Isle of Capri and who eventually retired there. Living near Munthe's house was a man who made a lot of money by netting birds as they flew northward in the migrating season. This man spread nets and caught thousands of birds, tightly packed them (still alive) into wooden boxes, and freighted them (without food or water) to Marseilles, and thence to Paris, where they were killed and devoured in restaurants.

A decoy bird was first obtained. The man would blind this bird, and it would then sing louder and attract others of its kind to land in the thickets where the nets had been placed. Only a few birds in a hundred survived the operation. Near Munthe's villa was an entire mountain owned by this man where he captured thousands of birds a day.

Munthe appealed to the secular and religious authorities to have the trapping stopped. But he was informed that nothing could be done; the man owned the mountain where the birds landed. Munthe tried to frighten the birds away by firing shots or by encouraging his dogs to bark. But he was fined for interfering with the man's lawful trade. Next Munthe offered to buy the mountain, and the man asked an exorbitant price. Munthe sold some of his goods and raised the money only to have the price doubled.

Then the trapper of the birds became mortally ill. Munthe was one of the few physicians on the island, and he was asked to attend to the man. He agreed only if the bird-trapper would swear that, if he recovered, he would sell the doctor the mountain at the first-stated price and that he would never again blind a decoy bird. The man refused; he preferred to take his chances. But after a few more days of illness the trapper accepted the terms. Munthe treated him and was able to buy the mountain on which the birds landed.

Munthe later wrote: "The mountain … is now a bird sanctuary. Thousands of tired birds of passage are resting on its slopes every spring and autumn, safe from man and beast."

Munthe's actions illustrate the love of God. He was prepared to buy a mountain at a much inflated cost. God was prepared to pour out the love of heaven in order to make man's eternal home safe. Munthe exhausted every known way in order to protect the birds he loved. God knew that there was only one way to save humankind. Munthe bought the mountain at considerable personal sacrifice. "God so loved the world that He gave His only begotten Son" (John 3:16). This was the greatest sacrifice of all. And this sacrifice was for you.

Acceptance of Jesus Christ as Savior and Lord results in a new sense of self-worth. Yet it is to be governed by reason and reality, not by some exaggerated concept of one's own abilities. Paul wrote in Romans, chapter 12: "For I say, through the grace given to me, to everyone who is among you, not to think of himself more highly than he ought to think, but to think soberly, as God has dealt to each one a measure of faith" (Romans 12:3). Paul urged his fellow Christians not to be "puffed up on behalf of one against the other" (1 Corinthians 4:6). He asked, "What do you have that you did not receive? Now if you did indeed receive it, why do you glory as if you had not received it?" (1 Corinthians 4:7).

Then in Romans 12, Paul speaks of the various spiritual gifts bestowed upon believers by the Holy Spirit. He writes: "For as in one body we have many members, and not all the members have the same function, so we, who are many, are one body in Christ, and individually we are members one of another. We have gifts that differ according to the grace given to us: prophecy, in proportion to faith; ministry, in ministering; the teacher, in teaching; the exhorter, in exhortation; the giver, in generosity; the leader in diligence; the compassionate, in cheerfulness" (Romans 12:4–8, NRSV).[3]

We all have one or more special gifts given us by the Holy Spirit, and we are to use them in the service of God.

Then Paul instructs us to turn away from evil. He writes: "Let love be without hypocrisy. Abhor what is evil. Cling to what is good" (Romans 12:9). And in verse 21 he repeats the counsel: "Do not be overcome by evil, but overcome evil with good."

How do we overcome evil? The Bible says: "Submit to God. Resist the devil, and he will flee from you. Draw near to God and He will draw near to you" (James 4:7, 8). The first thing to do when we are tempted by evil is to submit our minds to God. Then when we resist the devil, we know that it is not our strength that is overcoming, but God's power making it possible for us to overcome.

Jesus taught that apart from Him we can do nothing (John 15:5). That means that, apart from Jesus' spiritual power, we cannot overcome evil. But when we are in league with Jesus, we have the special strength to resist evil. Jesus taught: "If you abide in Me, and My words abide in you, you will ask what you desire, and it shall be done for you" (John 15:7). That means that when we ask for strength to resist and overcome our unholy desires and obsessions, Jesus is always willing to give us the victory. The Bible promises that we can "do all things through Christ who strengthens" us (Philippians 4:13). We can do all things He asks of us when we trust Him. The Bible also tells us: "This is the victory that has overcome the world—our faith" (1 John 5:4).

In Romans, chapter 12, verses 9–13, God gives us 12 positive commands: (1) Let love be without hypocrisy; (2) abhor what is evil; (3) cling to what is good; (4) be kindly affectionate to one another with brotherly love; (5) in honor giving preference to one another; (6) not lagging in diligence, fervent in spirit; (7) serving the Lord; (8) rejoicing in hope; (9) patient in tribulation; (10) continuing steadfast in prayer; (11) distributing to the needs of the saints; (12) given to hospitality.

If by the strength Christ gives us we follow each of those injunctions, we will be reflectors of His character.

Paul continues in Romans 12 by reiterating the teaching of Jesus in His Sermon on the Mount. Paul said: "Bless those who persecute you; bless and do not curse" (Romans 12:14). Jesus said: "Blessed are you when they revile and persecute you, and say all kinds of evil against you falsely for My sake. Rejoice and be exceedingly glad, for great is your reward in heaven, for so they persecuted the prophets who were before you" (Matthew 5:11, 12).

Paul said: "Rejoice with those who rejoice, and weep with those who weep" (Romans 12:15). Jesus said: "Blessed are those who mourn, for they shall be comforted" (Matthew 5:4).

Paul said: "Live in harmony with one another; do not be haughty, but associate with the lowly (Romans 12:16, NRSV). Jesus said: "Blessed are the poor in spirit, for theirs is the kingdom of heaven. … Blessed are the meek, for they shall inherit the earth" (Matthew 5:3, 5).

Paul said: "Repay no one evil for evil. Have regard for good things in the sight of all men" (Romans 12:17). Jesus said: "Blessed are the merciful, for they shall obtain mercy" (Matthew 5:7).

Paul said: "If it is possible, as much as depends on you, live peaceably with all men" (Romans 12:18). Jesus said: "Blessed are the peacemakers, for they shall be called sons [children] of God" (Matthew 5:9).

Paul said: "Beloved, do not avenge yourselves, but rather give place to wrath; for it is written, 'Vengeance is Mine, I will repay,' says the Lord. Therefore if your enemy hungers feed him; if he thirsts, give him a drink; for in so doing you will heap coals of fire on his head. Do not be overcome by evil, but overcome evil with good" (Romans 12:19, 20). Jesus said: "You have heard that it was said, 'You shall love your neighbor and hate your enemy.' But I say to you, Love your enemies and pray for those who persecute you, so that you may be children of your Father in heaven; for he makes his sun rise on the evil and on the good, and sends rain on the righteous and on the unrighteous. For if you love those who love you, what reward do you have? Do not even the tax collectors do the same? And if you greet only your brothers and sisters, what more are you doing than others? Do not even the Gentiles do the same? Be perfect, therefore, as your heavenly Father is perfect" (Matthew 5:43–48, NRSV).

What are the results in our lives of knowing Jesus? These Bible passages spell out the answer as clearly as anything could. Hating sinners become loving servants of God and others. Uncaring people become compassionate and kind. Proud people become humble. Bitter, revengeful people become forgiving. Contentious, belligerent people become gentle peacemakers. Selfish people become generous toward others less fortunate. Dishonest people become honest in all their dealings with others. Impure, immoral people become pure, never stepping over the boundaries that Jesus sets for meaningful human relationships.

Bob Butler lost his legs in a 1965 land mine explosion in Vietnam. He returned home a war hero. Twenty years later he proved once again that heroism comes from the heart. Butler was working in his garage in a small town in Arizona on a hot summer day when he heard a woman's screams coming from a nearby house. He began rolling his wheelchair toward the house, but the dense shrubbery wouldn't allow him access to the back door. So he got out of his chair and started to crawl through the dirt and bushes.

"I had to get there," he says. "It didn't matter how much it hurt." When Butler arrived at the pool there was a three-year-old girl named Stephanie Hanes lying at the bottom. She had been born without arms and had fallen into the water and couldn't swim.

Her mother stood there screaming frantically. Butler dove to the bottom of the pool and brought little Stephanie up to the deck. Her face was blue; she had no pulse and was not breathing. Butler immediately went to work performing CPR to revive her, while Stephanie's mother telephoned the fire department. She was told the paramedics were already out on a call. Helplessly, she sobbed and hugged Butler's shoulder.

As Butler continued with his CPR, he calmly reassured her. "Don't worry," he said. "I was her arms to get her out of the pool. It'll be okay. I am now her lungs. Together we can make it." Seconds later the little girl coughed, regained consciousness, and began to cry. As they hugged and rejoiced together, the mother asked Butler how he knew it would be okay.

"The truth is, I didn't know," he told her. "But when my legs were blown off in the war, I was all alone in a field. No one was there to help except a little Vietnamese girl. As she struggled to drag me into her village, she whispered in broken English, 'It okay. You can live. I be your legs. Together we make it.' Her kind words brought hope to my soul, and I wanted to do the same for Stephanie."

You see, my friend, as Bob Butler says: "There are simply those times when we cannot stand alone. There are those times when we need someone to be our legs, our arms, our friend."

The one willing to be our legs, our arms, our Friend, is Jesus. He says that He will never leave us or forsake us. His love and His strength make it possible for us to carry on and do the work He has called us to do. Moreover, just as Jesus gave His all for us, so He calls upon us to serve others. Knowing Jesus makes us like Jesus in character. Knowing Jesus makes us gentle, loving servants of God and humanity. Do you know Him? He waits at the door of your heart, longingly hoping that you will open the door and let Him in. Come to Jesus today; He has the answer to all your needs. And He will support you in every situation of life.

Endnotes

1. The Greek adjective is *logikos, e, on*, means "rational," "spiritual." (See Arndt and Gingrich's *Greek-English Lexicon.)* The spiritual person who is surrendered to Christ is "holy, acceptable unto God." (Compare Romans 6:17–19; 1 Peter 1:15, 16; 3:10–12.)
2. The Greek translated "transformed" is *metamorphoo*, which means "to change in form." From this Greek word comes our English word "metamorphosis." When we come to Christ, we experience a genuine metamorphosis. Our minds are renewed by the Holy Spirit.
3. Compare the list of spiritual gifts mentioned in Romans 12:6–8 with the lists in 1 Corinthians 12:27–31 and Ephesians 4:11–16. Every Christian has some gift or number of gifts, and his or her responsibility is to discover what they are. They are to be used for the edification of the church.

Chapter Sixteen

The Christian's Attitude to the State

Romans 13

Some years ago a letter addressed to "Santa Claus, North Pole" was received in the Washington Post Office. It was sent to the Postmaster General, who was touched by the urgency of the request. It was from a little boy who didn't want toys, but food and clothing for his destitute family. The Postmaster General, a cabinet member, addressed a reply to the little boy on official stationery, saying that Santa Claus had referred the matter to him, and the fifty dollars enclosed was a gift from the North Pole.

The following year another letter addressed to Santa Claus, written by the same boy, came to Washington, and was forwarded to the Postmaster General. When it was opened the cabinet member read the following: "Dear Santa, you were very kind to me last year, and I appreciate it very much. But next time you send me money don't forward it through the government. Those men always keep half of what they receive."[1]

We can understand a poverty-stricken little boy having negative feelings about the government. And many of us complain rather bitterly about the taxes we have to pay, and the various kinds of restrictions imposed upon us by the government. But all we have to do is to travel to other countries of the world to discover that we are better off than the citizens of most other places. We have more to eat, more conveniences, better homes and cars, and a much higher standard of living than most other places in the world.

Some few years ago, I spent time in the Far East. People in one city drank water out of the gutters. I saw people living in grass huts and shacks. I saw run-down buildings and roads full of potholes, and automobiles that you and I would never want to drive. I saw grinding poverty of a kind I have never seen in these United States. Even in our slums and ghettoes, our people are better off than most people in third world countries.

Some years ago, Henry Smith Leiper pointed up American affluence with some startling statistics. Imagine that we could compress the world's population into one town of 1,000 people, keeping proportions right. In this town there would be only 60 Americans. These 60 Americans would receive half the income of the entire town. They would have an average life expectancy of 70 years; the other 940 persons would have less than 40 years. The sixty Americans would own 15 times as much per person as all of their neighbors. They would eat 72 percent more than the maximum food requirements; many of the 940 other people would go to bed hungry every night.

Of 53 telephones in the town, Americans would have 28. The lowest income group among the Americans would be better off by far than the average of the other townspeople. The 60 Americans and about 200 others representing Western Europe and a few classes in South America, Australia, and Japan, would be relatively well off. The other 75 percent would be very poor.

In the light of these considerations, we Americans have every reason to take seriously the counsel of Romans, chapter 13. The first two verses read: "Let every soul be subject to the governing authorities. For there is no authority except from God, and the authorities that exist are appointed by God. Therefore whoever resists the authority resists the ordinance of God, and those who resist will bring judgment on themselves" (Romans 13:1, 2).

God allows persons and governments to come to power so that they might provide for the welfare of the people under their rule. Their continuance in power or their fall from authority is in God's hands. The Christian's duty is to support the authority of the existing government. As a citizen, the Christian will not assume the right to resist or depose the powers that be. He will loyally obey the laws of the land and so demonstrate that Christians are law-abiding citizens.

The only circumstance in which a Christian should, with God's approval, resist the government's requirements is when its laws conflict with the law of God. Under such circumstances, the Christian's duty is "to obey God rather than men" (Acts 5:29). And even then Christians will not become rebels and revolutionaries. They will offer nonviolent resistance only to those laws that require them to disobey God's law.

This was the attitude of the apostles who preached the gospel in Jerusalem after the death and resurrection of Jesus. When Peter and John were ordered by the Israelite government not to speak or teach about Jesus Christ, they answered: "Whether it is right in the sight of God to listen to you more than to God, you judge" (Acts 4:19). The book of Acts, chapter 5, describes how the apostles were imprisoned because of their teaching in Jerusalem about Christ and His salvation. When they were brought before the council to answer for their disobedience, "the high priest questioned them, saying, 'We gave you strict orders not to teach in this name, yet here you have filled Jerusalem with your teaching, and you are determined to bring this man's blood on us.' " But Peter and the apostles answered, "We ought to obey God rather than men. The God of our fathers raised up Jesus whom you murdered by hanging on a tree. Him God has exalted to His right hand to be Prince and Savior, to give repentance to Israel and forgiveness of sins. And we are His witnesses to these things, and so also is the Holy Spirit whom God has given to those who obey Him" (Acts 5:29–32). The chapter concludes by announcing that, after they were released, the apostles "daily in the temple, and in every house … did not cease teaching and preaching Jesus as the Christ" (Acts 5:42).

The apostles were loyal citizens, but when the religious and civil authorities demanded that they disobey God, they simply put God first and disobeyed those human laws that conflicted with His will.

The Old Testament book of Daniel effectively dramatizes these clear New Testament principles. In Daniel's prayer of gratitude to God for revealing to him Nebuchadnezzar's dream and its interpretation, he prayed: "Blessed be the name of God forever and ever, for wisdom and might are His. And He changes the times and the seasons; he removes kings and raises up kings; He gives wisdom to the wise and knowledge to those who have understanding" (Daniel 2:20, 21).

Daniel let Nebuchadnezzar know that the God of heaven had given him his kingdom, power, and glory (Daniel 2:37, 38). But Daniel also revealed that Nebuchadnezzar's kingdom would be progressively succeeded in the Mediterranean world by three other kingdoms. The fourth kingdom would be split into numerous divisions, "and in the days of these kings the God of heaven will set up a kingdom which shall never be destroyed" (Daniel 2:44).

The next few chapters in the book of Danie, illustrate the principles that Daniel had presented to Nebuchadnezzar. Daniel, chapter 3, tells the story of the great golden statue that Nebuchadnezzar set up on the plain of Dura in the province of Babylon. Anyone refusing to worship this image was to be thrown into a furnace of fire. Three Hebrews who were worshipers of the true God refused to bow down to this image. They resisted Nebuchadnezzar's authority in this instance because it conflicted with God's command that He only should be worshiped. The brave words of these three Hebrews are recorded in Daniel 3:16–18: "Shadrach, Meshach, and Abednego answered and said to the king, 'O Nebuchadnezzar, we have no need to answer you in this matter. If that is the case, our God whom we serve is able to deliver us from the burning fiery furnace, and He will deliver us from your hand, O king. But if not, let it be known to you, O king, that we do not serve your gods, nor will we worship the gold image which you have set up.' "

The three men were thrown bound into the fiery furnace, and were miraculously delivered by God. To Nebuchadnezzar's amazement, he saw four men, not three, walking around unhurt in the flaming furnace, even though the soldiers who had thrown the three in were killed as they had approached the fire. Nebuchadnezzar exclaimed: "Look! … I see four men loose, walking in the midst of the fire; and they are not hurt, and the form of the fourth is like the Son of God" (Daniel 3:25).

The king commanded the three unhurt Hebrews to come out of the furnace, and he was so impressed that their God had protected them that he issued the following decree: " 'Any people, nation, or language which speaks anything amiss against the God of Shadrach, Meshach, and Abednego shall be cut in pieces, and their houses shall be made an ash heap; because there is no other God who can deliver like this.' Then the king promoted Shadrach, Meshach, and Abednego in the province of Babylon" (Daniel 3:29, 30).

These three men were law-abiding citizens. They were willing to serve the king with full obedience to his laws, so long as those laws didn't conflict with the laws of God. And when his laws did conflict with God's laws, they didn't become flaming revolutionaries. They didn't become terrorists trying to wipe out those who disagreed with their convictions. They passively resisted the king's demand that they disobey their God, and passively submitted to the consequences. But God intervened to deliver them and finally to exalt them to high positions in the nation.

Chapter 4 of Daniel describes how God taught King Nebuchadnezzar that his power depended entirely upon Divine approval. Chapter 5 describes the fall of Babylon to the Medes and Persians because of the rank paganism of the last king of Babylon, Belshazzar. Daniel, chapter 6, tells the story of Daniel's deliverance from the den of lions because he refused to obey the Persian king's decree that no one should pray to any God except to the king.

These chapters in the book of Daniel illustrate the message of Romans, chapter 13, and other passages of Scripture. Christians are bound first to obey God. The principles of the Word of God are their guiding light. Insofar as the laws of the land are not contradictory to God's laws, the Christian's duty is to obey them. The Bible teaches that Christians are not to be political activists who are trying to depose the powers that be. If Paul and the Christians of his day had actively opposed the Roman Emperor and had attempted to depose him, they would have brought reproach upon the Christian church and its message of peace and brotherly love.

That's why the New Testament is so insistent that Christian believers should be loyal citizens of the countries in which they live. Paul instructed the young evangelist Timothy: "Therefore I exhort first of all that supplications, prayers, intercessions, and giving of thanks be made for all men, for kings and all who are in authority, that we may lead a quiet and peaceable life in all godliness and reverence. For this is good and acceptable in the sight of God our Savior" (1 Timothy 2:1–3).

Paul wrote to pastor Titus: "Remind them [the believers] to be subject to rulers and authorities, to obey, to be ready for every good work, to speak evil of no one, to be peaceable, gentle, showing all humility to all men" (Titus 3:1, 2).

The apostle Peter gave similar counsel. He wrote: "Therefore submit yourselves to every ordinance of man for the Lord's sake, whether to the king as supreme, or to governors, as to those who are sent by him for the punishment of evil-doers, and for the praise of those who do good. For this is the will of God, that by doing good you may put to silence the ignorance of foolish men—as free, yet not using your liberty as a cloak for vice, but as servants of God. Honor all people. Love the brotherhood. Fear God. Honor the king" (1 Peter 2:13–17).

This was the same Peter who told the council in Jerusalem that we should obey God rather than men. Peter was a loyal citizen, but above all he was a servant of Jesus Christ. No man-made decree could keep him, or Paul, or any of the other apostles from their God-given mission of making known Christ and His salvation. That's why ultimately both Peter and Paul were martyred in Rome, about A.D. 67 or 68.

If ever there was a time when we should pray for our country and for our national leaders, this is the time. As we have seen, the apostle Paul wrote: "Therefore I exhort first of all that supplications, prayers, intercessions, and giving of thanks be made for all men, for kings and all who are in authority, that we may lead a quiet and peaceable life in all godliness and reverence" (1 Timothy 2:1, 2). To lead our country in these times of crisis requires great wisdom, and only God can qualify our leaders with that necessary wisdom.

Some years ago there was placed upon the altar of the Washington Memorial Chapel at Valley Forge an exquisitely illuminated copy of Washington's prayer for the nation, a prayer that should be repeated often. Washington prayed:

> "Almighty God: We make our earnest prayer that Thou wilt keep the United States in Thy holy protection; that Thou wilt incline the heads of the citizens to cultivate a spirit of subordination and obedience to government, and entertain a brotherly affection and love for one another and for their fellow citizens of the United States at large.
>
> "And finally that Thou wilt most graciously be pleased to dispose us all to do justice, to love mercy, and to demean ourselves with that charity, humility, and pacific temper of mind which were the characteristics of the Divine Author of our blessed religion and with a humble imitation of whose example in these things we can ever hope to be a happy nation.
>
> "Grant our supplication, we beseech Thee, through Jesus Christ our Lord, Amen."[2]

Paul continues his counsel regarding the Christian's attitude to the state as follows in Romans, chapter 13, verses 3–5: "Rulers are not a terror to good conduct, but to evil. Do you want to be unafraid of the authority? Do what is good, and you will have praise from the same. For he is God's minister to you for good.

But if you do evil, be afraid; for he does not bear the sword in vain; for he is God's minister, an avenger to execute wrath on him who practices evil. Therefore you must be subject, not only because of wrath but also for conscience' sake."

Paul is speaking to God's purpose that secular rulers should enforce laws that are for the welfare of the people. The Christian's duty is to cooperate in every way possible with the laws of the state. Only when those laws conflict with the law of God is disobedience to human law justifiable. When Paul says that "rulers are not a terror to good conduct, but to bad," he is referring to the ideal situation in which rulers are truly functioning as God's servants to enforce laws that are thoroughly consistent with divine law. Under such circumstances the Christian has a duty to conform to the laws of the rulers not only because of fear of punishment but, as the Bible says, "because of conscience." We obey the laws of the land because our consciences tell us that they are for our best good and for the best good of the citizenry in general.

Then Paul touches on the subject of taxes. He writes, "For because of this you also pay taxes, for they are God's ministers attending continually to this very thing. Render therefore to all their due: taxes to whom taxes are due, customs to whom customs, fear to whom fear, honor to whom honor" (Romans 13:6, 7).

The Christian is to be faithful is paying taxes. Certainly none of us enjoy having such a large percentage of our income taken by the government. But when we consider the benefits involved in living in this country, with all the services that are provided for us, we realize that little of this would be possible if the people were not taxed.

Jesus emphasized the same point. Luke, chapter 20, informs us that the scribes and chief priests watched Jesus and "sent spies who pretended to be righteous, that they might seize on His words, in order to deliver Him to the power and the authority of the governor. And they asked him, saying, 'Teacher, we know that You say and teach rightly, and You do not show personal favoritism, but teach the way of God truly: Is it lawful for us to pay taxes to Caesar or not?' But He perceived their craftiness, and said to them, 'Why do you test Me? Show me a denarius. Whose image and inscription does it have?' They answered and said, 'Caesar's.' And He said to them, 'Render therefore to Caesar the things that are Caesar's, and to God the things that are God's' " (Luke 20:20–25).

The Bible in no way condones the attempt by people to evade paying their taxes. Deceiving the government is just as dishonest as deceiving any human being. We may feel that the amount of tax required of us is exorbitant. We may feel that the government doesn't deserve such a high percentage of our income. But we choose to live in this country, and we willingly absorb all the services and protections that the government provides. If we don't like what the government is doing, we have every right to vote against it at the next election. But we have a Christian and civic duty to pay our taxes.

Then the Bible expresses the principle on which all this counsel about our attitude to the government is based. The inspired apostle writes: "Owe no one anything, except to love one another; for he who loves another has fulfilled the law" (Romans 13:8). In other words, render what is due to the government and to anyone in whose debt you happen to be, because the principle of love to God and love to others demands faithful payment of debts.

Sometimes we hear people say, "But if I give the government what it asks and give offerings and tithes to the church, as the Bible says I should, I won't have enough left to live on." The simple fact is that God promises to provide for our daily financial needs. Jesus said: "Do not worry, saying, 'What shall we eat?' or 'What shall we drink?' or 'What shall we wear?' For after all these things the Gentiles seek. For your heavenly Father knows that you need all these things. But seek first the kingdom of God and His righteousness, and all these things shall be added to you. Therefore do not worry about tomorrow, for tomorrow will worry about its own things. Sufficient for the day is its own trouble" (Matthew 6:31–33).

When we trust Jesus as Savior and Lord, goodness and mercy follow us all the days of our lives (Psalm 23:6). We have reason to be at peace because Jesus is with us to guide, provide for, and protect us.

A comparison of Romans 13:8–10 with Matthew 22:37–39 reveals that the Ten Commandments are an expression of God's love. Paul does not teach that love replaces law for the Christian. In Scripture, love and law are not antagonistic to each other; they are complementary. The law of God is a law of love (Romans 13:9) and a "law of liberty" (James 2:12). As we conform to the principles of the law by the power of the Holy Spirit (Romans 8:3, 4), we demonstrate our love to God and to our fellow human beings.

Romans 13:11 urges us "to awake out of sleep; for now our salvation is nearer than when we first believed. The night is far spent, the day is at hand. Therefore let us cast off the works of darkness, and let us put on the armor of light. Let us walk properly, as in the day, not in revelry and drunkenness, not in licentiousness and lewdness, not in strife and envy. But put on the Lord Jesus Christ, and make no provision for the flesh, to fulfill its lusts."

We have salvation *now*, if we believe in Jesus (Titus 3:5; 2 Timothy 1:9). It is also true that we are "*being saved*" (1 Corinthians 1:18). And we *will be saved* ultimately at the second coming of Jesus (Romans 13:11). The "armor of light" (Romans 13:12) is also referred to in Ephesians 6:11–18. We are to "make no provision for the flesh, to fulfill its lusts (Romans 13:14). But pure sexual expression within marriage is taught in Scripture (see 1 Corinthians 7:1–7; Hebrews 13:4).

George Vandeman, the TV evangelist, used to tell the story of a little girl standing on a street corner in London with a torn dress and matted hair. She was lost and crying as if her heart would break. A couple of police officers found her and tried to find out where she lived. But none of the places they described rang a bell with the little girl. Then one of the officers asked her, "Do you know where that big white church is that has the high steeple with a cross on it?"

"Oh, yes, yes," responded the lost girl, "take me to the cross. I can find my way home from there."

Don't you see? When you come to the cross, you can find your way home from there. Jesus died to save us. When we accept Him and His sacrifice for us, everything else falls into place. We love God, we love one another, and we are loyal to the government of our country.

Endnotes

1. Adapted from Gerald Lieberman, "Letter to North Pole," in *Encyclopedia of 7,700 Illustrations* (Rockville, MD.: Assurance Publishers, 1979), p. 1637.
2. *Encyclopedia of 7,700 Illustrations*, p. 1540.

Chapter Seventeen

The Unity of the Weak and the Strong

Romans 14

Jim Stovall is a blind author. He has overcome his blindness to accomplish some great things in life. He is a national champion Olympic weight lifter, a successful investments broker, and an entrepreneur. He is the co-founder and president of the Narrative Television Network, which makes movies and television accessible for our nation's 13 million blind and visually impaired people and their families. Jim Stovall joined the ranks of Walt Disney, Orson Welles, and four United States presidents when he was selected as one of the "Ten Outstanding Young Americans" by the U.S. Junior Chamber of Commerce. He has appeared on *Good Morning America* and CNN, and has been featured in *Reader's Digest, TV Guide,* and *Time* magazine. He has written a number of books, including *You Don't Have to be Blind to See, Success Secrets of Super Achievers,* and *The Way I See the World.* The President's Committee on Equal Opportunity selected Jim Stovall as the 1997 Entrepreneur of the Year.

In 1999 Jim Stovall published a book entitled, *The Ultimate Gift.* This book tells the story of the death of a multimillionaire oil man named Red Stevens who died very disillusioned about his own family. He had given his children everything they wanted, only to see them become selfish playboys and playgirls with no concern for anyone but themselves. He left his companies and properties to his children, two boys and a girl, but his will provided that the companies and properties should be managed by others so that his children could not destroy themselves and others by their mismanagement.

The one heir for whom Red Stevens held out some hope was his grandnephew Jason. But Mr. Stevens wanted him to learn some important lessons before he received the ultimate gift. Jason was to meet with Red Stevens' lawyer on the first of each month for a year, at which time he would be given a significant assignment. If he fulfilled each of the 12 assignments satisfactorily to the lawyer, he would receive the ultimate gift.

Of course, Jason was furious. Why should he be put through all this inconvenience? Why couldn't his crazy uncle just bequeath him his share of the fortune without his first having to prove himself? The answer to that question came only as the year went on. During that year, Jason was obliged to work on a farm for a month as a posthole digger. For a second month he was required to find five needy people and distribute money to them. He was given $1,500 and told to use it to help others. For the third month, Jason was to investigate and discover the meaning of true friendship. During the fourth month, he worked in a library in South America that his uncle had built for the poor of a particular town. Jason was to learn the importance and value of learning. And so on. Each month he was given an assignment that would teach him an important lesson in human relationships, the value of money, the value of life and health, the importance of problem solving, the blessing of gratitude, and the joy to be found in giving to others less fortunate. The twelfth assignment required Jason to explore how love is involved in everything meaningful we accomplish in life. The lesson of love and its importance was Red Stevens' ultimate gift to his nephew and the most important lesson he could teach him. And Jason learned the lesson well.

Then and only then was Jason able to inherit his uncle's final gift. Red Stevens left for his newly educated grandnephew control of his charitable trust fund. This was valued at slightly more than $1 billion. The will read: "As my grandnephew has shown himself to be responsible and able in every area of life, he will have the sole control of this charitable trust fund which supports the Red Stevens Home for Boys, the Red Stevens Library Program, several scholarship programs, hospitals, and many other worthy institutions. I direct Jason to use the wisdom and experience he has gained as a recipient of The Ultimate Gift to manage these projects and any others that he deems significant."

We're not qualified to receive God's abundant gifts until we are willing to use them in His service and the service of our fellow human beings. When we have learned how to dispense love to others, then and only then are we truly equipped to receive the gifts of the Spirit that God wants to bestow upon us. When we recognize that our spiritual, intellectual, and material wealth are not given for us to hoard and to satisfy our own selfish desires, when we recognize that God's gifts are ours to relieve the sufferings of the less fortunate and to demonstrate tolerance and love for those who have not had our advantages, only then can God safely entrust us with the rich spiritual gifts that He dearly wants to give us.

And that, I believe, is the basic lesson of Romans, chapter 14. Paul begins by instructing: "Welcome those who are weak in faith, but not for the purpose of quarreling over opinions" (Romans 14:1, NRSV). In other words, those of us who have strong faith, and who have had the advantage of special gifts from God, are to be tolerant of, and loving toward, those less fortunate.

Then Paul illustrates what he means by referring to controversies that were afflicting the church of Rome at that time. In these controversies the stronger, more enlightened Christians were in danger of lording it over their weaker, less well-informed brothers and sisters, and the weaker brothers and sisters were in danger of harboring bitter, critical, judgmental thoughts toward those who were more enlightened. The ultimate gift of love was being ignored as Christians opposed one another and sat in judgment upon one another.

What were the specific problems that Paul identified as existing in the Roman Christian church? He tells us in Romans, chapter 14, verses 2–6: "Some believe in eating anything, while the weak eat only vegetables. Those who eat must not despise those who abstain, and those who abstain must not pass judgment on those who eat; for God has welcomed them. Who are you to pass judgment on servants of another? It is before their own Lord that they stand or fall. And they will be upheld, for the Lord is able to make them stand. Some judge one day to be better than another, while others judge all days to be alike. Let all be fully convinced in their own minds. Those who observe the day, observe it in honor of the Lord. Also those who eat, eat in honor of the Lord, since they give thanks to God; while those who abstain, abstain in honor of the Lord and give thanks to God" (Romans 14:2–6).

Now what exactly was the problem Paul was identifying? Some interpreters of the Bible would have us believe that Paul was opposing those who were insistent upon observing the seventh-day Sabbath. In answer to that false interpretation, we can point out that the Sabbath is not mentioned in the passage. There is nothing in the passage that indicates that the controversy over days concerned which day was the Sabbath. After all, Jesus kept the Sabbath regularly (Luke 4:16), and He encouraged His followers to observe the Sabbath after His death (Matthew 24:20). The apostle Paul himself regularly observed the Sabbath, as is indicated by his practice described in Acts, chapters 13, 16, 17, and 18.

Moreover, Paul accepted the authority of the Ten Commandments as the standard of righteousness. In the same letter to the Romans, he wrote: "Do we then overthrow the law by this faith? By no means! On the contrary, we uphold the law" (Romans 3:31, NRSV). Paul also wrote: "What then should we say? That the law is sin? By no means! Yet, if it had not been for the law, I would not have known sin. I would not have known what it is to covet if the law had not said, 'You shall not covet' " (Romans 7:7, NRSV). A few verses later, Paul wrote: "So the law is holy, and the commandment is holy and just and good" (Romans 7:12, NRSV). In verse 14, he wrote: "For we know that the law is spiritual; but I am of the flesh, sold into slavery under sin."

In Romans 8:3, 4 (NRSV), Paul tells us that Christ died, "so that the just requirement of the law might be fulfilled in us, who walk not according to the flesh but according to the Spirit."

Now the Ten Commandment law that Paul quotes and exonerates as the standard of righteousness and of Christian behavior includes the fourth commandment, the Sabbath command that reads: "Remember the sabbath day to keep it holy. Six days shalt thou labor, and do all thy work: But the seventh day is the sabbath of the Lord thy God: in it thou shalt not do any work, thou, nor thy son, nor thy daughter, thy manservant, nor thy maidservant, nor thy cattle, nor thy stranger that is within thy gates: For in six days the Lord made heaven and earth, the sea, and all that in them is, and rested the seventh day: wherefore the Lord blessed the sabbath day, and hallowed it" (Exodus 20:8–11, KJV).

Paul accepted this commandment along with all the other nine of the Ten Commandments, and moreover, according to the book of Acts, he was faithful in his Sabbath observance. So in Romans, chapter 14, Paul is not opposing Sabbath observance. In fact, there is no evidence at all that his discussion of days in Romans 14 involved a discussion of the Sabbath day.

There are a number of important considerations to keep in mind as you study Romans 14. First, Romans 14:1–12 is not speaking of issues that were, or are, a matter of right and wrong. The passage tells us that God accepts both parties, the weak and the strong. Verse 4 reads: "And they will be upheld, for the Lord is able to make them stand" (NRSV). And verse 6 clarifies: "Those who observe the day, observe it in honor of the Lord. Also those who eat, eat in honor of the Lord, since they give thanks to God; while those who abstain, abstain in honor of the Lord and give thanks to God" (NRSV).

Both groups, those who were eating certain foods and those who were abstaining from eating those foods, those who were observing certain days and those who were not observing those days—both groups were acceptable to God. The issue was not a matter of right and wrong, as it would have been if the Ten Commandments that Paul observed were being ignored and disobeyed.

The stronger Christians who were eating any kind of food were not eating anything physically harmful. To do so would have contradicted their Christian commitment. Paul had already written: "I appeal to you therefore; brothers and sisters, by the mercies of God, to present your bodies as a living sacrifice, holy and acceptable to God, which is your spiritual worship" (Romans 12:1, NRSV). Paul had written to the Corinthian Christians that our bodies are the temple of the Holy Spirit. "If anyone destroys God's temple, God will destroy that person. For God's temple is holy, and you are that temple" (1 Corinthians 3:16, 17, NRSV).

The issue referred to in Romans 14 was not a matter of health. Since God accepted both parties, the dietary issue among the Roman Christians was not a question of right and wrong. God exonerated both groups, as he never could have if one group were eating something harmful to their body temples.

At this point someone asks, how do you explain Romans 14:14? The passage reads: "I know and am persuaded in the Lord Jesus that nothing is unclean in itself; but it is unclean for anyone who thinks it unclean" (NRSV). Paul makes a similar statement in 1 Timothy 4:4 (NRSV): "For everything created by God is good, and nothing is to be rejected, provided it is received with thanksgiving."

Paul's point was that everything God created *as acceptable for food* may be partaken of. But Paul was not condoning the eating of that which would be harmful to health. Nor was he contradicting the dietary laws listed in Leviticus, chapter 11. God could not accept a person who was eating food harmful to health. That would have been a moral issue, a question of right and wrong. Vegetarians today who refrain from eating flesh for health reasons have a different motivation than did the vegetarians in the Romans' church.

In Romans 14:5, 6 Paul treats the controversy over days in a similar manner to the controversy over food. The question was not one of right and wrong, as it would have been if the fourth commandment was being ignored. The Lord accepted both parties; those who observed days and those who did not. In the light of Jesus' command in Matthew 24:20 that the Sabbath should be observed after His death, the Lord could not have accepted anyone who did not honor the Sabbath day.

Dr. Raoul Dederen has pointed out that there seems to have been a clear connection between the observance of days in Rome and the vegetarianism of the weaker Christians. In an article on the subject in the book *The Sabbath in Scripture and History*, Dederen points out that those who were abstaining from eating particular foods "in honor of the Lord" seem to have been those who were observing particular days in honor of the Lord. Dederen's suggestion is that there was a party in the Roman church that chose to refrain from certain foods on certain days that they regarded as religious days.[1]

In support of that interpretation is the fact that in the time of Jesus and in the early Christian church after Jesus' day there was a controversy over which days were the correct days for fasting. Matthew 9:14 tells us that the disciples of John asked Jesus: "Why do we and the Pharisees fast often, but your disciples do not fast" (NRSV)? Jesus explained that while He was with them, they did not fast and mourn, but after He was taken from them, then they would fast.

In the parable of the publican and the Pharisee, the Pharisee boasted: "I fast twice a week" (Luke 18:12, NRSV). The *Didache* or *Teaching of the Twelve Apostles* is a late first- or early second-century document. It says to Christians: "Your fasts must not be identical with those of the hypocrites. They fast on Mondays and Thursdays; but you should fast on Wednesdays and Fridays."[2] This document instructs early Christians not to fast on Mondays and Thursdays, because they were the fast days of the Jews. Christians were to fast on Wednesdays and Fridays.

You see, there was a controversy in the early Christian church over which days should be observed as fast days. Evidently there were Christians in the Roman church who were insisting on abstinence from certain foods on certain days. And Paul urged tolerance on the part of all parties involved in the controversy. If the ultimate gift of love is to prevail in the church, matters that are not matters of principle, matters that are not questions of right and wrong, should not divide us. If we truly love one another, we will pray for one another and not condemn those whose view of matters of indifference is not the same as ours. Even if the question happens to be a question of right and wrong, the Bible teaches that we are not to condemn others. Our task is to lovingly teach what God's Word teaches and allow the Holy Spirit to convict those who don't want to serve God by obeying His Word.

It's so easy to condemn others when we don't understand their beliefs and when we have little or no idea of the value of their contribution. For example, the day after Lincoln gave his Gettysburg Address in 1865, the *Chicago Times* commented: "The cheek of every American must tingle with shame as he reads the silly, flat, and dish-watery utterances of a man who has to be pointed out to intelligent foreigners as President of the United States." How the cheeks of those editors would tingle with shame if they could know how famous that address has become.

C. R. Hembree wrote the following verse:

"I dreamed death came the other night:
And heaven's gates swung wide.
With kindly grace an angel
Ushered me inside.
And there, to my astonishment,
Stood folks I'd known on earth.
Some I'd judged and labeled
Unfit or of little worth.
Indignant words rose to my lips,
But never were set free;
For every face showed stunned surprise …
No one expected me!"

Paul's following words are very pertinent. He writes: "Why do you pass judgment on your brother and sister? Or you, why do you despise your brother or sister? For we will all stand before the judgment seat of God. For it is written, 'As I live, says the Lord, every knee shall bow to me, and every tongue shall give praise to God.' So then, each of us will be accountable to God. Let us therefore no longer pass judgment on one another, but resolve instead never to put a stumbling block or hindrance in the way of another" (Romans 14:10–13, NRSV).

Then Paul states a vital principle. "If your brother or sister is being injured by what you eat, you are no longer walking in love. Do not let what you eat cause the ruin of one for whom Christ died" (Romans 14:15, NRSV). That principle is illustrated by 1 Corinthians, chapter 8. Some of the food purchased and eaten by the Corinthian Christians had been ceremonially offered to idols. Some of the new Christians had once been idol worshipers, and eating food offered to an idol was to them tantamount to worshiping the idol. So when they saw a Christian brother or sister eating food that had been offered to an idol, they were projected back into their idol-worshiping experience. Paul's instruction is that there is nothing wrong with the food offered to idols—it is good food, because the idol is nothing. But, he instructs, don't eat such food in the presence of the ex-idol-worshiper, because that might induce that person to lapse back into his earlier practice of worshiping idols.

The principle is important to a Christian. The Bible is telling us so to respect others that we should refrain from doing some things that are good in themselves, if our actions will cause another person to wander away from Christ. What we recognize as good behavior might be a stumbling block to another person. Our food, our music, our entertainment, our manner of life might very well cause another person to turn away from Christ. The Bible instructs us to consider other people's feelings and convictions, to walk in love, to allow our concern for others to influence the way we behave.

Romans 14 ends with the vital principle: "Whatever does not proceed from faith is sin" (Romans 14:23, NRSV). In other words, if our behavior is not motivated by faith and love for God and for others, we are sinning. But when faith and love are driving us to do the things we do, we can know that God is directing our lives and using us to serve others.

Twelve-year-old Chris and his father, Mike, were visiting an uncle's cabin six hours from their home. It was an exciting vacation for Chris; he enjoyed exploring the forest and fishing in the nearby stream. One day as Chris and his father, Mike, were fishing in a stream, Mike fell, hitting his head on a rock. "Ow!" he yelled, and starting wiping away the trickle of blood.

"I'll get some tissues!" Chris offered and scrambled up the bank to their truck. But when he returned, Mike was lying face down in the river, his body jerking wildly! Quickly Chris pulled his father's face out of the water. But his dad was unconscious, and he panicked inwardly as he wondered how he could drag him out of the river and up the steep bank to the truck. Chris was only twelve, and his dad had given him his first driving lesson only the day before.

Then the 120-pound seventh-grader began hauling his 185-pound father up the 75-foot bank. Taking a deep breath, Chris began pulling his dad to the top of the bank, pleading, "God, give me strength!" The mud often gave way beneath his feet, but he refused to give up. After twenty minutes, Chris was able to pull his dad to the top of the bank. But Mike began having another seizure; his body began jerking violently. Chris grabbed him under the arms from behind, and pushed him up into the truck. Then he strapped him in with the seat belt.

Then Chris rushed to the other side of the truck and climbed into the driver's seat. He could hardly see over the steering wheel. He turned on the ignition, put it in drive, and slowly pressed down on the gas peddle. The truck jerked forward and Chris pressed harder on the gas peddle. Slowly at first and then more rapidly, he drove the truck along the country road. When he came to a fork in the road, he didn't know which way to go, but uttering a prayer he turned to the left. His dad was sitting beside him, thrashing about as he had another seizure. The day before his dad had let him drive at 10 miles an hour. Now he was going 40. He wiped away his tears and pushed even harder on the accelerator. Minutes later he wheeled into his uncle's driveway and honked the horn.

Quickly his uncle called 911, and very soon they heard the sirens of an ambulance that took Mike to the hospital. The next day Mike regained consciousness, and the doctor told him: "You had seizures, but you're going to be okay, thanks to this little guy here." Mike listened in amazement as he was told what Chris had done. Mike hugged him and said, "I can't believe how brave you were—or how strong! You saved my life!"

You know, your willingness to come to the rescue of a person in need might very well save that person's life. The ultimate gift of love for others sometimes leads us to do special things for them. And that's what Romans, chapter 14, is all about.

Endnotes

1. Raoul Dederen, "On Esteeming One Day as Better Than Another—Romans 14:5, 6," in Kenneth A. Strand (ed.), *The Sabbath in Scripture and History* (Washington, D.C.: Review and Herald, 1982), pp. 333–337.
2. *Didache*, 8:1: in Cyril C. Richardson (trans. & ed.), *Early Christian Fathers* (Philadelphia: Westminster Press, 1953), p. 174.

Chapter Eighteen

Following Christ's Example

Romans 15

An Army chaplain described the terrible destruction from the World War II bombardment of Liège, Belgium. Four days and nights a rescue party worked desperately, trying to find those who might still be living under the rubble of the fallen buildings. Just when they thought they had discovered everyone, they heard a feeble cry. Surely no one could have survived so long in the cold, least of all a child—and yet it was a baby's cry. They dug deeper. Sure enough, the little fellow was there; and when they got him out, they found him to be still conscious, even though he hadn't had food or water for four days. How could he possibly have lived? It was because he was sheltered beneath his mother's body. It was a miracle of a mother's love and sacrifice. She curved her strong body above her child. The building collapsed, and she took the full weight of the crushing stones. Although she was dead, her child was alive.

As John Mansefield, the Poet Laureate of England, once wrote: "Oh, Mother, when I think of thee, 'tis but a step to Calvary." Just as that mother gave her life to save her little one, so Jesus gave His life to save us. The Bible says that He "was handed over to death for our trespasses and was raised for our justification" (Romans 4:25, NRSV). The Bible also says that "God proves his love for us in that while we still were sinners Christ died for us" (Romans 5:8, NRSV). It says: "He died for all, so that those who live might live no longer for themselves, but for him who died and was raised for them" (2 Corinthians 5:15, NRSV).

Because Jesus gave His life for us, He wants us, now that He is our risen Savior, to copy the way He lived. And that's what

Romans, chapter 15, is talking about. Verses 1–3 read: "We then who are strong ought to bear with the scruples of the weak, and not to please ourselves. Let each of us please his neighbor for his good, leading to edification. For even Christ did not please Himself; but as it is written, 'The reproaches of those who reproached You fell on Me' " (Romans 15:1–3).

That fact can be illustrated in many ways from the story of Jesus' life contained in the four Gospels: Matthew, Mark, Luke, and John. Jesus was constantly working for those who were weak. One day Jesus was surrounded by a crowd of people when the ruler of the synagogue, a man named Jairus, pressed through the crowd and begged Him to come to his house because his daughter was sick and dying. This man was one of those legalistic Israelites who didn't have much time for Jesus' teaching. But Jesus had just as much concern for him and for his dying daughter as He did for everyone else. Jesus began walking toward the ruler's house, but the people pressed around Him, and His progress was slow. Then a woman who had been hemorrhaging for twelve years came up behind him and touched the fringe of His garment. She knew Jesus had the power to heal, and she thought that if she could just touch the hem of His cloak, she would be healed. And sure enough it happened. The Bible says, "Immediately her flow of blood stopped" (Luke 8:44). Jesus turned around and said, "Who touched Me?" Peter said, "Master, the multitudes throng You and press You, and You say, 'Who touched Me?' " But Jesus said, "Someone touched Me; for I perceive power going out from Me."

Then the woman came forward trembling with fear. She fell down before Jesus and explained why she had touched Him, and she testified that she was immediately healed. Jesus was full of compassion for her. He said: "Daughter, be of good cheer, your faith has made you well. Go in peace" (Luke 8:48).

We too can reach out by faith and touch Jesus. He is just as powerful today to heal as He was two thousand years ago. It may be His will to heal our bodies as He healed that suffering woman in the throng that day. But it is certainly His will to forgive our sins and to give us the power to be overcomers. Jesus cares for you with infinite love. As the hymn writer put it so beautifully:

"We touch Him in life's throng and press, and we are whole again."

Jairus was distressed that it was taking Jesus so long to come to his home. His daughter was dying, and every moment counted. Then to his dismay, a servant from his house pressed through the crowd and informed him: "Your daughter is dead. Do not trouble the Teacher" (Luke 8:49). Jairus' spirits sagged. He was overcome with grief and frustration. But Jesus reassured him. He said: "Do not be afraid; only believe, and she will be made well."

When they arrived at Jairus' house, Jesus took Peter, James, and John, and the parents of the dead girl into the room where she lay. Taking her by the hand He commanded, "Little girl, arise." And she did! Jesus told them to give her something to eat. "And her parents were astonished" (Luke 8:56).

You see, Jesus was the great Healer. He was in the business of inviting people to accept the free gift of salvation. And in the process, He demonstrated His love and power by healing the sick and raising the dead.

That's why the apostle Paul invites us to "bear the infirmities of the weak, and not to please ourselves" (Romans 15:1, KJV). We don't have the same power to heal that Jesus had. But He gives us the power of His Holy Spirit to show love for the people around us. He motivates us to offer a word of encouragement to those who are struggling with sin and to those who are suffering physically. Jesus' love can be manifested through us as we minister to those less fortunate than we are.

Paul writes: "Now may the God of patience and comfort grant you to be like-minded toward one another, according to Christ Jesus, that you may with one mind and one mouth glorify the God and Father of our Lord Jesus Christ" (Romans 15:5, 6). There is no harmony between members of a family, a church, or a society, no harmony in our nation, or between nations unless the love of Jesus Christ is ruling. Jesus Christ is the one sure Source of unity, harmony, and love.

In His last wonderful prayer for His disciples, Jesus prayed, "I ask not only on behalf of these, but also on behalf of those who will believe in me through their word, that they may all be one. As you, Father, are in me and I am in you, may they also be in us, so that the world may believe that you have sent me. The glory that you have given me I have given them, so that they may be one, as we are one, I in them and you in me, that they may become completely one, so that the world may know that you have sent me and have loved them even as you have loved me" (John 17:20–23, NRSV).

There is no binding force in the world like the binding power of God's love. When God's love comes into the lives of an estranged husband and wife, they come together again. When God's love reigns in our community, we live in harmony and peace. When God's love takes possession of our national leaders, they pass laws, not for political reasons but for the welfare and blessing of citizens. If only the rulers of the nations would allow God's love to rule in their hearts, they would do all they could to promote peace and harmony in the world, instead of wrangling over coveted real estate and fighting over selfish, narrow national interests.

Oh, you say, that's not likely to happen! And undoubtedly in this world of sin it's not likely to happen. But it can happen for you and me. We can change our world by following the counsel of Romans, chapter 15. By God's grace, we can "live in harmony with one another, in accordance with Christ Jesus, so that together [we] may with one voice glorify the God and Father of our Lord Jesus Christ" (Romans 15:5, 6, NRSV).

Paul proceeds to urge us: "Receive one another, just as Christ also received us, to the glory of God. Now I say that Jesus Christ has become a servant to the circumcision for the truth of God, to confirm the promises made to the fathers" (Romans 15:7, 8). In other words, Christ lived and died for the Jews. Then Paul adds: "… and that the Gentiles might glorify God for His mercy" (Romans 15:9). In other words, Christ lived and died also for the Gentiles. He lived and died for everyone, irrespective of ethnic or national origin.

Paul adds his earnest hope: "May the God of hope fill you with all joy and peace in believing, that you may abound in hope by the power of the Holy Spirit" (Romans 15:13). "Joy and peace in believing" is ours "by the power of the Holy Spirit." What a difference that makes to our lives! The Holy Spirit living in our lives is the presence of Jesus. When Jesus was promising the Holy Spirit, He said: "I will not leave you orphaned; I am coming to you" (John 14:18, NRSV). Jesus lives with us. He dwells in our hearts by the presence of His Spirit. He keeps us from evil, and gives us daily the joy and peace we need. Our spiritual health and our mental health are dependent upon His soothing, saving presence in our lives. But when we turn away from Him and refuse to believe, His peace forsakes us, and we are left to struggle hopelessly against impurity, dishonesty, hatred, selfishness, and despair.

We all deeply appreciate Leonardo da Vinci's painting of the Last Supper. Da Vinci is reputed to have taken twenty years to paint that picture. He chose various men who, he felt, approximated the appearance and characteristics of the disciples.

The legend says that in the cathedral he noticed a young man in the choir who reminded him of what Jesus must have looked like—noble and kind, bright and responsive. He made arrangements with the young man to sit for the face of Christ. The young man's name was Pietro Bardinelli. Da Vinci was so pleased that he didn't care how long after that it took him to complete the painting. He now had the central figure.

But the most difficult character to find was someone who could represent Judas. Year after year he searched as he worked on the painting. Several years later he found a man whose face appeared to him to be as cunning and shrewd and deceitful as Judas must have appeared. Da Vinci made arrangements to paint this man's picture.

When it was completed, Da Vinci gave him an extra amount of money. Then he asked his name. The man replied: "My name is Pietro Bardinelli. I sat as you painted the face of Christ many years ago."[1]

The young man had turned away from Christ; he had given in to evil; he had made a wreck of his life. May God save us from that! Jesus wants to give us now and always throughout life "joy and peace in believing … by the power of the Holy Spirit."

Paul's great concern was that the peoples of all nations should have such joy and peace and power. He referred to himself as "a minister of Jesus Christ to the Gentiles, ministering the gospel of God, that the offering of the Gentiles might be acceptable, sanctified by the Holy Spirit" (Romans 15:16).[2]

Paul wanted the Gentiles to be sanctified. The last phrase of verse 16 translates literally: "… having been sanctified by the Holy Spirit." In the New Testament the verb *to sanctify* often refers to an experience of holiness in Christ enjoyed by believers now.[3] For example, Acts 26:18 records Jesus' words to Paul on the Damascus road. He commissioned him to open the eyes of the Gentiles, "so that they may turn from darkness to light and from the power of Satan to God, so that they may receive forgiveness of sins and a place among those who *have been sanctified* by faith in me."[4]

Those who believe in Jesus have been sanctified by faith in Him. The verb *to sanctify* means "to make holy." When you believe in Jesus Christ, He makes you holy by giving you the presence of the Holy Spirit in your heart.

In writing to the Corinthians, Paul spoke of "the church of God which is in Corinth, *having been sanctified* by Christ Jesus, called saints" (1 Corinthians 1:2).[5] They had received the gift of Christ's holiness by the Holy Spirit, and so were called "holy ones," or "saints." In the Bible, a saint is a believer in Jesus Christ. A saint is one who has accepted Jesus as Savior and Lord and who now has the presence of the Holy Spirit living in his or her heart.

The Corinthian Christians had been sanctified by Jesus Christ; they had received the gift of His holiness. But they were spoiling that gift by their divisiveness. They were fighting one another. Paul wrote to them precisely because he wanted to bring them together again. He wrote: "I plead with you, brethren, by the name of our Lord Jesus Christ, that you all speak the same thing, and that there be no divisions among you, but that you be perfectly joined together in the same mind and in the same judgment" (1 Corinthians 1:10).

That was exactly the message that Paul presented to the Roman Christians in Romans, chapter 15. He wanted both Jews and Gentiles to be sanctified by the Holy Spirit so that they could live in harmony. Moreover, he wanted them to grow in holiness. To the Corinthians he wrote these beautiful words: "We all, with unveiled face, beholding as in a mirror the glory of the Lord, are being transformed into the same image from glory to glory, just as by the Spirit of the Lord" (2 Corinthians 3:18).

In the latter part of Romans, chapter 15, Paul praises God for using him to preach the gospel in places where it had never been heard before (vs. 17–21). Then he tells the Roman Christians that he plans to visit them on the way to Spain (vs. 22–29). But he explains that first he must visit Jerusalem to take to the believers there the offering that had been collected for them in Greece. Writing about A.D. 58, Paul tells the Roman Christians that, after visiting Jerusalem, he will visit them on the way to Spain.

Paul appealed to the Roman Christians to pray for the success of his mission to Jerusalem. He wrote: "Now I beg you, brethren, through the Lord Jesus Christ, and through the love of the Spirit, that you strive together with me in your prayers to God for me, that I may be delivered from those in Judea who do not believe, and that my service for Jerusalem may be acceptable to the saints, that I may come to you with joy by the will of God, and may be refreshed together with you. Now the God of peace be with you all. Amen" (Romans 15:30–33).

The prayers of the Roman Christians on Paul's behalf were answered, but not in the manner that he had expected. He traveled back to Jerusalem as described in Acts, chapter 21. Stopping over in Caesarea on the way to Jerusalem, he was warned by the prophet Agabus that the citizens in Jerusalem would oppose him, arrest him, and hand him over to the Gentiles (Acts 21:10, 11).

Because of that, the believers in Caesarea pleaded with Paul not to go on to Jerusalem. But he answered courageously: "What do you mean by weeping and breaking my heart? For I am ready not only to be bound, but also to die in Jerusalem for the name of the Lord Jesus" (Acts 21:13).

Paul went on to Jerusalem as planned, but before long he was attacked by those who opposed his gospel. They dragged him out of the temple and were about to kill him when the Roman soldiers intervened.

The following day, Paul was tried before the Jewish Sanhedrin, but they were hopelessly divided. The Romans delivered him from the Sanhedrin and imprisoned him in their barracks. That night the Lord appeared to Paul in a vision and said, "Be of good cheer, Paul: for as you have testified for Me in Jerusalem, so you must also bear witness at Rome" (Acts 23:11).

Next, the Romans imprisoned Paul at Caesarea, where he was tried before the governor Felix, then by his successor, Festus, and finally by King Agrippa. But, as a Roman citizen, Paul exercised his right to be tried by Caesar in Rome. So it was that, after being in prison in Caesarea for two years, Paul was sent by ship to Rome. Acts, chapters 27 and 28, dramatically describes Paul's voyage to Rome, during which the ship on which he was traveling was wrecked in a storm.

Eventually arriving in Rome, Paul was given the right to live by himself with a Roman soldier guarding him. This gave him the opportunity to meet the Jewish leaders in Rome and to present to them the good news about salvation through Christ. "Some were persuaded by the things which were spoken, and some disbelieved" (Acts 28:24).

For the next two years as a prisoner in Rome, Paul lived at his own expense, "and received all who came to him, preaching the kingdom of God and teaching the things which concern the Lord Jesus Christ with all confidence, no one forbidding him" (Acts 28:30, 31). At the end of those two years, Paul was tried and released. He traveled again through the Mediterranean world preaching the gospel, until once again he was arrested by the Romans. Again he was imprisoned in Rome and finally was executed after being tried by Nero about A.D. 67 or 68.

Paul's entire evangelistic endeavors for the Gentiles of the Mediterranean world were directed by Jesus Christ. He was a faithful ambassador for the Lord in every situation, so much so that multitudes of lost sinners were saved. And today the same good news of salvation through Christ results in people coming to the Lord and finding deliverance from sin.

Harry Orchard was undoubtedly the most notorious criminal of his generation at the turn of the twentieth century. His name is linked with the desperate class struggle and lawlessness that marked the rugged history of our great Northwest. The West was sparsely settled in those days. Towns and cities were scattered. Gun slaying was frequent. Into this environment stepped Harry Orchard, a fugitive from justice, alone, unhappy, and desperate. He made money and spent it faster, until, deep in debt, he found himself employed by corrupted labor forces. Before long he was in the inner circle—actually planning organized crime. Harry Orchard had more than twenty notches on his gun, and for the crimes those notches represented he was hunted by the authorities. Now he undertook his last gruesome assignment—taking the life of Governor Frank Steunenberg of Idaho.

Mrs. Steunenberg was a devoted Christian, determined to teach her children the ways of the Lord. But the governor made no profession of Christianity. One morning late in 1905, Mrs. Steunenberg was conducting family worship, and the governor joined her and the children. "Frank," she said to him in her gentle manner, "the children and I have been praying for you. Won't you give your heart to Christ?"

The governor paced the floor for a few minutes and then began to sing, "Nearer, my God to Thee." Shortly after that, unknown to his wife, he contacted his friends and business associates and told them that from now on he wouldn't be doing some of the things he was used to doing.

That evening as Governor Steunenberg returned home, he opened his front gate and triggered the bomb that Harry Orchard had planted nearby. The Governor died within hours.

Harry Orchard was arrested and imprisoned. Dr. David Paulson of Chicago sent him a Bible, and he read it. Then Mrs. Steunenberg's son visited him just before one of his court sessions. The boy handed him a package from Mrs. Steunenberg, a copy of the little book *Steps to Christ.* The boy told Harry Orchard, "Mother says that she forgives you the terrible wrong you have done our family. She asks you to give your heart to Christ. She says her only hope is that you will be saved in God's kingdom."

Mrs. Steunenberg visited Harry in prison several times, and finally he confessed to the crime of murdering her husband and was sentenced to life in prison. Years went by, and he was permitted to establish prison industries. Now he was a converted man. Now he belonged to Jesus Christ.

After forty years in prison, Harry Orchard wrote:

"I well remember the day I walked into this penitentiary. As the jailer turned the key in my cell, I felt instinctively that I would never be a free man again. That was more than four decades ago. I am still incarcerated within that prison. But in spite of these years of confinement, I have … a freedom of soul that I never once knew in the days when I was physically at liberty. Stone walls and metal bars have held my body captive, but my soul has long been free."

That sounds like Lovelace's familiar old seventeenth-century hymn, "Stone walls do not a prison make, nor iron bars a cage."

There is no freedom like the freedom that Jesus gives you when you come to Him, confessing your sin, and accepting Him as Savior and Lord. Let me appeal to you to do what Harry Orchard did and come to Jesus today for forgiveness and salvation.

Endnotes

1. Adapted from George Vandeman, *Touch and Live* (Washington, D.C.: Review and Herald, 1958), pp. 30, 31.

2. The Greek of the last phrase of Romans 15:16 reads: *hegiasmene en pneumati hagio.* The perfect passive participle, *hegiasmene,* translates literally, "having been sanctified."
3. The Greek verb *hagiazo* means "consecrate, dedicate, sanctify, treat as holy, purify, make holy." (See Arndt and Gingrich, *A Greek-English Lexicon.*)
4. My translation. The phrase "who have been sanctified" literally translates the perfect, passive participle *hegiasmenois.* The believers had been sanctified, and the results of that sanctification still remained.
5. First Corinthians 1:2 translates literally from the Greek text: "To the church of God which is at Corinth, having been sanctified in Christ Jesus, called saints." The phrase "having been sanctified" translates the perfect, passive participle *hegiasmenois.* The believers were called saints (*hagiois*) because they had been sanctified. Paul's concern was that the Corinthian Christians were spoiling the sanctification of the Spirit by their divisiveness.

Chapter Nineteen

Trophies of Christ's Victories

Romans 16

In the early days of America, a family lived in their wilderness home on the bleak New England shores. They had built the home themselves and carved out their furniture with their own hands. There were two adult children in the family. One was a young doctor who was often away from home visiting the little towns and isolated settlements along the coast. The other child was a lovely girl about twenty years of age.

Each evening she would steal away to the quiet of the nearby wooded forest without the family knowing just where she had gone. There she would have her quiet devotions alone in nature's retreat. Always she would sing:

"When softly falls the twilight hour
O'er moor and mountain, field and flower,
How sweet to leave a world of care,
And lift to heaven the voice of prayer."

One evening she was enjoying her meditation, and had just completed the first two lines of her little song,

"When softly falls the twilight hour
O'er moor and mountain, field and flower."

At that moment, an Indian crept up behind her and struck her on the head with a tomahawk and then fled. She dropped to the ground unconscious. When the evening meal was served and the girl was missing, a party went out to search for her. They found her, but she remained unconscious for several days. Her doctor brother was called, and he performed an operation to remove the pressure on her brain.

When the operation was completed and she had regained consciousness, her lips began to move, and she finished the song so abruptly interrupted a few days before:

"How sweet to leave a world of care,
And lift to heaven the voice of prayer."

Her brain began to function just where it had left off. Just so, God's plan for mankind was interrupted—rudely interrupted by man's fall into sin. God's plan was delayed, but not changed. The song begun in Eden will again be taken up and finished when the earth is restored to its original beauty and men and women to their original happiness at the second coming of Jesus.[1]

The apostle John wrote these wonderful words: "Then I saw a new heaven and a new earth; for the first heaven and the first earth had passed away, and the sea was no more. And I saw the holy city, the new Jerusalem, coming down out of heaven from God, prepared as a bride adorned for her husband. And I heard a loud voice from the throne saying, 'See, the home of God is among mortals, He will dwell with them as their God; they will be his peoples, and God himself will be with them; he will wipe every tear from their eyes, Death will be no more; mourning and crying and pain will be no more, for the first things have passed away" (Revelation 21:1–4, NRSV).

Among those who will dwell with God for eternity are the trophies of Christ's victory on the cross. Because they accept Jesus as their Savior and Lord, multitudes will live for eternity. They will never experience sickness or death, sorrow or pain. God will wipe away their tears, and they will be His loyal, happy children for eternity.

Included with those trophies of Christ's victory will be the faithful people to whom Paul sent greetings in the final chapter of his letter to the Romans. Paul was in Corinth; the year was A.D. 57 or 58. Paul knew many of the Christians who lived in Rome, even though he had never had the opportunity of visiting there. Many Jews, Jewish Christians, and Gentile Christians had previously migrated to Rome. In those days, Rome was a little like America today. People wanted to live at the heart of the then-known world, just as today people of other countries covet the privilege of living in America.

All went well until the Jews and the Christians in Rome came to blows. In A.D. 49, the Roman emperor Claudius expelled the Jews from Rome, evidently because of riots resulting from the preaching about Christ. The historian Suetonius wrote: "Since the Jews constantly made disturbances at the instigation of Chrestus, he [Claudius] expelled them from Rome"[2] In his *Apology*, the North African church father, Tertullian, writing at the end of the second century, said that the Greek name *Christos* was often pronounced *Chrestos.*[3] So the trouble among the Jewish population of Rome evidently resulted from their rejection of Christ as the Messiah. Riots broke out, and Claudius expelled all Jews and Jewish Christians from Rome.

This is why Paul knew so many of the members of the Roman Christian church. They had traveled from Rome to the Roman province of Asia where Paul was evangelizing. Those who were already Christians joined his efforts for those who were not Christians. And many more accepted Jesus as the Messiah. Later after the death of Claudius in A.D. 54, they were able to return to Rome. So in A.D. 57 or 58, when Paul was writing from Corinth his epistle to the Romans, he was able to greet by name quite a number of the believers who had been in Asia Minor but who had returned to their homes in Rome.

We know Paul was writing from Corinth, because he recommended to the Roman Christians a lady named Phoebe (Romans 16:1, 2). She was a deaconess of the church of Cenchreae, which was the eastern seaport of Corinth, about 7 miles from the city. She had been a benefactor, or helper, of many people, including Paul himself, and she may have carried Paul's letter to Rome. Paul asked the Roman Christians to "help her in whatever she may require of you" (Romans 16:2).

Also included among those whom Paul greeted in the final chapter of his epistle, were Prisca and Aquila. They had traveled from Rome to Corinth in A.D. 49 when the Roman emperor

Claudius had expelled the Jews from Rome (Acts 18:1–3). Because they were faithful Christians and tentmakers, Paul, also a tentmaker, lodged and worked with them. Later Prisca and Aquila were with Paul in Ephesus (see 1 Corinthians 16:19; Acts 18:18, 19, 26). But when Paul was writing his letter to the Roman Christians, Prisca and Aquila were back in Rome. After the death of Claudius, they had returned.

Romans, chapter 16, verses 5–16, provide quite a list of people whom Paul had known in Asia Minor but who now were living back in Rome. He greets them as faithful believers and loyal supporters of his ministry to the Gentiles. Some were his own countrymen who had migrated to Rome. Undoubtedly these were among those who welcomed Paul the prisoner when he was taken to Rome to be tried early in the 60s.

The beautiful thought is that they were all trophies of Christ's victory on the cross. They had accepted Jesus' gift of salvation, and they were prepared to witness to others of His saving power. They will be among the believers whom Jesus will take to his heavenly kingdom when the interruption caused by sin is over and Jesus restores this earth to its Edenic beauty.

These faithful followers of Christ, whom Paul knew so well, had accepted the experience Paul describes in Romans 12:2. They had allowed the Holy Spirit to transform their minds, so that they could "discern what is the will of God—what is good and acceptable and perfect" (NRSV).

You see, the real battle going on in our world today is the battle for the mind. Jesus wants us to surrender our minds to Him so that He can give us the power to think pure thoughts, speak pure words, and act in ways that are loving and good. He wants our minds to be under His divine control. But the devil has the opposite intent. He wants us to be evil, to be reflectors of his hateful, malicious, unholy, impure character. The one who will win this war going on in your mind is the one to whom you yield allegiance.

Isaac Watts was a celebrated hymn writer. Most churches today use some of his great hymns. When he became a great public figure, people would throng the narrow streets in order to catch a glimpse of him.

On one occasion, Isaac Watts was to pass by in a parade in the city of London. A wealthy woman greatly desired to see him. So she hired an apartment overlooking the street and seated herself by a bay window where she might look down into his carriage. When the king passed, the bands played, and the people waved and cheered. But when Isaac Watts passed by in his carriage, everyone stood on tiptoe and remained strangely silent, out of sheer respect for this revered man.

The woman in the apartment overhead had expected to see a tall, manly figure with a noble forehead. How disappointed she was when she saw a little man wrinkled with age seated in the carriage. She was so surprised that she leaned out of the window and shouted, "What! You Isaac Watts?" And he heard her! He called for the carriage to stop, and standing in quiet dignity to his feet, spread out his short arms in a gesture of wideness and said:

"Could I in fancy reach the pole
Or grasp creation in my span,
I'd still be measured by my soul;
The mind's the measure of the man." [4]

How right Isaac Watts was! More important than the mental faculty that reasons; more important than the faculty that memorizes; more important than the everyday uses of our minds, there is that portion of the mind called the "heart." This part of the mind has the capacity for love or hate. This part of the mind has the ability to choose Christ and to be devoted to His service. This part of the mind is the part that God wants you to give Him when He asks you to surrender your heart to Him. This part of the mind is the measure of your character. The mind is, indeed, the measure of the person. God wants to transform our minds, our hearts, so that, like the people Paul greets in Romans, chapter 16, we won't be "conformed to this world, but … transformed by the renewing" of our minds (Romans 12:2).

In the second part of Romans, chapter 16, Paul gives believers a few words of final counsel. He writes in verses 17 and 18: "I urge you, brothers and sisters, to keep an eye on those who cause dissensions and offenses, in opposition to the teaching that you have learned; avoid them. For such people do not serve our Lord Christ, but their own appetites, and by smooth talk and flattery they deceive the hearts of the simple-minded" (Romans 16:17, 18, NRSV).

Throughout his epistles, Paul warns of the danger of disunity and divisiveness. Previously he had written to the Corinthian believers: "Now I appeal to you, brothers and sisters, by the name of our Lord Jesus Christ, that all of you be in agreement and that there be no divisions among you, but that you be united in the same mind and the same purpose" (1 Corinthians 1:10, NRSV).

To the Galatian Christians, Paul wrote: "I am astonished that you are so quickly deserting the one who called you in the grace of Christ and are turning to a different gospel—not that there is another gospel, but there are some who are confusing you and want to pervert the gospel of Christ. But even if we or an angel from heaven should proclaim to you a gospel contrary to what we proclaimed to you, let that one be accursed! As we have said before, so now I repeat, if anyone proclaims to you a gospel contrary to what you received, let that one be accursed!" (Galatians 1:6–9, NRSV).

Strong words coming from the beloved apostle! But necessary words for those who present their own theories in place of the true gospel of Jesus Christ. In every period of the Christian era, there have been those who have substituted human ideas and methods for those taught in the Word of God. There are always those who ignore the clear teaching of Scripture and promote ideas that are theirs, not God's.

For example, in every era there have been those who contradict the central thesis of the book of Romans. The Bible tells us that we are saved by God's grace, not by human works. But some religious leaders want us to believe that we should confess our sins to human priests and do works of penance before we can be forgiven. The Bible teachers clearly that "the righteousness of God … is through faith in Jesus Christ to all and on all who believe" (Romans 3:22).

On the other hand there are those who want us to believe that the Ten Commandment law of God was abolished at the cross. But Paul had reminded the Roman Christians that God's law is "holy and just and good" (Romans 7:12).

Some want us to believe that when we receive God's gift of grace, we don't have to keep the law any more, that the Ten Commandments are outmoded. But Paul pressed home the point that we don't destroy the law of God by faith, "we establish the law" (Romans 3:31).

Some people want to paddle along in their sins, believing that they are still saved. But that is a terrible fallacy. The whole message of Scripture is that we should forsake our sins, through the mighty power given us by Jesus Christ. Paul had written to the Roman Christians: "The mind that is set on the flesh is hostile to God; it does not submit to God's law—indeed it cannot, and those who are in the flesh cannot please God" (Romans 8:7, 8, NRSV). Only through the power of the Holy Spirit can we obey the law of God, and with His power victory over sin is assured.

An old legend says that a Portuguese monastery stood precariously on top of a three-hundred-foot cliff. Visitors were strapped in a huge wicker basket, then pulled to the top with an old ragged rope. As one visitor stepped into the basket for the descent, he asked anxiously, "How often do you get a new rope?" The monk calmly replied, "Whenever the old one breaks."[5]

How dangerous! That's like skidding through life with no real concern for fellowship with God. Sooner or later, the old habits will break us. Sooner or later the false philosophy of life we have espoused will destroy our peace of mind and our capacity to cope. We must have the sustaining presence of Jesus in our hearts if we are to live right lives now and make it through to the heavenly kingdom.

Paul urges the Roman Christians to "be wise in what is good and guileless in what is evil" (Romans 16:19, NRSV). Then he encourages them and us with the statement: "The God of peace will crush Satan under your feet shortly" (v. 20). That's a promise that means the day is coming when there will be no more evil in our world, no more temptation, no more hatred and bitterness. The book of Revelation tells us that Satan, the devil, the evil one, finally will be punished for his wickedness and will be destroyed in the fires of the last great day. Revelation 20, verse 10, says that the devil will be "thrown into the lake of fire and sulfur" (NRSV) and will be no more.

Paul concludes the letter to the Romans with an inspiring doxology. It reads: "Now to God who is able to strengthen you according to my gospel and the proclamation of Jesus Christ, according to the revelation of the mystery that was kept secret for long ages, but is now disclosed, and through the prophetic writings is made known to all the Gentiles, according to the command of the eternal God, to bring about the obedience of faith—to the only wise God, through Jesus Christ, to whom be the glory forever! Amen" (Romans 16:25–27, NRSV).

There are three parts to this doxology. First, the gospel provides strength to the believer in Jesus Christ. This is the message of the book of Romans. Chapter one introduces the theme: "I am not ashamed of the gospel of Christ, for it is the power of God to salvation for everyone who believes, for the Jew first and also for the Greek" (Romans 1:16). There is power in the gospel, and that power spells deliverance from sin and the ability to reflect the love of Jesus Christ.

The power in the gospel resides in the gift of God's righteousness by the bestowal of the Holy Spirit upon us. "For in it [that is, in the gospel], the righteousness of God is revealed through faith for faith; as it is written, 'The one who is righteous will live by faith'" (Romans 1:17, NRSV). The point is emphasized magnificently in Romans, chapter 8, that identifies the gift of Christ as the gift of the Holy Spirit to our hearts, which is the gift of righteousness (Romans 8:9, 10).

Second, Paul's doxology tells us that the gospel is the "revelation of the mystery that was kept secret for long ages" (Romans 16:25, NRSV). In a number of his epistles, Paul makes the same point. For example, 1 Corinthians 2:7 reads: "We speak the wisdom of God in a mystery, the hidden wisdom which God ordained before the ages for our glory." Again in Ephesians, chapter 3, Paul writes: "In former generations this mystery was not made known to humankind, as it has now been revealed to his holy apostles and prophets by the Spirit" (Ephesians 3:5, NRSV).

The fact is that people before the cross had ample knowledge of God and of His plan of salvation to be saved. But the details of the good news of salvation were understood only after Jesus died on Calvary. Paul identifies the mystery that is now known to believers as "Christ in you, the hope of glory" (Colossians 1:27). Certainly Old Testament humankind had ample opportunity for salvation. But those of us living since the cross and looking back have the wonderful assurance that our salvation has been purchased, that Christ lives in our hearts by His Spirit, and that we have the certain hope of a place in God's eternal kingdom.

Finally, Paul's doxology makes the point that God's wisdom and love are manifest through Jesus Christ. He writes: "… to God, alone wise, be glory through Jesus Christ forever. Amen" (Romans 16:27).

There was no doubt in Paul's mind that Jesus Christ is the Deity, equal in authority and power with the heavenly Father. He wrote to the Colossians: "In Him dwells all the fullness of the Godhead bodily" (Colossians 2:9). So the love and tenderness manifested by Jesus during His earthly ministry accurately demonstrated the love and tenderness of our heavenly Father. The wisdom of Jesus, manifested in all His dealings with humanity, is the infinite wisdom of the Deity. Praise God, the only wise God is manifested through Jesus Christ.

One of the most significant battles in world history was the battle of Waterloo, between the Duke of Wellington and Napoleon

Bonaparte. The news of the battle reached England by a sailing vessel that approached the south coast. The message was carried overland by semaphore to the top of Winchester Cathedral and on to London.

The people waited eagerly. The semaphore spelled out the words—"W-E-L-L-I-N-G-T-O-N D-E-F-E-A-T-E-D.

Just then a dense fog settled down over the harbor, as this incomplete message was waved on to London. The people were devastated. Streets were barricaded. People prepared to defend their country in the streets and in the fields if necessary. But finally the fog lifted and the semaphore signals came through again: "W-E-L-L-I-N-G-T-O-N D-E-F-E-A-T-E-D T-H-E E-N-E-M-Y.[6]

Imagine the paroxysm of joy that swept over the land, in contrast to the previous depression and discouragement!

And imagine how Jesus' disciples must have felt the day of His crucifixion! They had fondly believed that Jesus was the Messiah. They sincerely accepted the truth that He was God in human flesh. But here He was allowing Himself to be crucified. They stood off at a distance from the cross, mourning their loss and weeping bitter tears of discouragement. The message that came through to them was "Jesus defeated."

All through the following Sabbath day, as Jesus lay in the tomb, His disciples grieved. How could they face the world? How could they ever justify their previous faith in Him as the world's Redeemer?

But then a change came! The women followers of Jesus found His tomb empty the next Sunday morning, and the Savior they loved appeared to them. They hurried away to tell the unbelieving disciples that Jesus had risen. It was true, despite the doubts of the disciples! That very evening Jesus appeared to them in the upper room where they were hiding out. He assured them that He had indeed risen from the dead and that He was indeed the Resurrection and the Life.

The message was changed. Now it read: "Jesus defeated death!" And that's the message that you and I can accept with wholehearted devotion. Jesus is victorious. We are the trophies of His sacrifice. We serve a risen Savior! We don't have to reconcile ourselves to a life of disappointment now and to an eternity of separation from God. We are His children; He loves us; He will save us; heaven is our home; the fullness of joy will soon be ours. Praise God, His salvation is manifest through Jesus Christ.

Endnotes

1. Adapted from George Vandeman, *Touch and Live* (Washington, D.C.: Review and Herald, 1958), pp. 13, 14.
2. *Lives of the Caesars,* v.25.4; Loeb ed., *Suetonius,* vol. 2, p. 53.
3. Tertullian iii.5; Alexander Roberts and James Donaldson (trans. & eds.), *The Ante-Nicene Fathers* (Grand Rapids, Michigan: Eerdmans, 1963), vol. III, p. 20.
4. Adapted from George Vandeman, *Touch and Live,* pp. 121, 122.
5. *Ibid.,* p. 73.
6. *Ibid.,* p. 89.

AMAZING FACTS